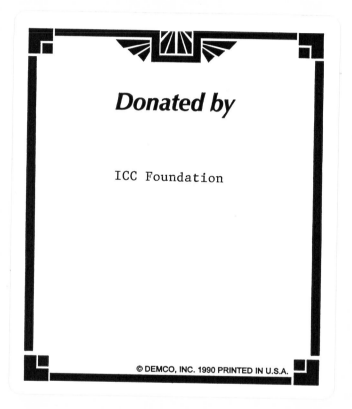

Donated by

ICC Foundation

Technological Empowerment

Technological Empowerment

The Internet, State, and Society in China

YONGNIAN ZHENG

Stanford University Press

Stanford, California

Stanford University Press
Stanford, California

Printed in the United States of America
on acid-free, archival-quality paper

Library of Congress Cataloging-in-Publication Data

Zheng, Yongnian.
  Technological empowerment : the Internet, state, and society
in China / Yongnian Zheng.
     p. cm.
  Includes bibliographical references and index.
  ISBN-13: 978-0-8047-5737-9 (cloth : alk. paper)
    1. Political participation—Technological innovations—China.
2. Internet—Political aspects—China.   3. Democracy—China.
4. Internet—China.   I. Title.
  JQ1516.Z4468 2007
  303.48'330951—dc22

                                                    2007019282

Typeset by Newgen—Austin in 10/12.5 Electra

For Katherine and Nevin

Contents

Tables and Figures   ix

Preface   xiii

Acknowledgments   xix

1 Politics of Technological Empowerment:
   Science vs. Democracy   1

2 Information Technology, Nation-State Building,
   and Social Movement   17

3 Regulatory Regime and Political Control   49

4 The Internet, Political Liberalization,
   and Political Democratization   79

5 The Internet, Civic Engagement, and
   Public Distrust   103

6 Interaction Strategies, Collective Action,
   and Political Consequences   135

7 Information Technology, Transformation of
   State-Society Relations, and Political Changes   166

Selected Bibliography   189

Notes   205

Index   231

Tables and Figures

TABLES

2.1 Local switchboard capacity in China, 1985–2002   28

2.2 Number of fixed-line phone subscribers in China, 1978–2002   29

2.3 Penetration rate and teledensity in China, 1985–2002   30

2.4 Number of mobile phone subscribers in China, 1988–2002   30

2.5 Social groups that benefited the most and least since the reform and open door policy (perceptions, 2002)   44

2.6 Fluctuations in the urban-rural income levels since 1995   45

2.7 The development of corruption among leading cadres in the 1990s   46

3.1 Heads of the Department of Propaganda   56

3.2 Major rules and regulations on the Internet in China, 1994–2005   59

4.1 Most important reasons for going online in China (%), 2002–2004   92

4.2 Information searched for by Internet users in China (%), 2002–2004   93

4.3 Services that were used most frequently (multiple choices, %), 2002–2004   95

5.1 Reasons for not using the Internet in China (percentage, 2003)   107

x

5.2 Reasons for not using the Internet in urban areas
(percentage, N: 1,382) 108

5.3 Trust on information available in the Internet among Internet
users and non-users in urban China (by percentage) 114

5.4 Public opinions of the Internet and politics in urban China
(percentage, 2003) 116

5.5 Public opinions on corruption in China (multiple
choice, percentage) 120

6.1 Popular concerns about the SARS in five Chinese cities on
May 24, 2003 (percentage) 159

6.2 "Were you aware of the SARS before such news became available
in official news media?" (percentage) 160

6.3 "What do you think of the performance of the central
government in battling the SARS?" (percentage) 162

6.4 "Has your confidence toward the government increased
or decreased after the SARS event?" (percentage) 163

FIGURES

2.1 Number of computer hosts in China 31

2.2 Growth of Internet users in China 32

2.3 Number of domains registered under CN,
October 1997–January 2004 33

2.4 Internet users by occupation, January 2004 33

2.5 Use of the Internet at work among business elites 34

2.6 Use of the Internet at home among business elites 34

2.7 "I am proficient in using the Internet" 35

2.8 Regional allocation of Internet users,
October 1997–January 2002 39

2.9 Location of Internet access, January 2004 39

2.10 Monthly income of Internet users in China,
January 2004 40

3.1 Party and state organizations responsible for the media
(central level) 55

3.2 Party and state organizations responsible for the Internet
(central level) 58

3.3 Internet arrests in China 67

5.1 "Using the Internet will enable people to work
more efficiently" 110

5.2 "The Internet keeps me up to date with
world developments" 111

5.3 "Using the Internet will invade one's privacy" 112

5.4 "Using the Internet will enable one to befriend
bad company" 112

5.5 "Using the Internet will subject one to bad influence" 113

5.6 The level of trust of the Internet 113

5.7 The Internet and interpersonal interaction in
China, 2003 114

5.8 "The Internet is a good way to keep in touch
with people" 115

5.9 "Do you think by using the Internet people like you
can better understand politics?" (all respondents,
18 and above), 2003 118

5.10 "Do you think by using the Internet people like you
can have more say about what the government
does?" (all respondents, 18 and above), 2003 119

5.11 Approval rate of the government's anti-corruption
performance 122

Preface

The rise of the Internet in China since the country was first "connected" in 1993 has been extraordinary. By mid-2006, the number of Chinese Internet users had reached 123 million, meaning that China now has more Internet users than any country but the United States. Over half of the Chinese Internet users have broadband. The number of Chinese using instant messaging systems has more than doubled in the past few years. By the end of 2005, Chinese blogs (online personal diaries) numbered more than 30 million, and search engines received over 360 million requests a day. The new information technology has also reached China's hinterland. Almost every county (and indeed many towns and villages) now has broadband. Internet cafés with high-speed connections are ubiquitous and cheap even in remote towns. Fixed-line Internet access is still uncommon in rural homes, but in many parts of the countryside, it is possible to surf the Internet at landline modem speeds using a mobile handset.

The development of the Internet in China has become an increasingly hot topic, not only in academic and policy circles, but also in business circles, especially in the United States. Never before has the rise of a new form of information technology stimulated such heated debates. It is not simply the speed of Internet development in China that is causing such consternation. Given the size of the Chinese population and the country's rapid economic growth, the use of the Internet and other forms of information technology will continue to increase. Central to all the debates related to the Internet are the potential sociopolitical consequences that this new technology could bring. It is widely believed that the development of the Internet is likely to have a great sociopolitical impact on authoritarian China.

From the very beginning, there have been high expectations of the Internet in China. Many have hoped that the Internet will facilitate political change and transform China not only into an open society but also into an open and democratic regime. But the reality lags far behind these expectations. The Internet has not been able to promote democratic development in China; instead, the new technology seems to have become an effective instrument of control for the Chinese Communist Party (CCP). Years ago, former U.S. president Bill Clinton described China's efforts to restrict the Internet as "sort of like trying to nail Jell-O to the wall." However, as China's Web-filtering technology has grown more sophisticated, many begin to doubt whether the Internet will ever be able to aid the democratization of China. At a U.S. congressional hearing in February 2006 on American companies involved in Internet business in China, a Republican congressman, Christopher Smith, said that the Internet there had become "a malicious tool, a cyber sledgehammer of repression."[1]

Some began to blame multinational firms that have facilitated Internet development in China, including Cisco, Google, Microsoft, and Yahoo! Some analysts suggest that China's sophisticated Internet infrastructure would not be possible without technology and equipment imported from U.S. and other foreign companies.

The Chinese government worries about the undesirable political consequences of the free flow of information. For decades, the government has ruthlessly suppressed any organized dissent inside China. It has also attempted to limit the activities of non-governmental organizations (NGOs). The government has now relaxed its control over NGOs in order to transfer to them certain functions that it used to perform itself. Chinese NGOs have grown steadily over the years. Yet, the significance of NGOs in China varies, depending on their nature and functions. In some areas, such as poverty reduction, charity, and environmental issues, NGOs are encouraged to play a greater role. But in other areas, such as religion, ethnicity, and human rights, the influence of NGOs is virtually absent. While NGOs are allowed and even encouraged to use information technology to perform their functions, their ability to criticize the government is extremely limited. They are expected to be a "helping hand" and nothing else.

While pessimists view the Internet in China as merely a tool for governmental control, optimists point out the almost unlimited potential of the technology to generate liberating effects. Chinese Internet users can always use newly developed technology to make government control less effective. Take blogs as an example. Blogs make the censors' work much more difficult, if not impossible. China's fast-growing population of blog users knows how to get past censorship by avoiding using taboo keywords, including those programmed into the Chinese version of MSN Spaces. As China's Internet companies engage in fierce competition to draw blog traffic to their portals, few checks seem to be made on who is writing them. A blog can easily and quickly be set up on a Chinese portal, and no one will ask for verifiable personal information.

Compared with more traditional media such as newspapers, television, and broadcasting, new information technology opens possibilities for Chinese users to communicate among themselves. The mobile phone, text and instant messaging, Windows Messenger (Microsoft's instant-messaging system), and QQ (a messaging service provided by a Chinese company, Tencent) have all helped people to form networks on a scale and with a speed that is beyond the government's ability to control.

The freedom of information associated with the Internet is also a reflection of contradictions between the market and politics. Due to various market factors, multinational firms and domestic firms alike have to cooperate with the Chinese government. But exactly for market reasons, firms have to "liberalize" the regulations and requirements set up by the government in order to be competitive in the market. For example, the Chinese government recently issued a regulation to limit phone-card sales. According to that regulation, sellers have to check buyers' ID cards. But the Chinese soon found that this regulation was extremely difficult to enforce. Limiting phone-card sales to just a few shops with the ability to process registration requirements would be a blow to mobile-phone companies and the huge number of private vendors who thrive on such business. Competition between the market and politics becomes intensive. The government can make frequent attempts to limit the functioning of the market, but the market tends to prevail over politics.

The government does control the Internet, but it also uses the technology to mobilize social support for its own cause. The pessimists seem to have focused excessively on the technical ability of the government to control the Internet. However, once the government uses the Internet for social mobilization, opportunities are created for other social forces to further their own causes, which are not necessarily in line with the government's. This can be exemplified by the rise of Internet nationalism. Because nationalism has become an increasingly important source of political legitimacy for the communist state, nationalist diatribes have a better chance of getting past the censors than other forms of political comment. But nationalism has also provided a convenient cover for experimenting with new forms of activism on the part of social forces. The power of instant messaging, for instance, became evident in April 2005, when it was used to organize anti-Japanese protests in several Chinese cities, including Beijing, Shanghai, Guangzhou, and Shenzhen.

In the buildup to the protests, Sina organized an online campaign aimed at demonstrating public opposition to Japan's bid for permanent membership of the United Nations Security Council. Some 20 million people submitted their names. In competing with Sina, Sohu also gathered more than 15 million names. These Internet-based nationalistic campaigns certainly provided strong support for the government's Japan policy. Nevertheless, the government soon found that it had to contain such nationalistic mobilizations because, once social forces were mobilized, they began to place high pressure on the government.

There are also many other cases in which the Internet was used by the government to mobilize social support. The government now desires to expose various forms of malfeasance, such as corruption and mine disasters. The shift to a more "people-centered" approach to governance has legitimated certain forms of exposure, which means that citizens can push those limits. The boundary between what is legitimate to expose and what is illegitimate to expose is always shifting, and this opens up possibilities for Internet activists to bring about political change. This is especially true when the government is divided. For instance, before the Sun Zhigang case, there were many internal discussions about changing the custody and repatriation regulations, but nothing changed until the case became known. Then those in favor of changing these regulations were able to prevail upon those who had resisted. Shifting issue and policy agendas have allowed reform to emerge in the interstices of the system. The Internet and other information technologies are certainly able to strengthen these tendencies.

Due to the Internet's fast-growing influence, even the party leadership now has to pay attention to the deluge of public comment. Eager to acquire some legitimacy but anxious to avoid democracy, the leadership is trying to appeal to populism via the Internet. Premier Wen Jiabao said during the National People's Congress in March 2006 that the government should listen extensively to views expressed on the Internet. With few other ways of assessing the public mood, the Internet is indeed a barometer, even though surveys suggest that users are hardly representative of the general population, being mainly young, highly educated, and male.

Both pessimists and optimists can find empirical evidence to support their arguments. In this study, I do not attempt to add more evidence to either the pessimistic view or the optimistic view. Information technology in general and the Internet in particular can stimulate certain types of political change but not others. For example, the Internet is more likely to promote what political science literature calls "political liberalization" than what is called "political democratization." Accordingly, certain types of Internet-facilitated challenges to the state are likely to facilitate political reform on the part of the government, but other types of challenges are likely to be repressed. At this stage, it is too early to say which actor, the state or society, will win the battle over the Internet. In the multiple Internet-mediated meeting grounds between the state and society, sometimes the state wins and sometimes society wins. Such a situation is likely to continue in China for the foreseeable future.

This study aims to provide a conceptual framework to assist our understanding of the political impact of the Internet in China. The Internet and related information technology are relatively new, and they have not been properly integrated into our theoretical considerations. Given its rapidly expanding influence on our daily life, the Internet must become a part of theoretical thinking on political changes in China. To conceptualize the role of the Internet in China's political life, I make the Internet a part of the literature of state-society relations. Such an approach will enable us to see the mutually transforming effects of the Internet when it comes to regulating relations between the state and society. The Internet is a new platform in which the state and society tend to interact increasingly frequently. The outcomes of the interactions between the state and society vary. Some interactions can create more power for both. In such cases, the relationship between the state and social forces can be mutually empowering. But other interactions vitiate the power of each side, and in these cases, the struggle is one marked not by mutual empowerment but by mutually exclusive goals.

To clarify the role of the Internet in mediating relations between the state and society, this study highlights three points. First, the state must be disaggregated. The state should not be mistakenly treated as a monolithic and unitary actor in interacting with society in Internet-mediated arenas. The state is composed of different blocks, such as key individual leaders, factions, bureaucracies, and levels of government. All these actors have different preferences and interests related to Internet development. Each actor might use the Internet for its own purpose. Complicated relationships among different actors of the state matter significantly when it comes to interactions between the state and society. Interest conflicts or power struggles within the state can create new opportunities for social forces to empower themselves and exercise their political influence on one hand or to lead the government to adopt a hard-line policy toward them on the other hand, depending on the nature of power maneuvers among different political forces within the state.

Second, society, like the state, must be disaggregated. There are different social forces with different Internet-related preferences and interests. In China's political context, social forces are not autonomous in pursuing their own development, because they depend on their relations with the government.

Some social forces are more autonomous and more politically influential than others, and some are more organized than others. For example, well-organized commercial forces are able to exercise more political influence over the government than less-organized workers and disorganized farmers. Accordingly, the political behavior and power capabilities of social forces in Internet-mediated public space vary. Even for the same social group, its political action and influence are contingent on the political weight that the government assigns it at a given time. For example, the power of workers and farmers was greatly weakened under the Jiang Zemin leadership when policy priorities were overwhelmingly given to newly rising social groups such as private entrepreneurs. But workers and farmers have become more influential under Hu Jintao because the leadership has attempted to implement its pro-people policy package. The complicated nature of the relations between social forces also complicates their relations with the government over Internet-mediated public space.

Third, the state and social forces are mutually transformative via their interactions in Internet-mediated public space. To overemphasize the Internet as a mere tool for the government's control over social forces demonstrates a misunderstanding of real-world power struggles between the state and social forces. The results of the engagement and disengagement of the state with social forces are tangible and even momentous, but outcomes rarely reflect the ultimate aims of either. Their interactions cumulatively reshape the state and social forces. The state might sometimes be able to impose its own version of political change onto social forces but not always. It might do so to some social forces but not others. More often than not, the state has to adjust itself in order to accommodate social forces. On the other hand, social forces might find that they need to adjust themselves in their interactions with the state. In all cases, the state and social forces are constantly transforming each other and it is in such interactions that the Internet plays its role in leading meaningful political change in China.

Acknowledgments

During my research and its writing up, I have benefited from many individuals and a number of organizations. To begin with, I thank my friend Wu Guoguang. Some initial ideas on this research project came from several discussions with him. I believe that he will see his influence on my thinking about the Internet in this book. Many of my ideas on state-society relations came from Atul Kohli, who taught me how to think about the state and society in developing countries like China during my years at Princeton. Lynn White taught me how to bring the effects of diverse social forces into our thinking on China's political development. I benefited tremendously from Wang Gungwu, particularly from his wisdom on technological progress and political change. John Wong often shared with me his insights on the impact of new information technology, such as the Internet, on socioeconomic development. Elizabeth Wright and Richard Pascoe shared their journalistic experience in China with me and provided me with a unique perspective on information technology as a source of political change. Cao Cong helped me to understand how the Chinese scientific mind-set influenced the leadership's science and technology policy. Liang Roubing, Lye Liang Fook, and Zhao Kai provided excellent assistance in different stages of this work. Thanks also go to Muriel Bell, Kirsten Oster, and Judith Hibbard at Stanford University Press. They guided me through the prolonged process of reviewing, editing, and production. Special thanks go to Yang Lijun, who has provided the strongest moral and intellectual support and companionship. For any remaining faults and errors in this study, I must assume sole responsibility.

This research was conducted at the East Asian Institute, National University of Singapore, and the China Policy Institute, University of Nottingham.

xx Both institutes provided me with a productive research environment. I also would like to acknowledge a grant for research and writing from the John D. and Catherine T. MacArthur Foundation.

Portions of Chapters Two and Five appeared in "Information Technology, Public Space, and Collective Action in China," *Comparative Political Studies*, 38:5 (2005). I am grateful to Sage Publications for permission to use that material here.

My thirteen-year-old daughter Katherine and my eleven-year-old son Nevin asked me the other day about China's Great Firewall—a project by the Chinese government for Internet censorship. They learned about this from a popular book on the Internet. They wanted me to explain why the Chinese government needs to have this sort of project since it makes it difficult for people to get information from the Internet. They are too young to understand why people in China cannot express their political views freely on and get information freely from the Internet. I believe that when people as young as my children begin to ask this sort of question, there is hope that information technology will bring more freedom to China. This book is dedicated to the people growing up in the age of information.

Technological Empowerment

1

Politics of Technological Empowerment: Science vs. Democracy

Will progress in science and technology lead to political liberalization and even political democratization in China? While the linkages between science and modern world polity have lately become an important research agenda among social sciences scholars,[1] it is especially meaningful and significant to raise this question in the context of China's political development. The Chinese Communist Party (CCP) has long claimed ideological legitimacy based on scientific socialism. The CCP is indeed not much different from other main political forces in modern China, and they all believe in the linkages between scientific and technological development and political progress. Almost a century ago during the May Fourth Movement, Chinese intellectual elites expected that only "Mr. Science" (*sai xiansheng*) and "Mr. Democracy" (*de xiansheng*) could rescue China from internal collapse and external imperialism.[2] During that movement, Chinese elites called for the establishment of a scientific and democratic "new culture" devoid of all relics of China's feudal past. That generation believed that China's core *traditional* and *unscientific* values should be totally repudiated because they were symbols and sources of the country's backwardness and weaknesses. On the other hand, the movement's followers also genuinely believed that Mr. Science and Mr. Democracy should be wholly accepted because they represented rationality, modernity, and progress.[3]

The idea of the linkages between Mr. Science and Mr. Democracy came from American philosopher John Dewey, who visited China at the beginning of the twentieth century and delivered some far-reaching lectures on pragmatism and democracy.[4] During the May Fourth Movement, Dewey's followers

2   in China, led by his student Hu Shih, attempted to put his pragmatism into political practice in their quest for democracy.[5] According to Dewey, science and democracy were inseparable values. The spread of scientific intelligence would lead men to analyze and deal efficiently with their collective problems in the real world and even to reconcile their clashing interests.[6]

Needless to say, Chinese political elites did not understand the values of science and democracy in the way Dewey did. For the latter, both science and democracy were powerful tools for human beings to use in pursuing truth. But for Chinese elites, they could be effective tools to pursue power and wealth. It is not so difficult to understand why both science and democracy became important parts of modern Chinese nationalism. They would be pursued as long as they enabled China to achieve the status of "rich nation, strong army" — the core of modern Chinese nationalism.

Mr. Science and Mr. Democracy were soon differentiated from each other due to their different roles in helping Chinese political elites in pursuing power and wealth. The radicalization of the discourse on Mr. Democracy during the May Fourth Movement soon led to the belief in populism and proletarian dictatorship, which later became the core of the ideology of the CCP.[7] In their struggle for a modern nation-state, Chinese political elites, be they nationalists or communists, gradually renounced Western liberalism and turned to nationalism for help. The fate of Mr. Science is rather different. Despite the controversies within the May Fourth Movement, all parts of the movement seemed to have established a semi-religious belief that science and technology must be an integral part of China's nation-state building. This is particularly reflected in the CCP's efforts in linking "scientism" to "socialism" to establish the so-called "scientific socialism" (kexue shehui zhuyi) as the backbone of its ideology. By bringing them together, the Chinese leadership has attempted to justify the scientific nature or rationality of the political course of socialism that the CCP has pursued.

Fortunately, the spirit of Mr. Democracy seems to have survived decades of communist rule. On the eve of the People's Movement on the Tiananmen Square in spring 1989, a new "May Fourth Movement" suddenly arose within China. Chinese intellectual communities as well as reformist political leaders published enormous essays on the legacies of the May Fourth spirit, challenging the monopoly of power by the CCP.[8] Among others, one major theme of the 1989 enlightenment movement was the appeal to the young generation of Chinese intellectuals to strive for liberty, democracy, and science by inheriting the May Fourth spirit.[9]

Interestingly, the Chinese scientific community played a far more important role in initiating the new May Fourth Movement. This was reflected in the fact that scientists such as Fang Lizhi, Wen Yuankai, and Xu Liangying were the key leaders of this movement. This community ardently believed that progress in science and technology would not be possible without political democracy. In their search for intellectual freedom, they found that the first priority is to advocate political liberalization and democratization.[10]

With the dawn of information technology, the century-old question related to science and democracy is as relevant to China today as before. On the side of Mr. Science, the Chinese government has not had much difficulty in embracing the age of information technology. Indeed, the development of information technology has been regarded as an important project of nation-state building. With the diffusion of science and technology, China as a nation-state is continually reshaped by the global expectation of what a nation-state ought to be. Standardization and rationalization have been main themes in the restructuring of state political and economic organizations since the reform and open door policy of the late 1970s. An obvious example is the restructuring of the state bureaucratic system, financial and taxation systems, and a modern system of corporate governance.[11] The political legitimacy and authority of the current regime has increasingly been justified in scientific terms, and scientific management has permeated virtually every corner of the political domain. It is safe to argue that the scientific mind-set has become prevalent among a new generation of technocrats that has come to dominate the Chinese political scene since the late 1980s. This mind-set is particularly reflected in the new policy agenda of the so-called scientific development set up by the Hu Jintao–Wen Jiabao leadership since the early 2000s.[12]

Despite the apparent impact of the world scientific culture on the Chinese polity, China seems to have emerged unscathed from the expanding world democratic culture. Scholars have observed a general cultural model in many countries; that is, with the spread of modern and democratic political arrangements worldwide, science has gone right along.[13] The spread of science and technology in China seems to have empowered the nation-state and its organizations but not individuals. This has cast doubts on the impact of progress in science and technology on political changes and democratization in China. Some scholars tend to believe that scientific and technological developments are tools for certain political groups to preserve and advance their interests and thus are instrumental only in nature.[14]

Nevertheless, the issue is not all that simple. Progress in information technology has also empowered social forces in their interaction with the state. Both the state and society can use information technology in their favor. In the contemporary world, there have been cases in which less organized social groups and disorganized underclasses succeeded in bringing about collective

4   actions that challenged the power of organized interests, especially the state. In these cases, information technology enables marginalized groups to overcome resource limitations and other, more serious barriers to gain political power. The successful overthrow of the Suharto government in Indonesia is a dramatic and clear-cut case.[15] Another example is the "Zapatista Effect" in Mexico. Since 1994, revolutionaries opposing the Mexican government in the state of Chiapas have benefited substantially from the decentralized, inexpensive, and self-organizing nature of communication facilitated through new information technology. Such a trend has also developed in China. While the communist regime still exercises tight control over information technology, especially the Internet, social forces have organized successful collective actions to expand their political influence. The question is how the political impact of scientific and technological progress can be explained.

TECHNOLOGY AND POLITICS IN SOCIAL SCIENCES

The impact of scientific and technological progress on politics is generally regarded as underestimated and undertheorized in the social sciences.[16] This is especially true in the studies of Chinese politics. Although China scholars have identified the claim by the CCP of "scientific socialism" as the core of its political legitimacy, they have treated scientific development and socialism as two separate research areas. There is an enormous body of literature on China's progress in science and technology.[17] The same is true of literature on the development of socialism in China.[18] To a great degree, in the existing literature of China studies, the impact of scientific and technological progress on China's political development has been unduly underestimated. This is inevitable somehow because there is no essential linkage between "scientism" and "socialism" in the tradition of intellectual exploration. The rationale to bring the two together in China has been political.

Several bodies of literature in social sciences in general and China studies in particular are relevant to this study on technology and politics. First, the impact of information technology on political liberalization and democratization must be examined in terms of the changing relations between the state and society. Therefore, the growing body of literature on state-society relations in post-Mao China becomes relevant here.[19] Nevertheless, the linkages between information technology and political changes are not the focus of this body of literature. Some scholars have paid attention to how the Chinese scientific community, as a powerful interest group, has played an important role in facilitating changes in the relationship between the state and society and how key leaders in this community use their networks with the top leadership to have their "scientific" inputs in making important decisions for China.[20]

This body of literature is useful in explaining how the scientific community has been able to persuade the leadership to accept a "scientific" approach to development and why the leadership has placed so much emphasis on scientific and technological development in post-Mao China. However, to say that the scientific community is becoming increasingly significant politically does not tell us how science and technology have actually affected the interaction between the state and society in China. The impact of scientific and technological progress on political changes cannot be too narrowly defined. The scientific community has obviously played an important role in facilitating political changes in China. But this approach is not able to show how other social forces or communities can make use of scientific and technological development to make their inputs in politics. The political impact of science and technology goes far beyond the realm of the scientific community.

A second relevant body of literature is that of the so-called technocracy movement. *Technocracy* refers to a system of governance in which technically trained experts rule by virtue of their specialized knowledge and positions in dominant political and economic institutions.[21] The rise of technocracy as a system of governance is believed to be a result of the complex nature of modern political systems and governance.[22] In the vein of Max Weber, scholars have argued that contemporary politics are shaped by two groups of elites—namely, technically trained career administrators and professional party politicians—and different skills are required for each role. So, by definition, technocrats are technically trained elites who are selected into power, in contrast to politicians, who are elected. The recruitment and promotion of technocratic elites are determined by universalistic, impersonal, and achievement-oriented standards. Needless to say, technocrats are believed to be able to employ their scientific knowledge and technical methods to solve socioeconomic problems. Their scientific approach to social problems is unique, speaks the language of science, and recognizes no authority but the facts. Therefore, technocrats are more interested in technical matters than political issues, and they concern themselves more with tasks than power.[23]

Similarly, China scholars have focused on how the mind-set of scientific management has affected China's elite politics, that is, how the reform policy has led to the rise of the movement of technocracy.[24] Technocracy rather than democracy became acceptable for China's leaders in the post-Mao era due to its virtues. First of all, technocracy is a political system in which an educated elite rules. Such a system is in accordance with China's Confucian political tradition. For more than two thousand years, education served as the main social ladder to success in China. Certainly, by adopting a system of technocracy, the Chinese leadership tends to readily establish a natural base of political legitimacy. Second, to accept the technocratic governance is to react to the

6   Maoist elite recruitment policy. One major theme in Maoist China was the conflict between "red" and "expert." Mao initiated waves of campaigns against intellectuals and professionals in the first three decades of the People's Republic of China, particularly during the Cultural Revolution (1967–1977). This elite recruitment policy was reversed after Deng Xiaoping came to power. The leadership began to appreciate the role of the "expert" and downplayed that of the "red." To promote the country's economic development, the "expert" had to be placed at the center of the political system. Third, the need to reduce the role of ideology in policy making also required technocracy. With generational changes in the leadership, the basis of authority needed to be redefined. The old revolutionaries could use their charisma and ideology to incite mass mobilization, but the new leaders did not have such powerful resources and had to turn to more secular and pragmatic forms of political authority. For technocrats, ideology cannot be taken as a dogma that provides specific and infallible solutions to immediate political and economic issues. Because of their pragmatism, technocrats are able to overcome difficulties to reach a consensus. They can "evaluate even political decisions in terms of actual outcome rather than ideological value. In developing a range of policy options — each of which carries different costs, benefits, and feasibility — this way of thinking inclines the bureaucratic technocrats toward compromise and bargaining."[25]

Scholars have found that the technocratic movement has a deep impact on Chinese elite politics, such as in developing scientific approaches to decision making and establishing a scientific policy of elite recruitment and scientific management of party cadre and government officials.[26] Other scholars have also tried to spell out the impact of the technocratic movement on state–society relations. They have found that the technocratic leadership is more pragmatic in embracing capitalism and newly rising social forces. This is so because technocrats are able to share an ideology of modernization, an aversion to politics, a belief in the free enterprise system, and a commitment to development. For technocratic leaders, political reforms and democratization are instrumental, and as long as they can improve and enhance the legitimacy of the regime, they are acceptable.[27]

Like the literature on the scientific community as an interest group, this body of literature on scientific mind-set helps explain why the Chinese leadership has given the highest priority to scientific and technological development and how such a mind-set has facilitated changes in elite politics. This body of literature, however, has two main weaknesses in exploring the linkages between scientific development and political changes in China. First, the literature does not pay sufficient attention to how technological progress has affected the interaction between the state and society as a whole — not only the scientific community. Second, the technocratic leadership is not disaggregated. While technocratic leaders can reach consensus in their problem-solving based on their scientific knowledge, they have different political interests, which often motivate them to adopt different approaches to problem-solving. Take Zhao Ziyang and Li Peng for example. Both were regarded as technocrats, but they had different approaches to engaging the reforms in the 1980s and eventually adopted different approaches to the pro-democracy movement in 1989. While it would be questionable whether Zhao and Li had different ideological orientations, it is safe to say that their political interests differed. Different political interests matter in explaining political changes in China.

While the approach of the scientific community as an interest group enables us to look at how this community has affected political changes from below, the technocratic approach helps us to explore how the scientific mind-set has provided a dynamic of political change from above. Nonetheless, neither of the approaches is able to show us how the state and society interact over the new political realms that modern information technology has created and how their interaction has affected political changes in China.

The most relevant body of literature is media studies in general and China's media reforms in particular. As will be discussed in later chapters, scholars in media studies have put much emphasis on how the development of new information technology can provide new channels for political participation from below and thus affect political changes. This is a main theme for scholars who have worked on civic engagement in advanced Western democracies. Nonetheless, their studies are helpful in our reflections on media politics in China.

Media reform has also been a focus among China scholars. Since the reform and open door policy, quite substantial changes have occurred in China's media. On the part of the media, it has long faced increasingly greater pressure from marketization and commercialization and thus has to operate based on market principles. On the part of the regime, the CCP has to reform its media policies in order to cope with changing socioeconomic circumstances and to satisfy social demands on information. Scholars have looked at how the media reform from above and media commercialization from below will affect China's political changes. Voluminous works have been published, but no consensus has been reached among scholars on the political impact of the media reform. While many have argued that the media reform is only to strengthen, not to weaken, the CCP, others see that such reforms could lead to political liberalization.[28] This body of literature covers a wide range of media, including print (newspaper, magazines, and books), broadcasting, and television. The focus of most scholars in this school is on more traditional forms of media technology such as print, broadcasting, and television and less on the latest information

8   technology, namely the Internet. Given the fact that the Internet has drastically distinguished itself from all traditional forms of media technology, we have to go beyond the existing media studies to examine in detail how the Internet as a new form of information technology has affected political development in China. Furthermore, scholars on media reforms in China have put much emphasis on how different media communities have interacted with the state, and the issue of how information technology per se can affect the interaction between the state and society is not given much attention.

Different forms of information technology affect politics in different ways. In this study, I attempt to explore how the Internet affects political development in China. I shall show how the Internet distinguishes itself from traditional media such as television, broadcasting, and print. By doing so, I shall be able to demonstrate how the Internet as a form of information technology per se can have an important impact on politics. The next task is to explore how the Internet affects political actors — that is, the state and society — and the relationship between the two. In other words, this study attempts to examine the impact of the Internet on state-society relations from three dimensions: 1) how the Internet affects the state, 2) how it affects society, and 3) how it affects the interaction between the state and society.

THE INTERNET IN THE CONTEXT OF STATE-SOCIETY RELATIONS

As briefly discussed above, China scholars have actually attempted to explore the political impact of the Internet in the context of state-society relations. Nevertheless, these studies hardly examine how the Internet has introduced changes into state-society relations, and their focus is on how the state or society is affected by the Internet.

First of all, there is the argument of the empowerment of the state by the Internet. Scholars have drawn ideas from Lawrence Lessig, James Boyle, and others who have applied Michel Foucault's analysis of formal and informal forms of coercion to show how the Internet can empower the state.

Lessig argued that governments anywhere can most certainly regulate the Internet, both by controlling its underlying code and by shaping the legal environment in which it operates.[29] According to him, the "code" — which is the combination of the four basic elements of regulations, social norms, the market, and the architecture of the Internet itself — can shape behavior in cyberspace. The code writers set up most Internet features, which can be used to constrain some behavior by making other behavior possible or impossible. Needless to say, there will always be ways to circumvent the constraints imposed by architecture. But what is important is the fact that effective control is possible only because complete control is not.[30] To find out how cyberspace is regulated, it is important to discover how the code regulates, who the code writers are, and who controls the code writers.[31] Apparently, any investigation into the nature of Internet control must extend to the ways in which governments are able to indirectly regulate the Internet by directly regulating intermediary actors like Internet service providers (ISPs) and Internet content providers (ICPs).[32]

Similarly, drawing on Foucault, Boyle argued that the government can build various "surveillance" techniques into the Internet and thus achieve effective censorship.[33] According to Foucault, the early modern state imposed control formally on its inhabitants from without and with a hard hand. It set strict controls on certain behaviors and threatened draconian punishments for their violation. By contrast, the modern state enlists its subjects as participants in their own governance. In this process, it shifts the locus of control internally. Although the state and civil society, public and private, are clearly distinguished from each other, in fact the two are more interpermeated than ever before. Citizens govern themselves not just in terms of suffrage and political control but also in terms of their own moral, instinctual, and emotional economy, limiting their actions before the fact and moderating their impulses. Thus the harshness of the early modern state is rendered unnecessary. The modern state no longer instructs, commends, and punishes. It educates, informs, persuades, and discourages.[34]

Following this logic, some scholars have argued that the Internet is likely to consolidate China's authoritarian regime rather than undermine it. In their study, Shanthi Kalathil and Taylor Boas conclude that "the authoritarian state is hardly obsolete in the era of the Internet."[35] This is so because the authoritarian state plays a crucial role in charting the development of the Internet and in conditioning the ways it is used by societal, economic, and political actors. The very fact that the Chinese state acts as a designer of Internet development makes it less likely that non-state actors will exert political impact because Internet users "may back away from politically sensitive material on the web, and entrepreneurs may find it more profitable to cooperate with authorities than to challenge their censorship policies."[36] A similar conclusion is reached by Gudrun Wacker in a study of Internet censorship in China.[37] In Wacker's case, the CCP is apparently believed to be able to employ both what Foucault called "formal" and "informal" means to control the political effect of the Internet. All these early arguments seem to have been confirmed by a recent empirical study by the OpenNet Initiative (a collaboration between Harvard Law School, University of Toronto Citizen Lab, and Cambridge Security Program). According to the report generated by that study, "China's Internet filtering regime is the most sophisticated effort of its kind in the world."[38]

10   There is also the argument of the empowerment of society by the Internet. Policy makers in the West like U.S. President George W. Bush and former president Bill Clinton believe that the Internet will bring freedom and democracy to China because, by giving rise to civil organizations, the Internet tends to undermine the very infrastructure on which the CCP regime is founded. It is believed that technology can frustrate censorship and central control and that instant communications spread the truth, the news, and courage across borders.[39] Such a belief also appears in many scholarly writings. One popular argument is that the Internet will reduce the influence of the CCP over the ideational and organizational monopoly.[40] After surveying major Web sites created by Chinese dissidents, Michael S. Chase and James C. Mulvenon contended that despite the counterstrategies by the Chinese state, dissidents both in and outside China have made extensive use of the Internet in voicing dissent.[41] Similarly, while recognizing the existing tightened political control over the Internet, Eric Harwit and Duncan Clark pointed to the potential for independent group formation via newly available information technology.[42] Empirical evidence also supports the argument of the empowerment of society by the Internet. For example, based on his empirical study, Guobin Yang found that the Internet empowers civil society in China by different means. First, the social uses of the Internet have fostered public debate and problem circulation. The Internet has demonstrated the potential to play a supervisory role in Chinese politics. Second, the Internet has shaped social organizations by expanding old principles of association, facilitating the activities of existing organizations, and creating a new associational form — the virtual community. And third, the Internet has introduced new elements into the dynamics of protest.[43]

Without a doubt, scholars in both camps (empowering the state vs. empowering society) have their own logic and have found empirical data to support it. Two factors that have led to such different views can be identified. First, the Internet has empowered the state but not society in some areas; but in other areas, it has empowered society but not the state. Second, in some areas, the Internet can empower both the state and society.

These two factors have been greatly underestimated by scholars in both camps. The Internet is not only a tool that can be used by both the state and society in their interaction. More importantly, the Internet is a new and unexplored political realm where both the state and society try to expand their own political space. In doing so, the game between the two actors is not always a zero-sum one. One major problem for scholars in both camps is that inherent in their argument is an implicit assumption that Internet development is a zero-sum game between the state and society.

This study argues that Internet development is mutually empowering and 11 transforming between the state and society when some conditions are present. My initial findings are fourfold. First, the Internet empowers both the state and society because both benefit from Internet development. While the state can use the Internet to improve its governance, an improved governance system also benefits society. Second, Internet development has had effects of decentralization; namely, its benefits are distributed in a decentralized way. Despite the existence of a digital divide, Internet development benefits not only middle and upper classes but also lower-middle classes in their efforts to improve their economic and social well-being. Third, the Internet has created a new infrastructure for the state and society in their engagement with (and disengagement from) each other. It is a new forum for conducting politics. Compared with other settings, the Internet is more likely to exert a constraint on the state. Fourth, the Internet produces a recursive relationship between the state and society, mutually transforming interactions between the two. In other words, the interactions between the state and society over the Internet end up reshaping both the state and society. Consequently, in China, while it is too early to tell whether the Internet can lead to democratization, it has played an important role in facilitating political liberalization in different aspects such as political openness, transparency, and accountability. Such political liberalization also benefits both the state and society.

A mutually empowering and transforming argument requires us to reconsider state-society relations. For many years, scholars treated the state and society as a dichotomy.[44] The state was regarded as a critical agent of socioeconomic transformation. A condition of strong states and weak societies was believed to facilitate socioeconomic transformation, and that of strong societies and weak states was thought to pose a severe structural barrier for such a transformation.[45] In the state-centered literature, the state is regarded as a unitary actor that assesses its situation strategically and then acts accordingly to maximize its interests. Furthermore, the strength of the state is often equated with its autonomy from society and with its ability to ignore other social actors or to impose its will on society. The state-centered theory had an impact on policy makers and scholars in developing countries like China. Apparently, it greatly influenced a Chinese version of statism.[46] Frequently, for political elites in the third world, it is a simple solution to centralize all powers in order to engage in socioeconomic changes, even though centralization might not be an effective solution.

In the recent decade, scholars have revised their earlier argument. They found that in the real world, states are seldom the only central actors in societies and are almost never autonomous from social forces. In any political setting, some dimension of state power has more to do with the state's ability to work through and with other social actors, and a state's apparent disconnection from social groups turns out to be associated in many cases with weakness rather than strength. The state itself is a part of a given society, and it needs society to achieve its objectives. Increasingly, scholars have realized that when certain conditions are present, states and social forces can become mutually empowering, and interaction, not separation, between the state and social forces can have the effect of creating more power for both sides.[47]

State capacity is important in most developing countries where, more often than not, states are facing the tasks of socioeconomic transformation and political liberalization simultaneously. On one hand, rapid and sustained economic development requires a strong state capable of going beyond the shortsightedness of special interest groups with long-term developmental strategies. On the other hand, political development often requires and depends on the emergence of a robust sphere of civil associational life and the consolidation of social power in state organizations. Political reforms often entail weakening the power of the pre-existing state during a period when these states are promoting economic transformation and providing for effective governance.[48] Nevertheless, socioeconomic transformation and political liberalization are not necessarily in conflict with each other in certain circumstances. For instance, it is found that transition to democracy does not necessarily reduce the role of the state and weaken its capacity; instead, a capable state is an important condition in sustaining substantial democracy.[49] Joint efforts on the part of civil society and the state might offer the most efficient way of carrying out political reforms. Strong and robust civil associations can go hand in hand with powerful and resilient states.

While states have to engage with social forces in pursuing socioeconomic transformation, socioeconomic transformation often has the effect of mutual transformation of the state and society. Because states are parts of societies, during the process of interacting with each other, "states may help mold, but they are also continually molded by, the societies within which they are embedded. Societies affect states as much as, or possibly more than, states affect societies."[50]

I believe that the Internet provides such an arena for mutual empowering between the state and society to take place. It is also true that the degree of mutual empowering is rather different in different areas of state-society relations because the impact of the Internet varies in those different areas.

The argument of mutual empowering does not mean in any sense that there are no conflicting interests over the Internet between the state and society. Technological empowerment is also a form of politics between the state and society. There are areas in which the state and society clash. As will be seen in later chapters, even in the areas with conflicting interests, who will win the game between the state and society is not a straightforward question. There are cases in which social groups lost their battles in challenging the state, but there are also cases in which social groups successfully challenged the state. In an Internet-mediated political setting, the interaction between the state and society often becomes recursive and leads to a mutual transformation.

To understand the nature of mutual empowering and transforming of the Internet, it is imperative to disaggregate the state and society. The Chinese state is hardly a fixed ideological entity or an undifferentiated, unitary, rational actor. The state consists of different components, including the top party and government leaders, different political factions, party organizations and bureaucratic bodies in the capital city, and their counterparts at different levels of government (i.e., province, city, county, and township).[51] The various components of the state have different interests and identities over different policy areas, including the Internet. So does the Chinese society. Like elsewhere, the Chinese society consists of different social groups with different interests and identities. The role of the Internet in facilitating political changes hinges on the numerous junctures between diffuse parts of the state and social groups. The interactions between various components of the state and those of society often lead to unanticipated patterns of empowering and transforming.

Because the relationship between the state and society is characterized by recursiveness, interactive strategies matter in deciding the empowering effect of the Internet. Scholars have so far largely ignored such interactive strategies used by various components of the state and key social groups in their interaction over Internet-mediated public space. I will show that whether a given challenge can succeed depends not only on the areas in which the state and society interact but also on the strategies these actors employ in engaging with each other.

THE ORGANIZATION

The book is divided into seven chapters. Following this introduction, Chapters Two and Three focus on the Internet and the state. In these two chapters, I attempt to answer two important questions: 1) why has the Chinese leadership made even greater efforts to promote the development of information

14   technology, and 2) how has the leadership coped with unexpected political consequences resulting from the development of information technology?

Chapter Two examines the development of information technology in the context of nation-state building in China. As discussed in the context of Mr. Science and Mr. Democracy, science and technology have been an integral part of China's state building in modern times. Scientific and technological development was the cornerstone of Chinese nationalism, and "technonationalism" has been a main theme in China's nation-state building throughout the modern age. After the People's Republic was established in 1949, science and technology became even more significant politically. Without Mr. Democracy, the CCP has to rely on science and technology to promote rapid economic development. The regime's economic performance becomes the most important source of its political legitimacy. It is in this context that the post-Deng CCP leadership has given the highest priority to the development of information technology. A neo-technonationalism came into being so that globalization could be accommodated.

However, the rapid development of information technology as the infrastructure of the modern Chinese state has had unexpected political consequences. While nation-state building has generated social grievances, the Internet has served as an effective tool for social groups to voice their grievances. Therefore, the rise of Internet-mediated social protests and collective actions has been associated closely with the rapid development of information technology.

How has the Chinese leadership promoted a rapid development of information technology while coping with its unexpected political consequences? This is the question Chapter Three attempts to answer. The CCP leadership has made great efforts to establish a regulatory regime to facilitate development on one hand and to set up control mechanisms to cope with its political consequences on the other. In today's world, regulation of the Internet is an important issue facing all governments, be they liberal, democratic, or authoritarian. No government would deny the need to regulate certain aspects of electronic communication in order to protect state sovereignty. Needless to say, the CCP government has made great efforts in establishing such a regulatory regime to govern the Internet. But more importantly, the CCP government has also exercised political control over the Internet. China has thus developed two Internet regimes: the regulatory regime and the political control regime. The fact that both are established by the CCP state does not imply that there is no conflicting interest between the two regimes. An examination of the two regimes and the conflicts between them will enable us to see how the tensions between information technology and political control have developed.

Chapter Four explores how the Internet can lead to political changes rang-ing from political liberalization to political democratization. Whether the Internet can promote political changes in China depends on how "political changes" is defined. In this chapter, I distinguish two key concepts, liberaliza-tion and democratization, and show that although the Internet has not been able to lead to democratization in China, it has greatly promoted political lib-eralization by empowering social groups in organizing collective action and creating opportunities for reformist leaders to form an implicit coalition with civil society. This chapter examines how the Internet, as a new form of infor-mation technology, has made it possible for social groups to initiate collective action and challenge unjustified policy practices on the part of the state. It also highlights some positive linkages between the state and society and thus shows the mutually empowering and transforming effects of the Internet.

Chapters Five and Six focus on the Internet and society. Chapter Five examines Internet-based civic engagement. In Chapter Four, I examine posi-tive, or mutually empowering, linkages between the state and society, but in Chapter Five, I focus on some negative linkages between the two, namely, that the Internet might empower society but not the state in some political realms. I demonstrate that while the Internet has greatly promoted civil engagement, it has had a destructive impact on popular confidence in public institutions and the state. The decline of popular confidence poses a serious challenge for the state. Nevertheless, such a challenge is not necessarily detrimental to the state. It can create great political pressure for the regime, and the regime can make use of the challenge to improve its governance.

Chapter Six focuses on the strategic interaction between the state and so-ciety over Internet-based public space. We have witnessed successful cases of Internet-mediated collective action, but we have also seen failed ones. How to explain their success or failure? I argue that interaction strategies matter. Whether the Internet empowers social groups to organize successful collective actions in challenging the state depends on the interaction strategies between the state and society. This chapter examines how interaction strategies affect the results. I show that the best result of collective action can be achieved when an implicit coalition forms between various components of the state and those of society, while the worst result occurs when a given collective action is perceived by the regime as a whole as threatening to its survival.

In concluding, Chapter Seven summarizes the major findings of this study. The chapter attempts to provide an overview of the linkages between scien-tific and technological development and political changes in contemporary China. The emphasis is on the nature of the mutual transformation of the In-ternet. This chapter shows that it is not the Internet per se (or any other form of

16   information technology) but the interactions between various components of the state and society over the Internet-mediated public space that have created the dynamic of political changes in China. Socioeconomic forces are main actors in promoting political changes. Employed by these socioeconomic forces, the Internet is a powerful resource in leading to the transformation of the Chinese state. In this chapter, I first identify some main scenarios of regime changes in China and then examine what role the Internet can play in each of these scenarios.

Information technology is part of nation-state building efforts on the part of the Chinese leadership. Information technology promotes nation-state building on one hand and creates opportunities for new types of collective action that challenge the state on the other hand. In this sense, the Internet provides a new platform where the state and society compete for power. The Internet empowers both the state and society in some realms, while in other realms, it empowers one actor but not the other. Furthermore, information technology, especially the Internet, is an effective tool for both the state and society. For social groups, it is a tool to organize collective action; for the state, it is a tool to regulate and control Internet behavior on the part of society. The interaction between the state and society over Internet-based public space has transformed both actors and provided the dynamics for political changes in China.

2

INFORMATION TECHNOLOGY, NATION-STATE
BUILDING, AND SOCIAL MOVEMENT

INFORMATION TECHNOLOGY AND NATION-STATE BUILDING

This chapter examines the development of information technology in the context of nation-state building in China. The development of science and technology is an integral part of the modern Chinese state. I attempt to highlight two major aspects of nation-state building. First, the development of science and technology has long been embedded in the mind-set of the Chinese elite regarding nation-state building. In other words, it is a way of thinking among Chinese elites on how a modern nation-state should be built. For Chinese elites, science and technology are instrumental and are tools for China to become a strong and modern nation-state. Second, policies and practices related to nation-state building more often than not provide opportunities for the rise of social movements. This is especially true in the case of the latest form of information technology, namely, the Internet.

How can the impact of information technology on nation-states be explained? In answering this question, some scholars often cite events such as the August 1991 uprising against the Soviet Union. During that event, university faculty members in Moscow used email to inform and update the global community, circumventing Soviet censorship. Domestic forces, together with external ones, thus were able to exert an influence on Boris Yeltsin and help bring about a peaceful conclusion to the political drama. Needless to say, one also can refer to the Falun Gong (FLG) event in China and the overthrow of the Suharto government in Indonesia. In all these cases, scientific activities and linkages, such as the availability of academic email, shaped political events and led to political changes and the transformation of nation-states

18   from authoritarianism to democracy. Nevertheless, according to Drori et al., such an interpretation of the link between science and political openness is too narrow because it connects the specific actions of scientists to political events rather than emphasizing the general and cultural influence of science on local politics.[1]

According to Drori et al., "science, as the authoritative voice of modern thinking, codifies rational thinking and rational order."[2] In other words, "science provides the cultural scripts for nation-states to act on or support action. . . . Nation-states are obliged by their role as actors/agents to move toward the achievement of social goals. In their search for successful paths to achieve these goals, they rely on the available cultural scripts."[3]

As will be discussed later, what Drori et al. called "cultural scripts" have actually been reflected in the mind-set of Chinese political elites in their efforts to build a modern Chinese nation-state. Cultural scripts helped Chinese elites acquire knowledge on what a modern nation-state should look like. An obvious example is that their efforts in nation-state building are based on their perceptions of successful models of nation-states. In this regard, science and technology helped them in rationalizing and standardizing the frame of the Chinese nation-state.

Such a mind-set of science and technology has guided the Chinese leadership in developing information technology, especially the Internet. In post-Mao China, the development of information technology becomes particularly meaningful for China's nation-state building. Information technology is not only perceived as the most modern indicator of scientific and technological progress but also as a symbol of the modernity of the Chinese state. More importantly, it is also perceived as one of the core pillars of sustainable economic growth, which has been the foundation of the "political" legitimacy of the ruling party (CCP). By resisting Mr. Democracy, the leadership has to turn to Mr. Science for its legitimacy. This explains why the leadership has placed so much emphasis on the development of information technology.

"SCIENTIFIC" MIND-SET AND TECHNONATIONALISM IN MODERN CHINA

When discussions include the modern state, they usually refer to the state that originated in the West and then spread to the rest of the world. It is almost impossible to talk about the state in developing countries without referring to the modern Western state. As French scholar Bertrand Badie argued, globalization is a process of the westernization of the political order — "the establishment of an international system tending toward unification of its rules, values, and objectives, while claiming to integrate within its center the whole humanity."[4] Therefore, before I discuss how the Chinese leadership has made efforts to develop modern information technology, I shall take a brief look at how science and technology affected the choice that Chinese elites made in their efforts of nation-state building and how a "scientific" mind-set was formed throughout modern Chinese history.

The world system of modern nation-states was mainly shaped by the expansion of European states. The expansion of Europe led to the dismantling of older, non-European types of interstate connections. Some key features of the modern state system — the centralization of political power, the expansion of state administration, territorial rule, the diplomatic system, the emergence of regular, standing armies — became prevalent features of the global order. The main vehicle for this was, to begin with, the European states' capacity for overseas operations by means of military and naval forces capable of long-range navigation.[5]

Ever since the rise of modern nation-states in Europe, the rest of the world has had to follow the European model. With the spread of ideas on modern nation-states, nation-states became structurally similar in many unexpected dimensions and changed in unexpectedly similar ways. As John W. Meyer and his colleagues found, nation-states are theorized or imagined communities drawing on models that are lodged at the world level.[6] They further found that many features of the contemporary nation-state are derived from worldwide models constructed and propagated through cultural and associational processes. These models and the purposes they reflect are highly rationalized, articulated, and often surprisingly consensual. Worldwide models define and legitimate agendas for local action, shaping the structures and policies of nation-states and other national and local actors in virtually all of the domains of rationalized social life — business, politics, education, medicine, science, even the family and religion.[7]

So, as raised in the last chapter, the question is why Chinese elites in modern times have chosen to emphasize the technological aspect of the modern nation-state but not its democratic aspect. In other words, why and how did the scientific mind-set–based technonationalism develop and become dominant in guiding China's development in the modern era?

Before the arrival of the concept of the modern nation-state from the West, the Chinese Confucian state had existed for thousands of years. Despite the rise and fall of different dynasties, the basic political structure of this Confucian state remained intact. What brought down this Confucian imperial order during the course of the nineteenth century was the Western power, a new power based on superior science and technology, political and economic

20   organizations, and a revolutionary vision of indefinite progress. Against this power, mere Chineseness, however confident, was no match. It was the coming of this Western power that triggered a century-long process of nation-state building in China.

The development of the mind-set on science and technology is reflected in changing intellectual discourses on nation-state building since the middle of the Qing dynasty. When modern European nation-states came to China, Chinese intellectuals were shocked by the superiority of Western science and technology. While they tried to absorb such achievements into their culture, they still believed in the basic soundness of the foundation of their own traditional culture. The representative of this discourse is Zhang Zhitong (1837–1909), who advocated "Chinese learning for *ti* (substance, essence) and western learning for *yong* (function, utility)." But gradually, the Chinese intellectuals became thoroughly disappointed with their own tradition as they could not find anything valuable in it. They began to believe that tradition served only as a stumbling block to obstruct any move toward future progress, and the hope lay only in a quick and totalistic westernization process. The representative of this discourse is Hu Shih (1891–1962), who advocated wholesale westernization or wholehearted modernization. But the westernization project did not result in any positive fruits for Chinese nation-state building. Again, gradually, the Chinese intellectuals came to realize that the West was not all positive and that their own tradition was not all negative. The Western culture, as well as the modernization process, had its problems. Although many traditional habits of the heart had to be eradicated, some cultural insights deeply rooted in tradition needed to be reconstructed in such a way that they might make significant contributions in moving toward the future. A synthesis based on the realistic understanding of the problems of humanity and its environment had to be sought. The representative of this discourse may be said to be Mou Tsung-san (1909–1995), who advocated the revitalization and reconstruction of traditional Chinese philosophical insights.[8] Despite different discourses on nation-state building, modern Western science and technology occupied a unique place in all these discourses. Most Chinese intellectuals would agree that while it is debatable whether China should give up its own tradition, it is a must for China to learn Western science and technology in order to build a strong nation-state.

At the political front, the development was quite similar to the intellectual front. In facing the Western power, the Chinese political elite had to do something about the old form of the state in order to cope with and survive changing external and internal circumstances. In doing so, they faced enormous constraints. According to Karl Bunger, the Chinese rulers faced three choices: 1) to reform the institutions that had grown up in the course of Chinese history; 2) to copy the Western model; or 3) to develop China's own new institutions, drawing, where appropriate, on foreign examples.[9]

The first option no longer existed because the old order had not been able to counter the Western power. Once they realized their limitations, Chinese political elites began to make efforts to rebuild the state by learning from the West. Nevertheless, when Chinese leaders started to struggle to modernize China's political institutions in the late nineteenth century, they found that they had to give priority to military and technology modernization simply because the international system then was characterized by an age of imperialism. Among the European states and the United States, a nation's power was measured almost invariably in terms of its ability to wage war successfully. The intrusion of Western powers into East Asia shattered the traditional Chinese idea of a world order centered on the Middle Kingdom. Western powers brought the idea of the nation-state to China, but they were not prepared to recognize China as a sovereign state. Such an international system had a significant impact on China's choice of state-building alternatives. It seemed to the Chinese elite that only a modernized military force could prevent further intrusion of Western powers. They realized that if China were to gain respect abroad and protect itself, it had to first strengthen its armed forces. Military modernization was thus accorded the highest priority.

Like Japan, Chinese elites developed a mind-set of "rich nation and strong army" (*fuguo qiangbing*) in their interaction with the outside world.[10] Such a mind-set was reflected first in the "self-strengthening movement" of the 1870s and then the attempted reforms of 1898. All these reform efforts, despite ultimately failing, set the Chinese state on the paths of modern industrialization, military modernization, scientific inquiry, and Western educational reform. These reform movements were inspired by studying a combination of Japanese Meiji reforms, European industrial and military strategies, and American science and education.

Following the importation of various schools of Western ideas such as nationalism, liberalism, anarchism, and socialism, the Chinese intellectual-political elites became radicalized. By the early twentieth century, westernization had become a prevalent paradigm for China's state building. As Jacques Gernet correctly pointed out, "The [Chinese] imitation of western institutions was inspired simply by the desire to copy those things which led to the success of the West."[11] In this context, Japan was regarded by the Chinese, at the end of the nineteenth and the beginning of the twentieth century, as the most exemplary model. For the Chinese elite, if Japan had become a powerful state, this was because it had copied Western institutions.

22   The 1911 revolution was inspired by Western ideas; hence, the Republic was established after the revolution. After 1911, China undertook a series of attempts to import Western political institutions. As a matter of fact, as Karl Bunger pointed out, imitating and importing Western models of the state became a major theme of China's state building during the greater part of the twentieth century.[12] The various constitutions of a Western type bear witness to this. But all these efforts were without any success and did not help bring about a modern and strong China. Instead, the importation of Western state ideas led to China's rapid disintegration in the 1920s and 1930s in the form of warlordism.[13]

The failure of westernization projects led to the third option, that is, to devise China's own new institutions while learning from the outside world. It has been a long and difficult process, but it has become the most promising for the Chinese leadership. Following the radical May Fourth Movement was very serious criticism of modern Western ideas in the 1920s. Nevertheless, the mind-set on science and technology was apparently deeply rooted among Chinese elites. They disagreed with one another on what "ism" China should follow in its efforts of nation-state building, but they all agreed that only by learning from Western science and technology could China build a strong nation-state. The emphasis of the scientific foundation of a modern Chinese nation-state is explicitly reflected in the goal of achieving a "rich nation and strong army," which has been pursued by generations of the Chinese through-out the modern era. Despite their differences in political ideologies, all political forces, be they nationalists or communists, have placed their emphasis on the scientific foundation of a modern nation-state.

Such a scientific mind-set existed among elites in the Republican era. Great efforts were made in building institutions such as scientific societies (e.g., the Science Society of China and the Geological Research Institute) and universities. As early as 1924, Dr. Sun Yat-sen planned to establish a central scholarly academy in China. The Academic Sinica was founded in 1928, one year after the establishment of the nationalist government in Nanjing. Although Chiang Kai-shek, Sun's follower, was quite resistant to Western liberalism, his appreciation of science and technology should not be underestimated. Chiang attempted to redefine the Chinese state by combining Western science and technology with Chinese values.[14] For instance, the Peiping Academy was founded in 1929, a major step in the establishment of China's independent system of scientific research.[15] Such a scientific mind-set was also apparent in the New Life Movement that Chiang initiated in the 1930s. The movement was regarded as anti–Western liberalism, but Chiang actually attempted to establish and spread a scientific way of life in China.[16]

While the elite aspiration for a "rich nation and strong army" was frequently frustrated by civil war and foreign invasions, the victory of the communist revolution in 1949 led to a new stage of scientific and technological progress in China. The scientific mind-set is even more explicitly embedded in the CCP regime. Mao Zedong and his communist comrades built the People's Republic based on the Soviet model. The leadership rejected not only the Western components of democracy but also Chinese traditions, especially Confucianism. However, Mao Zedong redefined the Chinese state by accepting the so-called scientific socialism as the pillar of the communist system. What scholars have termed technonationalism actually guided the leadership in its efforts to build a new nation-state. This is the notion that "technology is fundamental to both national security and economic prosperity, that a nation's development policy must have explicit strategic underpinnings, and that technology must be indigenized at all costs and diffused system wide."[17] The new commitment to technological development by the new regime led to the rapid expansion of the higher education system and the building of an extensive network of research institutions in the early years of the People's Republic. Nevertheless, due to the unfriendly international environment, the regime tended to place an overwhelming emphasis on the strategic weapons programs.[18] It is worth noting that Mao even somewhat established a cult of science-technology. His religious belief in the relentless contribution of science and technology to social progress actually became the foundation of his rapidly implemented policies, which contributed to the disaster that followed the Great Leap Forward in the late 1950s and early 1960s.[19]

POLITICAL LEGITIMACY AND NEO-TECHNONATIONALISM
IN THE POST-MAO ERA

It is apparent that the Chinese elites have not changed much in their perceptions about a modern state; that is, a modern state should be able to pursue wealth and power in the most efficient way and to serve the needs of the people. They believe that a strong modern state can be built with advanced science and technology. In the post-Mao era, major efforts to promote scientific and technological development involved reforms of the system of research institutions, the revitalization of the higher education system, the expansion of enrollments in science and engineering fields, the sanctioning of institutional experimentation and innovation leading to the creation of new high-technology enterprises, and the introduction of a series of national programs for the support of research and development and of technology extension services.[20]

This is also the case of information technology. Scholars have found that the development of information technology under Mao was closely linked to China's nation-state building. For instance, Alan Liu examined China's efforts in developing information technology (at that time, broadcasting and TV) in

24   the context of national integration.[21] This policy orientation continues in post-Mao China. For the leadership, the development of information technology is still a means of moving toward a "rich nation and strong army."[22]

More importantly, in contemporary China, scientific and technological development becomes even more meaningful and significant politically. It is not only part of the leadership's continuous efforts in nation-state building but also a strong foundation of political legitimacy of the CCP and its state. This point deserves special attention because it explains why the post-Mao leadership has put so much emphasis on scientific and technological development as one of the pillars of the country's sustainable economic growth.

Max Weber long ago observed that power can be based on different sources such as individual charisma, traditions, and rational institutions, so the political legitimacy of the ruling elite varies.[23] For political leaders who are not able to rely on the old base of political legitimacy, it is vital to discover and explore new sources of legitimacy; otherwise, effective governance can hardly be established. Because the base of political legitimacy varies, leaders have to create new sources of political legitimacy in accordance with changing social and economic contexts. In other words, political legitimacy is dynamic: once a certain type of legitimacy is established, it will generate new challenges and thus exert pressure on political leaders to search for new sources of legitimacy.

Searching for a new base of political legitimacy has been a major driving force behind China's reform in the past decades. While various reform measures have been implemented in accordance with changing economic, social, and political circumstances, one major theme has stood out and remained unchanged — all reforms have to enable the CCP and its state to increase or strengthen their political legitimacy.

Even though Deng Xiaoping called the post-Mao reform and opening a second revolution, he did not intend the reform to undermine the Leninist state structure, let alone overthrow it. Instead, he meant that the old system needed to be reformed and new economic and political order be established so that China would be able to pursue economic development internally and international influence externally.[24]

When Deng took power in the late 1970s, he inherited a Leninist state from Mao Zedong. This state seemed to have been undermined seriously by waves of political movements during Mao's time, especially the Great Leap Forward and the Cultural Revolution. Politically, it was no longer able to provide a stable order for Chinese society, while in economic terms, it failed to deliver goods to the people. Not only social members but also party cadres and government officials lost their confidence in the state, and a crisis of state identity became deeply rooted in Chinese society in the aftermath of the Cultural Revolution.

How could the CCP government regain its legitimacy? One major approach was to engage in economic reform. The state introduced the agricultural reform first in the late 1970s and then the industrial reform in the early 1980s. These initial reforms soon met with success.[25] It is worth noting that the leadership under Deng overwhelmingly emphasized the importance of science and technology in facilitating the country's economic development. The scientific community became influential in decision making.[26]

In the mid-1980s, when it came to a new stage, China's economic reform encountered great difficulties. The reform was trapped in a vicious circle of centralization-decentralization-recentralization.[27] Resistance from vested interests was strong, and social dissatisfaction became apparent. To overcome the resistance and find new sources for political legitimacy, the leadership under Deng began to put much emphasis on political reform. Deng discussed on several occasions why political reform was important for China's ongoing economic reform. He indicated that political reform had to be democratization-oriented by stating that "without democracy, there would be no socialism."[28] It is hard to doubt the leadership's sincerity on the necessity of political reform. During the Thirteenth Congress of the CCP in 1987, political reform became a major agenda item for the leadership. In the following years, political leaders, especially Zhao Ziyang, devoted themselves to vigorous debates on what political reforms China should engage in and how they could be implemented.

Needless to say, China's political leaders perceived political reform differently. For Deng Xiaoping, to engage in political reform was to increase the country's productivity and efficiency. He often interpreted "democracy" in terms of economic decentralization and believed that decentralization would promote economic efficiency because party cadres and government officials would be able to make economic decisions scientifically and rationally. But Zhao Ziyang believed that, while economic decentralization was important, political reform should go far beyond economic decentralization. It should aim at introducing changes into China's political system.[29]

Regardless of how the leadership perceived political reform, one thing was certain: political reform was to be initiated from the top and managed by the leadership. The leadership somehow encouraged social groups to engage in heated debates about political reform, but it did not allow social discourse on political reform to become a public discourse, let alone to affect the leadership's decision making. Therefore, the leadership initiated waves of so-called anti-bourgeois campaigns, and eventually it cracked down on the pro-democracy movement in 1989.[30]

In the 1990s, when the Deng-centered second generation of leadership was passing away, the search for new sources of legitimacy became even more

26   important for the emerging leadership. While the second generation of leadership could base its political legitimacy on the revolutionary experience of individual leaders, the Jiang Zemin–centered third generation of leadership did not have such qualifications. Nevertheless, the third generation of leadership did not go beyond the development framework set forth by Deng. What happened inside and outside China still led the new leadership to opt to continue economic reform rather than turn to political reform.

First of all, the leadership perceived the 1989 pro-democracy movement as the outcome of loosening political control after the Thirteenth Party Congress in 1987. This perception led the leadership to tighten political control after the movement. In effect, the crackdown on the movement meant a failure of not only nascent democratic forces but also of democratic-oriented reform. This failure made the leadership unlikely to initiate any new political reform.

Second, the collapse of communism in the former Soviet Union and Eastern Europe in the early 1990s reinforced such a perception among Chinese leaders. The initial failure of political reform in China and radical democratization in the Soviet Union and Eastern Europe not only led to the collapse of communism there but also led to the breakup of the Soviet Union. The impact of what happened in the Soviet Union and Eastern Europe on the Chinese leadership could not be underestimated. Since then, no single political leader, whether conservative or liberal, could undertake initiatives to reform the country's political system.

Finding new sources of political legitimacy became the leadership's highest priority in the early 1990s. Deng and other reformist leaders were realistic and imaginative enough to conclude that the rise of people's power in the Soviet Union and Eastern Europe was due to the failure of economic reform and the opening of political space for the people. The former led the populace to lose confidence in the communist regime and led the regime to lose its sources of political legitimacy, while the latter provided the people a legitimate channel to overthrow the party and government.[31]

To avoid the fate of regime collapse, the leadership adopted two main approaches. First, it undertook radical economic reform, which enabled the government to continuously provide the people with economic goods and thus expand the sources of political legitimacy. Second, the regime was wary of political reform, so it sought to deprive social forces of an avenue to participate in the political process and express their political demands. The Chinese leadership believed that economic changes would lead to the rise of social forces, but it was the leadership that provided social forces with opportunities to make themselves politically powerful. This did not mean that the leadership did not need to do anything politically. Instead, the leadership needed to adjust its political system in accordance with the changing social and economic situation. Nevertheless, such adjustments would be initiated from the top and would be independent of pressures from any social forces.

Scientific and technological development was perceived as the foundation of rapid economic growth and thus was linked to the survival of the communist state. Scholars have observed that China's new strategy of scientific and technological development began during the period of political transition from the leadership of Deng Xiaoping to that of Jiang Zemin as the core of the third-generation leadership, which started after the government's crackdown on the Tiananmen protesters in June 1989 and ended with the death of Deng in 1997. During this period, the government launched its Informatization of the National Economy (INE) program. Informatization of the national economy and society was given a strategic priority in the Tenth Five-Year Plan (2001–5).[32]

The mind-set on science and technology is most explicitly expressed in the strategy formulated by the third-generation leadership, that is, *kejiao xingguo* ("revitalizing the nation through science, technology, and education").[33] Jiang Zemin reiterated that "scientific research and education are both national priorities and are incorporated into all of China's development strategies" and that "information science, life science, material science, and resources and environmental studies will be crucial to China's sustained development in the future."[34] It is not an exaggeration to say that Jiang was a key political figure behind China's revolution of information technology.[35] His preference for information technology has been reflected in all aspects of development in this area (see discussions below). Among other things, Jiang certainly recognized the importance of information technology in building a strong army.[36]

The strategy for scientific and technological progress developed by the third-generation leadership has been characterized by a neo-technonationalism. According to Richard Suttmeier and Yao Xiangkui, in such a strategy, technological development in support of national economic and security interests is pursued through leveraging the opportunities presented by globalization for national advantage. Different from other forms of technonationalism, neo-technonationalism requires attention to international norms, cooperation with foreign partners, and recognition of the need for new forms of public–private accommodation.[37]

To a great degree, such a neo-technonationalism departs from the Maoist technonationalism. In the post-Mao era, especially after the passing of the second-generation leadership, Chinese leaders have shown a genuine interest in joining the WTO and other international organizations in their efforts to make scientific and technological progress. They believe that by joining the world, China could more efficiently and quickly realize the nationalistic

28   goal of "rich nation and strong army."[38] The neo-technonationalism matters in China's progress in information technology, and it provides the Chinese leadership with a huge incentive to make efforts to connect China to the rest of the world.

THE FORMATION OF AN INFORMATION SOCIETY

With such a scientific mind-set, the Chinese leadership began to focus on building an information society after the mid-1980s in order to lay the foundation of the nation-state in an age of information while spurring economic growth. China made very impressive progress in a short period of time. The average growth rate of the number of main telephone lines from 1988 to 1991 doubled the rate of gross domestic product (GDP) growth. In line with the acceleration of investment in the 1990s, the growth rate of the number of telephone lines exceeded that of the GDP; on average, it was three to four times higher.[39] The buildup of telecom infrastructure in China was staggering after the mid-1990s. Table 2.1 shows the growth in switchboard capacity, and

TABLE 2.1

Local switchboard capacity in China, 1985–2002

	LOCAL SWITCHBOARD CAPACITY	
Year	Million lines	% Change
1985	6.134	
1986	6.724	9.62
1987	7.739	15.10
1988	8.872	14.64
1989	10.347	16.63
1990	12.318	19.05
1991	14.922	21.14
1992	19.151	28.34
1993	30.408	58.78
1994	49.262	62.00
1995	72.036	46.23
1996	92.912	28.98
1997	112.692	21.29
1998	138.237	22.67
1999	158.531	11.01
2000	178.256	16.16
2001	205.695	15.37
2002	283.584	37.86

SOURCES: *China Statistical Yearbook* and *Yearbook of China Transportation and Communications,* various issues. Also, see Ministry of Information Industry Web site, http://www.mii.gov.cn.

TABLE 2.2

Number of fixed-line phone subscribers
in China, 1978–2002

	FIXED-LINE PHONE SUBSCRIBERS	
Year	No. of subscribers (million)	% Change
1978	1.925	
1979	2.033	5.61
1980	2.141	5.31
1981	2.221	3.74
1982	2.343	5.49
1983	2.508	7.04
1984	2.775	10.65
1985	3.120	12.43
1986	3.504	12.31
1987	3.907	11.50
1988	4.727	20.99
1989	5.680	20.16
1990	6.850	20.60
1991	8.451	23.37
1992	11.469	35.71
1993	17.332	51.12
1994	27.295	57.48
1995	40.706	49.13
1996	54.947	34.99
1997	70.310	27.96
1998	87.421	24.34
1999	108.716	24.36
2000	144.829	33.22
2001	180.368	24.50
2002	214.419	18.88

SOURCES: *China Statistical Yearbook* and *Yearbook of China Transportation and Communications*, various issues. Also, see Ministry of Information Industry Web site, http://www.mii.gov.cn.

Table 2.2 demonstrates the growth in the number of fixed-line phone subscribers. By 2002, the penetration rate (total number of fixed-line and mobile telephones per 100 persons) reached 34 percent, while teledensity (number of main telephone lines per 100 residents) was 17 percent (Table 2.3).

China's telecom growth was driven by the expansion of mobile telephony. There were only 1 million mobile subscribers in 1994, but the number increased to 5 million in 1996, passed the 20 million mark in 1998, and surpassed 206 million in 2002 (Table 2.4).

The government sought to create islands of information technology excellence, namely, software parks in many regions such as the Yangtze River (*Changjiang*) Delta and the Pearl River (*Zhujiang*) Delta. Many e-parks were

TABLE 2.3

Penetration rate and teledensity in China, 1985–2002

Year	Penetration rate	Teledensity
1985	0.60	
1986	0.67	—
1987	0.75	—
1988	0.86	—
1989	0.98	—
1990	1.11	—
1991	1.29	—
1992	1.61	—
1993	2.20	—
1994	3.20	—
1995	4.66	3.36
1996	6.33	4.49
1997	8.11	5.68
1998	10.53	7.00
1999	13.00	8.64
2000	20.10	11.45
2001	25.90	14.14
2002	33.74	16.80

SOURCES: *China Statistical Yearbook* and *Yearbook of China Transportation and Communications*, various issues. Also, see Ministry of Information Industry Web site, http://www.mii.gov.cn.

TABLE 2.4

Number of mobile phone subscribers in China, 1988–2002

	MOBILE PHONE SUBSCRIBERS	
Year	No. of subscribers (million)	% Change
1988	0.0032	
1989	0.0098	206.25
1990	0.0183	86.73
1991	0.0475	159.56
1992	0.177	272.63
1993	0.639	261.01
1994	1.568	145.38
1995	3.629	131.44
1996	6.853	88.84
1997	13.233	93.10
1998	23.863	80.33
1999	43.238	81.20
2000	84.533	96.51
2001	145.222	71.80
2002	206.616	42.27

SOURCES: *China Statistical Yearbook* and *Yearbook of China Transportation and Communications*, various issues. Also, see Ministry of Information Industry Web site, http://www.mii.gov.cn.

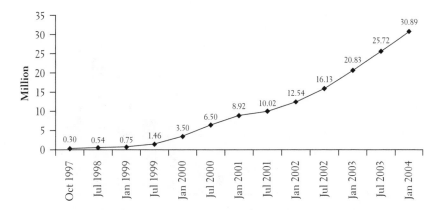

FIGURE 2.1   Number of computer hosts in China

SOURCE: *Survey Report on China's Internet Development*, CNNIC, January 2003. http://www.cnnic.net.cn.

established; among others, the Zhongguancun E-Park in Beijing, where high-tech enterprises mushroomed from 11 in 1983 to some 12,000 at the end of 2002, is well known.[40] The rapid development of information technology infrastructure in China laid a solid foundation for the emergence of its new economy.[41] All economic sectors, including state-owned enterprises, private enterprises, and foreign companies, benefited from the rapid development of the new infrastructure.[42]

A solid telecom infrastructure gave rise to an information society. Figure 2.1 shows a rapid growth of the number of computer hosts, and Figure 2.2 shows that of Internet users. By the end of 2003, China had 30.9 million networked PCs and 79.5 million Internet users. China's Internet users composed only 6.2 percent of its total population, but the number of China's Internet users was already the second largest in the world, next to that of the United States. By the end of 2003, one out of every nine Chinese people used the Internet.[43]

ECONOMY, POLITICS, AND SOCIETY

The formation of an information society benefits all actors. By the turn of this century, the Internet per se had become an important source of economic growth and had helped open up significant opportunities for entrepreneurship.[44] The development of information technology led to the invigoration of an independent private sector or the emergence of new domestic business elites.[45] As of the end of 2003, almost all big, state-owned enterprises had used the Internet to develop their businesses. The use of the Internet had also spread among small and medium-sized enterprises (SMEs). Some 47 percent

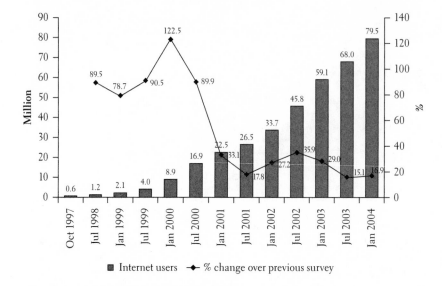

FIGURE 2.2   Growth of Internet users in China

SOURCE: *Survey Report on China's Internet Development*, CNNIC, January 2003. http://www.cnnic.net.cn.

of 8.3 million SMEs in China, mostly private firms, had connected to the Internet. Although only 11 percent of these SMEs had engaged in e-business, that percentage increased quickly.[46] Indeed, the dot-com.cn domains had the second largest share among total domains in China. Their number increased dramatically from 2,131 in 1997 to 140,779 in 2003 (Figure 2.3). A survey conducted at the end of 2003 (Figure 2.4) showed that the biggest share of total Internet users was made up of those in the manufacturing sector (12.8 percent), followed by education (12.7 percent), public administration and social organizations (12.4 percent), and information technology (10.2 percent).[47]

A survey by *Far Eastern Economic Review* in 2002 (Figures 2.5 and 2.6) also shows that business elites had used the Internet both at work and at home.[48] There was no big difference among businesspersons in major Chinese cities — namely, Beijing, Shanghai, and Guangdong — or among businesspersons with different income levels. However, as Figure 2.5 shows, the larger the company was, the more likely its manager tended to use the Internet. Figure 2.7 demonstrates that most business elites were proficient in using the Internet.

The impact of Internet-driven economic development is mutual empowerment between the state and enterprises. Economic development has enabled the Chinese government to deliver goods to people and thus to maintain and even enhance its legitimacy. Although the government has attempted to limit

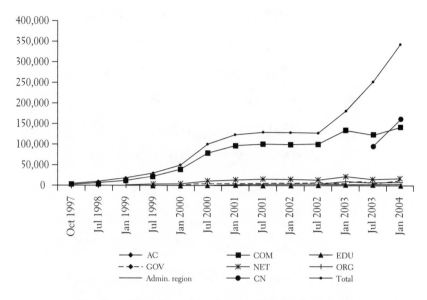

FIGURE 2.3   Number of domains registered under CN, October 1997–January 2004

SOURCE: *Survey Report on China's Internet Development*, CNNIC, January 2003. http://www.cnnic.net.cn.

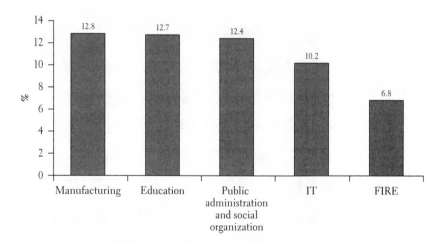

FIGURE 2.4   Internet users by occupation, January 2004

NOTE: FIRE includes financial, insurance, and real estate sectors.

SOURCE: *Survey Report on China's Internet Development*, CNNIC, January 2003. http://www.cnnic.net.cn.

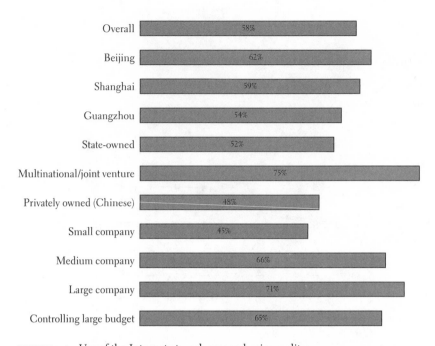

FIGURE 2.5 Use of the Internet at work among business elites

SOURCE: Adapted from *Far Eastern Economic Review, China's Elite 5: A Study of Affluent and Influential People in China* (Hong Kong, 2003).

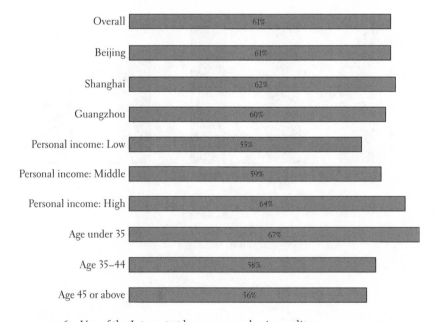

FIGURE 2.6 Use of the Internet at home among business elites

SOURCE: Adapted from *Far Eastern Economic Review, China's Elite 5: A Study of Affluent and Influential People in China* (Hong Kong, 2003).

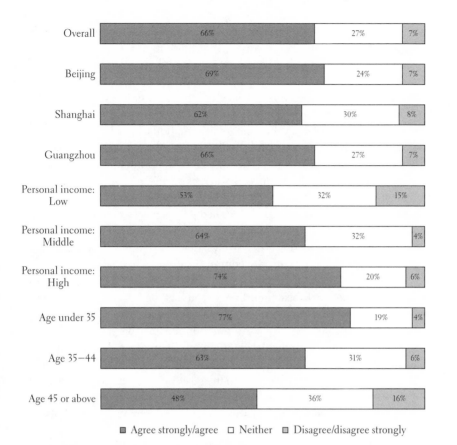

■ Agree strongly/agree □ Neither ▣ Disagree/disagree strongly

FIGURE 2.7   "I am proficient in using the Internet"

SOURCE: Adapted from *Far Eastern Economic Review, China's Elite 5: A Study of Affluent and Influential People in China* (Hong Kong, 2003).

the political impact of the Internet by various means, there is no substantial evidence to support the argument that the government is able to control the political preferences and political influence of Internet-based enterprises and new entrepreneurs. The fact that the government has promoted the development of Internet infrastructure does not necessarily mean that the government is always able to exercise control over it. Once such an infrastructure is established, it belongs to the category of public goods in the public domain. Newly rising entrepreneurs can actually articulate their voices over and above government policies. As a matter of fact, private entrepreneurs have become the most politically influential group in China. They are highly organized and

36   have access to government decision-making processes. Given the fact that the private sector is becoming increasingly important in promoting the country's economic development, the Chinese government has continuously made efforts to accommodate the sector's political demands and provide institutional, even constitutional, protections for its property rights since the late 1990s.[49]

The state has also benefited from an emerging information society. As discussed earlier, the rapid development of information technology can improve the state's legitimacy because information technology enables it to sustain economic growth. Furthermore, the state can use information technology to achieve more efficient governance. To a great degree, governance is a matter of information. Karl Deutsch highlighted the importance of information for governance several decades ago. He argued, "It might make sense to think of government somewhat less as a problem of power and somewhat more as a problem of steering. Steering is decisively a matter of communication, and information is absolutely essential for communication."[50] In China, information technology has become crucial in helping the government build a modern system of governance. Researchers have found that the Internet has been used for e-government and propaganda.[51] Propaganda has been interpreted as a form of political control.[52] While this function remains, propaganda has gone beyond mere control with the development of the Internet. The government uses the Internet to spread its policy agendas to the public, and the public uses the Internet to give its feedback to the government. The Internet is virtually a two-way communication process, not the traditional one-way process of propaganda. The Internet serves as an infrastructure of political conduits; no government officials are able to restrain the public from discussing a given government policy agenda or policy. The government can revise its policies based on the feedback from the public. Such two-way communication helps form a broader consensus among the public on the government's policy agendas. During the National People's Congress in March 2006, Chinese Premier Wen Jiabao publicly stated that political leaders also pay attention to public discussions on the Internet and that public opinions had played an important role in helping the government initiate and modify new policies.[53] Needless to say, the two-way communication is more favorable for the strengthening of government legitimacy than one-way propaganda. Despite Internet users' dissatisfaction with government censorship over Internet information, a 2003 survey among users in five major Chinese cities found that most of them continue to trust Internet information that is largely managed by governmental or semi-governmental organizations.[54] This was also confirmed by a 2005 survey conducted by the same organization.[55]

The Chinese leadership has aggressively promoted the e-government project.[56] In the Chinese context, e-government has three main components: office automation within a given government organization, information sharing via intranet among government organizations, and interactions between government bodies and citizens and between government bodies and enterprises. As early as the mid-1980s, some governmental departments began to use Computer Aided Office (CAO) to deal with basic government activities such as documentary processing and archive management. As of the 1990s, many government bodies at the central level had developed intranet capabilities. For example, the State Administration of Taxation launched the *Jinshui* (Taxation Intranet System) project, the Customs General Administration launched the *Jinguan* (Customs Intranet System), and the State Economic and Trade Commission built its intranet with World Bank aid.

In 1999, the State Council launched the Government Online Project (GOP), aimed at establishing Web sites on the Internet for government departments by means of computer communication technology. The project was expected to enable the government to provide policy information to citizens and push forward office automation of government departments and their public services. Key political leaders, including State President Jiang Zemin and Premier Zhu Rongji, showed great interest in such projects, and they repeatedly emphasized the importance of using information technology in government management. This gave a big push to the GOP. For instance, within a few months—from the end of 2000 to March 2001—ten provincial governments announced their own plans for government digitalization such as "Digital Beijing," "Digital Shanghai," and "Digital Fujian." On July 3, 2001, the State Information Leading Group, which was led by Primer Zhu Rongji, issued two important documents, *The Informatization Plan for National Economy and Society* and *Instructions on Building E-Government*. These two documents, which included measures for enforcement, served as a blueprint for China's national informatization.

The preference of the leadership on information technology led to heavy state investment in this sector and accounted for the huge achievements being made.[57] The Internet has been widely used by the government. As of early 2000, sixty-six government bodies—including the National People's Congress (NPC); the Chinese People's Political Consultative Conference (CPPCC); and all ministries, commissions, and bureaus of the State Council—had joined the GOP, establishing fifty-two government Web sites. At the provincial level, thirty provincial governments established their own Web sites. In some regions, all government organizations are connected to the Internet. For

38   example, by 2002, in eighteen prefectures in the Henan province, all 2,084 townships had realized the goal of e-government.[58]

As shown in Figure 2.3, dot-gov.cn domains increased from 323 in 1997 to 11,764 in 2003, about 3.5 percent of the total registered dot-cn Web sites.[59] China is now among the most highly ranked nations in terms of overall e-government performance. The wide use of e-government measures is beneficial for the government because it increases the state's capacity to provide citizen services efficiently, thus enhancing public satisfaction with the government.[60] The use of the Internet also makes public administration more efficient, and it increases openness and transparency by widening the radius of information. For example, the Internet has been used by social groups to expose rampant corruption in the public sector, which often causes crises of legitimacy on the part of the government.

Society also benefits from the Internet in the political realm. As already mentioned, different economic sectors have used the Internet widely for their economic activities. This is also true for non-government organizations (NGOs) and other social organizations. As shown in Figure 2.3, social organizations have used the Internet extensively. The Internet enables them to access information that is not available from more traditional media channels such as newspapers, TV, and broadcasting or from other channels controlled by the government. Social groups can also use the Internet to make their organizations more efficient via Internet-based communication and to broaden their social bases by recruiting e-members.

The government has played a leading role in laying down the Internet infrastructure. But once it is built, it can be regarded as public goods. The distribution of the benefit associated with this infrastructure is very decentralized. It has been found that by creating a digital divide, Internet development has widened the distribution gap of economic benefits among different social groups and different regions. Digital divides exist among different regions in China. For example, by the end of 2000, there were thirteen provincial regions that had per capita incomes above the national average. There were eleven provincial regions with a fixed-line telephone penetration rate or a mobile phone penetration rate above the national level. Most of the thirty-one provinces were below the national average in terms of telecom penetration rate.[61] Figure 2.8 shows that most Internet hosts are located in rich, east coastal regions such as Beijing, Shandong, Shanghai, Jiangsu, Zhejiang, and Guangdong. Such a situation has not changed since the Internet began to develop in China and is unlikely to change in the near future.

Nevertheless, the existing digital divide does not mean that different social groups cannot benefit from information technology. In terms of the distribu-

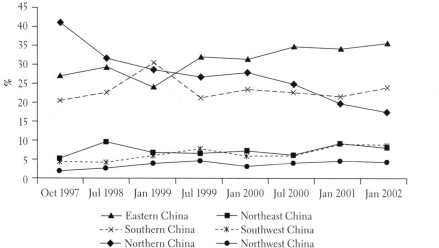

FIGURE 2.8   Regional allocation of Internet users, October 1997–January 2002
SOURCE: *Survey Report on China's Internet Development*, CNNIC, January 2003. http://www.cnnic.net.cn.

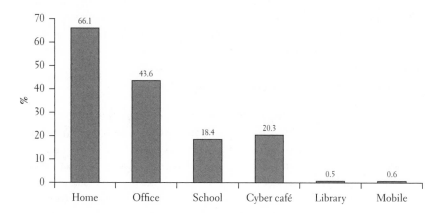

FIGURE 2.9   Location of Internet access, January 2004
SOURCE: *Survey Report on China's Internet Development*, CNNIC, January 2003. http://www.cnnic.net.cn.

tion of Internet users, the benefits have been decentralized. With the rapid development of the telecom industry, the Internet is increasingly becoming affordable for most families, especially in urban areas. As shown in Figure 2.9, by the end of 2003, more than 66 percent of users had access to the Internet from their home computers. Figure 2.10 shows the distribution of Internet

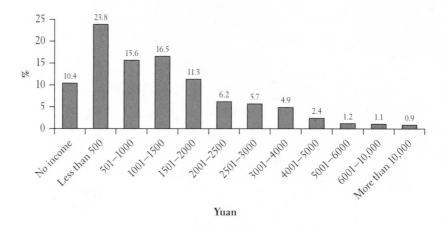

Yuan

FIGURE 2.10   Monthly income of Internet users in China, January 2004
SOURCE: *Survey Report on China's Internet Development*, CNNIC, January 2003. http://www.cnnic.net.cn.

users in terms of their income levels. Interestingly, most Internet users are in middle to lower social classes. More than 10 percent of users do not have any income, while nearly 24 percent of users — the biggest share — earn less than 500 *renminbi* (RMB) per month. Low-income users usually access the Internet in cyber cafés, and, accordingly, there has been an Internet bar boom in China since the mid-1990s.

INFORMATION TECHNOLOGY AND SOCIAL MOVEMENT

So far, I have discussed China's Internet development in the context of the country's nation-state building in an age of information technology. But the nation-state building is not without any unexpected political consequences. The development of information technology has provided a sound infrastructure for social and political changes. Any Chinese citizens with good IT knowledge can now engage in discussion with one another on practically any issue on the Internet platform. The Internet has allowed for the rapid transfer of ideas between persons who are connected to it. The Internet not only carries messages of economic opportunities to the masses but also accommodates voices beyond the economic realm. The Internet today is an increasingly important source of social and political awareness among Chinese.

Among others, one major sociopolitical consequence of Internet development is the rise of Internet-based political protests. Like other forms of social protests, there are no official statistics on Internet-facilitated social protests.

Due to political sensitivity, the Chinese authorities are reluctant to release any information on Internet protests. Nevertheless, we can observe Internet protests via an important indirect indicator, namely, Internet arrests, which have taken place frequently since the late 1990s. Frequent Internet arrests imply that the authorities have tightened control over the Internet, but they also indicate that Internet activism is growing continuously. How social groups engage in Internet-based popular protests will be examined in detail in the following chapters, but it is imperative to first look into how state building, of which Internet development is a part, can lead to social movements by generating various forms of social grievance among members. The Internet as a form of technology itself does not produce social movements, but it is a tool that can be used by various social actors to facilitate social movements. Apparently, Internet-facilitated social protests are only one of the many forms of social movement in China. Before social protests, including Internet-based ones, can be organized, there must exist socioeconomic environments that motivate individuals or social groups to organize such protests.

According to Sidney Tarrow, social movements can be defined as "collective challenges by people with common purposes and solidarity in sustained interaction with elites, opponents and authorities."[62] Then, why do social movements take place? No social movement is defined by a single factor. Social movements have various sources, and many scholars have pointed to the state itself, finding that social movements have been associated with state making or building.[63] This is particularly true in Europe, where "the coming of the national state coincided with the birth of national movement."[64] How social movements and state making are correlated has been a central question for scholars on social movements such as Tarrow, Charles Tilly, and Doug McAdam.[65]

To these scholars, the roots of social movements are found in the process of state making. State making is a process of interaction between the state and society. In the "statist" paradigm, the state is regarded as "an autonomous, irreducible set of institutions."[66] Nevertheless, scholars have also found that the state is a part of society, and it is not an "internally rationalized bureaucracy immune to popular influences or governed by self-generated rules." Instead, the state can be regarded as "the arena of routinized political competition in which class, status, and political conflicts, representing both elite and popular interests, are played out."[67] According to Bright and Harding,

> The state *is* autonomous in the sense that it is not reducible to economic and social struggles and is *not* autonomous in the sense of being self-contained or self-directing, since it is continuously penetrated by social and economic struggles that

ensure that no political process is purely political and that the logic by which bureaucracies develop is never simply rational (*emphasis original*). States are neither static givens lording over society nor subserviently by-products of historically specific processes structuring power relations in a society.[68]

From this point of view, state making "not only involves states' initiatives and the reactions of social groups towards them, but also social mobilizations which target the state and trigger responses by its governors."[69] Even though the state serves as a major actor in socioeconomic transformation, it does not do so without any social challenges that affect the state itself. Instead, "state-making does not end once stately institutions emerge, but is continuous. . . . Contentious processes both define the state vis-à-vis other social and economic institutions and continually remake the state itself."[70] In other words, "the boundaries between legitimate state politics and the activities of challengers, dissidents, and rebels 'outside' the sphere of the state are defined and redefined by contestatory actions."[71] Therefore, popular protests can be better understood by looking at how the state and society interplay in the process of state making. The state defines or redefines itself in accordance with changing relations between state institutions and society.

State making creates opportunities for social movements. According to Tarrow, modern state building involves three basic state policies: making war, collecting taxes, and provisioning food. Opportunities for social movements are embedded in all these policies. Tarrow told us, "States made war and collected taxes; war and taxes required the infrastructure of a consolidated state; social movements emerged from the conflicts and opportunity structures surrounding the process of state consolidation."[72] Surely, the state engaged in all three policies not to support social mobilization but to ensure and expand its power. Nevertheless, "each new policy initiative produced new channels of communication, more organized networks of citizens and more unified cognitive frameworks around which insurgents could mount claims and organize."[73] Tarrow concluded that "these policies shaped arenas for the construction of social movements, and these movements — or the fear of the movements — shaped the way the national state evolved."[74]

According to Tilly, while state making provided social actors with opportunities for collective action, the modern state was forged by tremendous contention not only in the countless wars fought among various emergent states but also in the struggle between state managers and the population during the process of subjugation. As state structures were nationalized and electoral politics evolved, popular agitation also underwent profound changes. Different and deliberately constituted groups came to make claims on the state, pre-

senting organized, sustained, and self-conscious challenges to state authori-   43
ties. As popular movements managed to gain access to and control over state
resources, they also reshaped the political arena and altered the activities of
the state itself.[75]

It seems that what happened to Europe and North America in the process
of nation-state building in the past centuries is also taking place in China
today. Nation-state rebuilding in the post-Mao era has generated enormous
grievances among different social groups and thus has led to the rise of collective actions against the state.[76] While nation-state rebuilding produces grievances, grievances themselves do not sufficiently explain the occurrence of
collective actions. To transform grievances into collective action, there must
be agents and a platform on which collective actions are carried out. The
Internet serves as both the agent and the platform.

As discussed earlier in this chapter, in post-Mao China, the communist
state has relied on economic performance for its legitimacy. In the past two
decades, China has managed to achieve spectacular economic growth at a rate
of above 9 percent. Such a sterling economic performance has now become
a major source of legitimacy for the party and its state. It is not far-fetched to
argue that the CCP has so far been able to remain at the helm of power due
to its success in delivering economic goods, such as employment and material
benefits, to the people. According to official statistics, with robust economic
growth, China succeeded in reducing the number of people living below the
poverty line from a high of 250 million to a low of 29 million in one generation
(from 1978 to 2003).[77] This represents one of the largest and fastest reductions
of poverty in human history.

Without a doubt, political legitimacy that is based on economic performance has enabled the state to resolve a number of pressing problems. As
many of these problems are developmental in nature, they can in large part
be resolved through the pursuit of economic growth. But China's remarkable
economic growth has unwittingly led to the emergence of other challenges
that are not easily resolved through economic measures alone. After the Asian
financial crisis of 1997, the idea of the "economic miracle," a phrase that had
been variously used to describe the economic successes of the countries in
the region, was somewhat damaged. It became more apparent that the wholehearted pursuit of economic growth was not a panacea for society's problems.
There were major limitations to this economic development model approach,
which the top leaders in China became aware of.

Nevertheless, rapid economic growth has also generated enormous social
grievances. In any society, the ability to participate in or even influence poli-

TABLE 2.5

Social groups that benefited the most and least since
the reform and open door policy (perceptions, 2002)

SOCIAL GROUPS THAT BENEFITED THE MOST		SOCIAL GROUPS THAT BENEFITED THE LEAST	
Types of social groups	Choice as a %	Types of social groups	Choice as a %
Party and government cadres	59.2	Workers	88.2
Private enterprise bosses	55.4	Farmers	76.3
Acting personnel	43.0	Teachers	15.3
Urban and rural self-employed	33.0	Professionals	14.2
State-owned enterprise managers	29.3	State-owned enterprise managers	8.8
Professionals	24.3	Urban and rural sole proprietorships	7.7
Teachers	14.9	Party and government cadres	5.1
Farmers	3.4	Private enterprise bosses	4.7
Workers	1.5	Acting personnel	2.5
Others	0.5	Others	2.7

SOURCES: Adapted from Zhou Jiang, "2002 nian zhongguo chengshi redian wenti diaocha" ("Investigation of the Hot Issues in Chinese Cities in 2002"), in Ru Xin, Lu Xueyi, and Li Peilin (eds.), *Shehui lanpishu 2003 nian: Zhongguo shehui xingshi fenxi yu yuce* (*Blue Book of the Chinese Society in 2003: An Analysis and Forecast of the Chinese Social Situation*), Beijing: Shehui kexue wenxian chubanshe, 2003, pp. 159–160.

tics is usually confined to the group that controls the economic resources. In China, the rich and the powerful will have an advantage over their poorer counterparts such as the peasants, workers, and other less privileged groups in pressing for their interests to be heard and acted upon by the top leaders.[78]

There is a perception among urban residents in China that only a select group of privileged individuals have been able to reap the most benefits from the reform and open door policy. According to a 2002 survey, the results of which are in Table 2.5, Chinese urban residents are of the view that the group that has benefited most from the reform and open door policy is the party and government cadres, followed by the bosses of private enterprises and actors. Not surprisingly, farmers and workers were ranked the lowest among the various social groups. The same survey also confirmed that farmers and workers benefited the least from the reform and open door policy.

Those groups that have consistently benefited the most or the least from the reform and open door policy have remained largely the same over the years.[79] There is therefore an urgent need for the top leadership to find ways and means of spreading the benefits of economic reforms in a more even manner so that the less privileged can see the benefit of supporting the existing system. Otherwise, there will be a widening gap between those who consistently benefit the most from a market economy and those who consistently benefit the least from it. This would pose a threat to the continued viability of the reform and open door policy in the long run.[80]

Such perceptions reflect the fact that the Chinese state has not been able to ensure a better distribution of wealth accumulated under a market economy. In a full-fledged market economy, an undue amount of emphasis is placed on the pursuit of development and accumulation of wealth, and less is placed on the distribution of such wealth. Also, the degree of wealth distribution would depend on whether the leaders under such a market-oriented system see it as in their interest to introduce wealth distribution policies and ensure that they are implemented.

It may be the case that those members of society who really want to see a better distribution of wealth are not in a position to convey their views effectively to those in power. On the other hand, those societal members who do not want to see an even distribution of wealth are better able to convince policy makers not to take any effective action. If the uneven distribution of wealth were to persist and even worsen, it would pose a long-term threat to the sociopolitical stability of the country. Table 2.6 shows the ever-widening income gap between the urban and rural residents over the years. According to the National Bureau of Statistics, the Gini coefficient indicating the gap between the rich and poor had risen from 0.3 in 1978 to 0.46 in China in 2003, at which point it was above the internationally recognized warning level of 0.4.[81] The main cause of the rise in the Gini coefficient is the increasing income gap between urban and rural residents. In 1995, the income of urban residents was 2.51 times that of rural residents, but this figure had increased to 3.23 by 2003.

TABLE 2.6

Fluctuations in the urban-rural income levels since 1995

Year	Per capita rural income (*Yuan*)	Increase in real income (%)	Ratio of urban-rural incomes
1996	1,926	8.99	2.51
1997	2,090	4.59	2.47
1998	2,162	4.35	2.51
1999	2,210	3.79	2.65
2000	2,253	2.11	2.79
2001	2,366	4.20	2.90
2002	2,476	4.80	3.11
2003	2,622	4.03	3.23

SOURCES: Adapted from Yang Yiyong and Huang Yanfen, "Zhongguo jumin shouru fenpei xinjumian" ("The New Situation of Income Distribution among China's Residents"), in Ru Xin, Lu Xueyi, and Li Peilin (eds.), *Shehui lanpishu 2003 nian: Zhongguo shehui xingshi fenxi yu yuce* (*Blue Book of the Chinese Society in 2003: An Analysis and Forecast of the Chinese Social Situation*), Beijing: Shehui kexue wenxian chubanshe, 2003, pp. 226–34; *China Statistical Yearbook 2003* and *China Statistical Abstract 2004.*

TABLE 2.7

The development of corruption among leading cadres in the 1990s

	1993	1994	1995	1996	1997	Jan–Sept 1998	1999
Punished by party & gov. disciplines							
Provincial level	6	17	24	23	7	10	17
Prefectural level	205	309	429	467	576	219	327
County level	2,793	3,528	4,880	5,868	6,585	2,955	4,029
Investigated by procuratorial organs							
Provincial level	1	1	2	5	3	3	3
Prefectural level	7	88	145	143	148	85	136
County level	1,141	1,826	2,306	2,551	2,426	1,462	2,200
Sentenced by law							
Provincial level		1		1	5	2	2
Prefectural level	7	28	35	43	58	30	65
County level	69	202	396	364	403	271	367

SOURCE: The Research Group of the Department of Organization, the CCP Central Committee, (ed.), 2000–2001 *Zhongguo diaocha baogao: xin xingshi xia renmin neibu maodun yanjiu (China Investigation Report, 2000–2001: Studies of Contradictions within the People under New Conditions)*, Beijing: Zhongyang bianyi chubanshe, 2001, p. 86.

Corruption is another major cause of social grievances. Table 2.7 shows official statistics on corruption committed by leading party cadres at different levels in the 1990s. Despite waves of anti-corruption campaigns by the state, the situation continued. According to the Corruption Perception Index (CPI) of 2003, China was given a CPI score of 3.4 out of a possible 10, with 0 being the most corrupt and 10 being the least corrupt.[82]

Corruption generated unhappiness in the people about the inability of the CCP to ensure fairness and also cast doubts on the CCP's legitimacy to rule the country. Various surveys have shown that since the early 1990s, "serious corruption committed by government officials" and "public disorder" were two issues of concern among ordinary citizens in China.[83] When the government is perceived as corrupt and there is a breakdown of public order, people tend to be worrisome. According to a 1998 survey, nearly 93 percent of people did not believe that China was a country ruled by law. When asked what they would do if conflicts or disputes with others happened, 74.7 percent said they would turn to legal means for a resolution. Nevertheless, they also believed that such means would be ineffective because those in power were still above the law in China, so they indicated they would appeal through other, non-legal means. About 49 percent believed that they would seek help from the media and 24.7 percent from individual leaders. Furthermore, about 16 percent of the people were likely to turn to some form of collective action to seek justice such as petition, demonstration, and collective visit to higher authorities for their intervention (*shang fang*).[84]

Serious corruption in the public sector has greatly affected social morale. Ordinary citizens see the abundance of wealth accumulated by party cadres and government officials and find it difficult to understand why they should restrain themselves. Gradually, they regard the system in which they live as being unfair to them. Meanwhile, government officials at different levels have also found that it is increasingly difficult to maintain a sense of morality and social community among both urban and rural residents. As corruption among party cadres and government officials becomes rampant, crime has also become widespread among ordinary citizens.[85] Robbery and armed assault, which were unthinkable during Mao's time, have become a part of people's daily lives.

We will see in the following chapters that the rise of different types of Internet-based social protest is closely associated with the presence of such social, economic, and political conditions. Rapid economic development associated with state building has benefited social groups unevenly, and widening income disparities and worsening social and political injustice have created grievances. The lack of the rule of law and other legitimate channels to influence government policies make the Internet a choice for disgruntled social groups to "voice" their grievances. The Internet here serves as an infrastructure for social protests.

CONCLUSION

What role does information technology play in transforming social grievances into collective action? In his study of social movement, Tarrow pointed to the impact of the development of commercial print media and new models of association and socialization on social movements. According to him, such developments "did not in themselves produce new grievances and conflicts but diffused ways of mounting claims that helped ordinary people to think of themselves as part of broader collectivities and on the same plane as their betters."[86]

In China, the Internet seems to have performed these two functions as a new form of media and as a new form of association. The Internet is not only a means of communication that diffuses social grievances; it also helps the formation of new social organizations. The Internet is a new area in which the state and society interplay in pursuing their interests. There are areas in which both the state and society can benefit from the Internet, but there are also areas in which the interests of the two actors clash. The following chapters

48   will examine how the two actors cooperate with or contest each other over Internet-based public space. More specifically, these chapters attempt to look at the two important issues—first, how the Chinese state attempts to regulate Internet-based public space in order to manage this growing information society, and second, how social groups and Internet-based civil communities initiate collective action to challenge the state.

3

REGULATORY REGIME AND POLITICAL CONTROL

DIFFICULT DOUBLE TASKS

As discussed earlier, the development of information technology is part of the leadership's continuous efforts in building a strong Chinese nation-state. It is especially important in the post-Mao era because the new generation of leadership has to rely on economic performance for its political legitimacy, and information technology is among the most important sources for sustainable economic growth. Nevertheless, the new public space created by information technology is also an area in which the state and society interact and contest for power. While the state tries to impose its will in this new area, social forces attempt not only to resist state control but also to use this new political realm to challenge the state.

The Chinese leadership faces unenviable dual tasks. On one hand, it has to implement effective policies to promote rapid development of information technology, and on the other hand, it has to control, manage, and minimize political risks brought about by the new technology. These two tasks, however, are not always cooperative; more often than not, they are in conflict. While development requires decentralization, with market principles and policies that are not guided by political ideology, political control requires centralization, with political priorities and policies that conform to political ideology. Effective management becomes even more problematic due to the fact that the responsibilities for development and control belong to two different government bodies with conflicting interests.

This chapter attempts to look at the issue of how the leadership performs these two contradictory tasks, namely, promoting rapid development while

50   maintaining political control. In doing so, the leadership has attempted to establish two regimes, one for promoting the development of information technology and another for exercising political control. The two regimes are managed by two separate bodies of personnel with some overlaps. This does not mean, however, that these two bodies can coordinate well in terms of their decision making and implementation. Tensions exist between them.

This chapter also aims to disaggregate the state at the bureaucratic level. As discussed in Chapter One, the state must be disaggregated to allow for the exploration of the political impact of the Internet. The impact of the Internet on the interaction between the state and society can be better understood by disaggregating the state than by treating it as a unitary unit because tensions among different state organizations often affect how the two actors interplay.

THE RISE OF THE MII AS A REGULATORY REGIME

While China's economy increasingly operates on market principles, the government has actively created a new role for itself by establishing various regulatory regimes—new institutions, rules, and methods of regulation. The Ministry of Information Industry (MII) is the regulator of the development of information technology in China. By examining the rise of the MII, one can see how the Chinese government has struggled to promote the development of information technology in accordance with market principles while continuously playing an important role in this strategically significant sector.

Before the post-Mao economic reform, the telecom sector was state owned and managed by the Ministry of Post and Telecommunication (MPT), which was a functional organ of the State Council. Like all other ministries, the MPT was highly centralized, and all enterprises under its jurisdiction did not have much autonomy or financial accountability.

China's early economic reforms were guided by the principles encouraging decentralization and enterprise autonomy. In 1979, when the reform first started, the State Council tried to introduce an incentive mechanism for post and telecom enterprises (PTEs). Administration of the daily business operation was decentralized, and primary financial accountability was given to enterprises managed by different levels of government. PTEs were allowed to have their own accounts and a degree of financial independence. In the middle 1980s, when Zhao Ziyang was premier, the State Council introduced a new accounting system under the MPT, which allowed PTEs to retain an essential portion of profits they made. Consequently, all PTEs established their independent accounts and started to operate on a system of contractual responsibility in which their earnings were linked to their business performance.[1]

With all these reform measures, a vertically organized hierarchy emerged as the administrative structure of China's telecommunications. The MPT at the top was responsible for overall planning and management of the industry. It controlled international and interprovincial communications. It also set and enforced technical standards and formulated key policies and plans. At the provincial level, post and telecom administrations (PTAs) performed a similar role within each province. Below them were hundreds of municipal and prefecture bureaus of post and telecom (PTBs). At the county level, more than 2,000 PTEs operated local service networks in the county capitals and extended lines into the surrounding rural areas. Below them were tens of thousands of branch offices operating exchanges at the village level. There were also many non-public branch exchanges owned and operated by work units and rural villages.

In 1988, after Li Peng became premier, the State Council initiated a new wave of bureaucratic restructuring. Departments of manufacturing, construction, and purchasing under MPT jurisdiction were granted separate legal entities with greater autonomy in financial accounting and human resource management. The Directorate General of Telecommunications (DGT) and the Directorate General of Posts were set up to incorporate business enterprise functions. The DGT comprised twenty-nine provincial PTAs, providing local and long-distance services. In 1995, the DGT was restructured as a corporate group, China Telecom. Accordingly, all PTEs under China Telecom were corporatized and became autonomous accounting entities that conform to the Corporation Law, which came into effect in 1994.

In reforming the telecommunications sector, China's reformist leaders faced a dilemma. On one hand, in order to provide enterprises with incentives, decentralization was needed. On the other hand, centralization seemed necessary in order to regulate their services. Scholars have long observed that China's authoritarian political structure is actually very fragmented.[2] Fragmentation is also the main pattern in the telecommunications sector. Even during the era of planned economy, the telecom service market was under a fragmented administrative structure. The governments at the levels of province, municipality, and prefecture had actual control over the planning of postal and telecom business in their domains. The MPT at the central level did not have exclusive power in regulating the whole telecom sector.

In the 1980s, when decentralization measures were introduced to provide an incentive for enterprises, the MPT had actually begun to make great efforts in rebuilding its centralized control over the public telecom sector and overseeing the whole telecom industry. But these reform efforts were not able to change the nature of fragmentation. Over the years, several government

52   ministerial branches developed a number of non-public communication networks (vis-à-vis the MPT-managed public network) for their own internal uses, including the networks under the Ministry of Railways, the Ministry of Electrical Power, and the China Academy of Sciences and State Education Commission, as well as the People's Liberation Army. These ministerial branches and their telecom systems went beyond the MPT's jurisdiction. To a degree, such developments made the system even more fragmented.

The MPT was the only ministry that combined the functions of policy regulation and public telecom service provision under its umbrella. With their growing interests in the telecommunications sector, other ministries began to challenge the MPT's monopoly over the public service market. To reduce the tension, the State Council decided to award a basic telecom license to the China United Telecommunication Corporation (or Unicom) in 1993. It was set up by three powerful ministries — the Ministry of Electronic Industry, the Ministry of Railways, and the Ministry of Electric Power — and thirteen major state-owned companies. The carrier intended to compete with the MPT in the long-distance and international services market.

While the move introduced competition into the telecom sector, the regulatory function of the MPT was weakened further. It was not able to intervene effectively in the domains managed by other ministries, which were at the same administration rank as the MPT in China's bureaucratic hierarchy. Whenever there were conflicts between the MPT and Unicom and its backing ministries, the MPT had to turn to the State Council for a resolution. To cope with the problem, the State Council created a national Joint Conference on State Economic Information (JCSEI) in 1994, an informal coordination body chaired by Vice Premier Zou Jiahua. Two years later, it was formalized and renamed the National Information Infrastructure Steering Committee (NIISC), which was charged with responsibilities for the formulation and implementation of plans, policies, and regulations in the information industry. The committee continued to be chaired by Vice Premier Zou, with ministers of the MPT, Ministry of Electronic Industry, the State Planning Commission, the State Science and Technology Commission, and the People's Bank as the committee's deputy directors. Nevertheless, the NIISC was still an interim task force for interministry coordination and negotiation, lacking the legislative status, financial means, and administrative power to effectively enforce regulations.

In 1998, when Zhu Rongji became premier, the leadership initiated massive efforts to reorganize the whole bureaucratic system under the State Council to mold the foundation of its regulatory state in order to meet the requirements for China's entry into the World Trade Organization.[3] The restructuring of the telecommunications sector was one of the priorities because this sector was identified as one of the "network industries" that were strategically vital to the nation in terms of national and economic security. In China, it is often 53 referred to as the "commanding heights" (*"jingji mingmai,"* or literally "economic lifeline").

Under the 1998 restructuring, a new ministry, the MII, was created during the Ninth National People's Congress through the merger of the former MPT; the former Ministry of Electronics Industry (MEI); and the Network Department of the former Ministry of Radio, Film, and Television. Two former rivals, the MPT and the MEI, were thus integrated. In addition, the new ministry took over information and network administration, handled previously by the former JCSEI/NIISC and the former State Council's Commission on Radio Frequencies; the former Ministry of Radio, Film, and Television (MRFT); the China Corporation of Aerospace Industry; and the China Corporation of Aviation Industry. Meanwhile, the former MRFT, which previously regulated the television industry, was downgraded to a sub-ministerial body under the State Council and became the State Administration of Radio, Film, and Television (SARFT). Wu Jichuan, the minister of the former MPT, became the first minister of the MII.

The newly formed MII was declared the "autonomous regulator" for telecom. It became a "super-ministry." An important rationale behind the formation of the MII was to further separate the regulator, previously the MPT, from China Telecom, as the MPT had shown extensive favoritism toward China Telecom over China Unicom — its competitor formed in 1994. It was expected that competition could be developed under the supervision of a single and supposedly impartial regulatory authority, the MII.

POLITICAL CONTROL

This chapter has so far examined how the Chinese government has attempted to establish a regulatory regime of information technology. Needless to say, this regime is aimed at promoting and managing a rapidly growing sector, and its main objectives are development and growth. It can be reasonably assumed that the main functions of the MII are administrative and managerial, not political. The rapid development of information technology infrastructure in China has been closely associated with the progress of this regulatory regime.

While the MII is the regulator of the information technology sector, the issue becomes complicated when it comes to the regulation of the Internet. Confusions and conflicts arise here. As the primary regulator for the info-communications industry, the MII has been the authorized agency to review, approve, and grant operation licenses to Internet service providers (ISPs). In an interview in December 1999, Wu Jichuan, the then-minister of the MII, stated, "Internet service providers will be regulated by the Ministry of Information

54   Industry. Internet content providers will be regulated by other government agencies."[4] Wu was absolutely correct. The information technology industry is not an ordinary industry but a special industry with enormous economic and political significance. This characteristic of the industry determines its "attractiveness" not only to various bureaucratic interests but also to political ones. Because of the industry's political significance, other bureaucratic agencies (under the State Council) and political bodies (under the Central Committee of the CCP) can claim their legitimacy in interfering in its operation and management. Because the MII, as a nascent regulatory regime, has not been fully institutionalized, it has to share power with other bureaucratic and political agencies.[5]

Scholars have observed that bureaucratic agencies like the SARFT have stepped into the information technology sector to share its growing economic interests.[6] The rationale for the involvement of bureaucratic interests like the SARFT and the Department of Propaganda is that while the info-communications sector has a huge impact on traditional media like radio and television, it is also vital for the propaganda of the CCP and national security. Although the regulatory regime (MII) is responsible for promoting and sustaining the development of the info-communications sector, other interests have to step in to serve the interests of the communist regime in the areas of propaganda and national security. In these areas, even though the MII is still relevant, it has to relinquish its control over many sections to other agencies. This is especially true in managing the Internet.

Therefore, it is important to take a look at how the CCP manages the traditional media before one can understand how such management techniques have been extended to new information technology, especially the Internet. Despite differences between the Internet and traditional media such as radio, broadcasting, and television, their political significance is similar in the areas such as propaganda and national security.

Propaganda Machinery

The institution that governs China's media industry as a whole can be largely divided into two broad categories: state agencies and CCP organizations. Figure 3.1 illustrates such a system. Under the State Council, the key organizations involved include the Ministry of Culture; the Xinhua News Agency, the SARFT, the State Council Information Office (SCIO), and the State Press and Publication Administration (SPPA).[7]

Although all of these are national-level organizations, each of them has provincial or lower-level bodies. For instance, under the Ministry of Culture

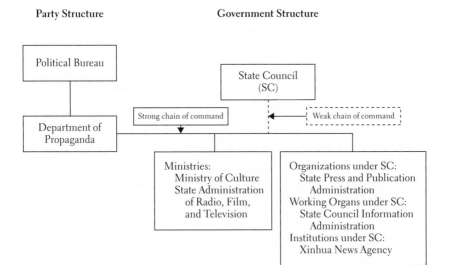

FIGURE 3.1   Party and state organizations responsible for the media (central level)
SOURCE: Compiled by the author.

are separate departments handling films, publishing, and theatre with their provincial and local equivalents. Also, under the Xinhua News Agency is its vast network of local branches, and under the SARFT comes the provincial equivalents, which themselves have lower-level operations below them.[8]

On occasions, these state organizations may collaborate or work with other government departments to mount national campaigns. For example, in the run-up to the Sixteenth Party Congress in April 2002, eight government bodies—the Ministry of Culture, the State Council Information Office, the Ministry of Public Security, the Ministry of Education, the Ministry of State Security, the Ministry of Information Industry, the State Administration for Industry and Commerce, and the State Bureau of Secrecy—came together to launch a nationwide campaign to curb the spread of undesirable information on the domestic Internet network, which was believed to affect national security and social stability.[9]

Running parallel to the state media institutions, the foremost organization for media control under the CCP is the Department of Propaganda (DOP) of the Central Committee of the CCP. The DOP reports directly to the Standing Committee of the Political Bureau on matters related to information dissemination and control and is currently headed by Liu Yunshan, concurrently a

TABLE 3.1

Heads of the Department of Propaganda

Name	Date of appointment	Concurrent appointment
Zhang Pinghua	October 1977	Central Committee Member
Hu Yaobang	December 1978	Political Bureau Member
Wang Renchong	February 1980	Secretary, Secretariat of the Central Committee
Deng Liqun	April 1982	Secretary, Secretariat of the Central Committee
Zhu Houze	July 1985	Central Committee Member
Wang Renzhi	January 1987	Central Committee Member
Ding Guan'gen	November 1992	Political Bureau Member
Liu Yunshan	November 2002	Political Bureau Member; Secretary, Secretariat of the Central Committee

SOURCE: Compiled by the author.

member of the Political Bureau. Table 3.1 shows the present and past leaders of the DOP. The head of the DOP usually holds a concurrent appointment in other party institutions, such as Secretary of the Secretariat of the Central Committee or, more importantly, the Political Bureau. Since the Fourteenth Party Congress in 1992 in particular, the head of the DOP is concurrently a member of the Political Bureau, indicating the level of importance the CCP attaches to the role played by this organ.

The DOP has an extensive network of departments at the lower administrative levels that exercise overall responsibility for the various newspapers and other media channels under their jurisdiction. Despite the parallel organizations at both the state and party levels, it is the DOP that wields real control of the media under the rule known as the Party Principle, according to which the media must adhere ideologically to the party line, propagate the party message, and obey its policies. In fact, not only are the local propaganda departments answerable to their central bodies, so are other central bodies with important supervisory roles over the media.

The DOP guides and supervises the work of several state bodies within the central government, including the SARFT, SPPA, and SCIO. In Chinese administrative terms, these bodies lie within the network, or *xitong*, of the DOP.[10] Any directive from the DOP has to be adhered to. For instance, just before the Sixteenth Party Congress in June 2002, the DOP instructed its lower branches to ensure that the various media channels under their jurisdiction either exercised caution in or refrained entirely from reporting on issues in thirty-two subject areas, such as protection of private property, tax reform in rural areas, and the adverse impact of China's WTO membership.[11]

Control Machinery over the Internet

Due to its political nature, the Internet certainly cannot be managed by the MII alone. Partly because of the economic significance of information technology and partly because of its political significance, the info-communications sector has been given a high priority by the leadership. Besides the efforts in establishing the MII as the regulatory regime, the leadership has also established two higher-ranking State Council organizations, overseeing MII's work and technology policy.

First, there is the State Information Leading Group (SILG). The SILG was formed within the State Council in 1996 and was headed by six senior officials involved in the sector, with the participation of twenty-four commissions, ministries, and other groups. As is characteristic of a "leading small group" (*liangdao xiaozu*),[12] SILG is a joint party-state endeavor with the job of devising strategies for the information technology sector, including telecom. Zhu Rongji led the SILG until March 2003, when he stepped down from his premiership, together with other members such as Hu Jintao, Li Lanqing, Wu Bangguo, Zeng Peiyuan, and Ding Guan'gen — all high-ranking officials then in charge of science, education, research, economy, and party propaganda.

Among its members, it is particularly important to highlight the involvement of Ding Guan'gen. Ding was then the director of the DOP, responsible for overseeing all traditional media. With the onset of the Internet age, the DOP naturally expanded its jurisdiction over the Internet. Of course, there are other administrative authorities involved in Internet management such as the Ministry of Public Security (MPS) and the State Secrecy Bureau (SSB). The responsibilities of these bodies somehow overlap and are intertwined. The MPS and the SSB are empowered with a wide range of administrative and quasi-judicial authorities over the Internet.

The SILG is entrusted with a wide range of powers, including making detailed rules for the implementation of the regulations; regulating the rights and duties of channel providers, Internet service providers, and users; and supervising and inspecting the international wiring of networks.

There is also the SCIO, which is under the SILG. The SCIO was formed in 2001. This organization has increasingly taken over the executive function of driving the telecom policy agenda.

Figure 3.2 shows the CCP and state control over the Internet. It is a complicated machine. In addition to many economic bodies such as the MII, Ministry of Commerce, and State Administration for Industry and Commerce, CCP and security organizations are also involved, such as the DOP, Ministry of Culture, SARFT, State Secrecy Bureau, and Ministry of Public Security.

58

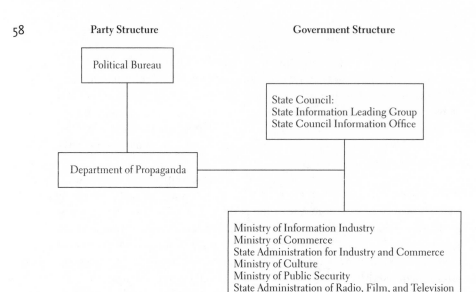

FIGURE 3.2   Party and state organizations responsible for the Internet (central level)
SOURCE: Compiled by the author.

RULES AND REGULATIONS ON THE INTERNET

The government has made enormous efforts to regulate the Internet through laws and administrative means. Table 3.2 summarizes major rules and regulations on the Internet issued between 1994 and 2005. These rules and regulations can be divided into three general categories in terms of political control.

Rules for Internet content censorship. In this category are the administrative provisions on secrecy of computer information systems, which deal with state secrets on the Internet. The administrative provisions ban individuals and institutions from discussing or disseminating any information that is considered a "state secret." Though the administrative provisions fail to provide any definition of "state secrets,"[13] the State Secrecy Law states, "State secrets are matters relating to national security and benefits whose access is, in accordance with the legal procedures, limited to persons of a certain scope in a certain period."[14] Furthermore, the administrative provisions provide that state approval should be obtained from relevant authorities for the distribution of information on the Internet.[15] It administers as tight a censorship on Internet contents as on

TABLE 3.2

Major rules and regulations on the Internet in China, 1994–2005

Rules and regulations	Year	Organization	Main contents
Safety and Protection Regulations for Computer Information Systems	Feb. 1994	The State Council	Giving the Ministry of Public Security overall responsibility for policing the Internet "to supervise, inspect and guide the security protection work . . . investigate and prosecute illegal cases . . . and . . . perform other supervising duties."
Interim Regulations on Management of Computer Information Networks—International Connections	Feb. 1996	The State Council	All Internet users, individuals, and organizations must obey relevant state laws and strictly follow the State Secrecy System; must not use the Internet to undermine state security or disclose state secrets; and must not make, access, copy, or disseminate information that is harmful to public security or pornographic.
Article 285 of the Criminal Law: "Crime on illegal access to state computer information system," *and Article 286: damaging computer information system*	Mar. 1997	National People's Congress	The two articles attempt to provide a legal base for punishing various forms of crimes related to computer information systems.
Interim Regulations on Management of URL Registration	May 1997	State Information Leading Group of the State Council	All Internet users must register at the China Internet Network Information Center (CNNIC) and accept the CNNIC's guidelines.
Rules and Regulations on Implementation of URL Registration	Jun. 1997	China Internet Network Information Center	Implementing *Interim Regulations on Management of URL Registration.*

(continued)

TABLE 3.2

(continued)

Rules and regulations	Year	Organization	Main contents
Computer Information Network and Internet Security, Protection, and Management Regulations	Dec. 1997	The State Council	All Internet Service Providers (ISPs) and other enterprises accessing the Internet are responsible to the Public Security Bureau. ISPs are also required to assist the Public Security Bureau in investigating violations of the laws and regulations. Serious violations of the regulations will result in the cancellation of the ISP license and network registration.
State Secrets Protection Regulations for Computer Information Systems on the Internet	Jan. 2000	State Secrecy Bureau	Prohibiting the release, discussion, or dissemination of "state secrets" over the Internet. This also applies to individuals and organizations when making use of electronic bulletin boards and chat rooms.
Measures for Managing Internet Information Services	Sep. 2000	The State Council	Regulating the Internet services and promoting the "healthy" development of these services. All ISPs and Internet content providers have to keep records of all subscribers' access to the Internet, account numbers, and the addresses or domain names of the Web sites and telephone numbers used.
Telecommunications Regulations of PRC	Sep. 2000	The State Council	Information is prohibited: 1) that goes against the basic principles set out in the State constitution; 2) that endangers national security, divulges state secrets, subverts the government, or undermines national unification; 3) that is detrimental to the honor and interests of the state; 4) that instigates ethnic hatred or ethnic discrimination or that undermines national unity; 5) that undermines the state's policy for religions or that propagates heretical organizations or feudalistic and superstitious beliefs; 6) that disseminates rumors, disturbs social order, or undermines social stability; 7) that disseminates pornography and other salacious materials; 8) that promotes gambling, violence, homicide, and terror or that instigates the commission of crimes; 9) that insults or slanders other people or that infringes upon other people's legitimate rights and interests; and 10) other information prohibited by the law or administrative regulations.

Regulations on Internet News and Bulletin Boards	Nov. 2000	MII and State Council Information Office	Regulations that place restrictions on foreign news and the content of online chat rooms and bulletin boards. The State Council Information Office supervises Web sites and commercial Web portals, and media organizations may only publish information that has been subject to controls in line with the official state media.
The Decision of the NPC Standing Committee on Safeguarding Internet Safety	Dec. 2000	National People's Congress	Under these regulations, those spreading rumors, engaging in defamation or publishing "harmful" information, or inciting the overthrow of the government or division of the country on the Internet will be punished according to the law. Prison sentences can be passed against those who promote "heretical organizations" and leak "state secrets."
The Death Penalty for Offenses Related to Use of the Internet	Jan. 2001	The Supreme People's Court	The Supreme People's Court ruled that those who cause "especially serious harm" by providing "state secrets" to overseas organizations and individuals over the Internet may be sentenced to death.
Regulations on Internet Domain Management	Aug. 2002	MII	Regulations require ISPs to monitor more closely people's use of the Internet. Software should be installed to ensure that messages are recorded, and if the user violates the law, the ISP must send a copy of the message to the MII, the Ministry of Public Security, and the State Secrecy Bureau.
Regulations on Internet Access and Cafés	Nov. 2002	Ministry of Culture	Restricting access to the Internet and the operations of Internet cafés. Proprietors of Internet cafés are obliged to install software preventing users from accessing information considered "harmful to state security," as well as disseminating, downloading, copying, or browsing material on "heretical organizations," violence, and pornography.
Notice on Improving Internet Domain Management	July 2003	MII	All organizations that provide domain services (.com, .net) within China must be registered in the MII, and only those that meet the *Regulations on Internet Domain Management* can continue to provide such services. Those that cannot meet the *Regulations* must stop providing such services before the deadline; otherwise, they will be disciplined.

(continued)

TABLE 3.2
(continued)

Rules and regulations	Year	Organization	Main contents
Explanations on Requirements to Provide Domain Registration Services	Nov. 2003	MII	Explaining the details of the requirements for the organizations that provide domain registration services.
Regulations on Internet Domain Management	Nov. 2004	MII	A revised version of *Regulations on Internet Domain Management* passed in 2002 integrating new rules stated in the *Notice on Improving Internet Domain Management*.
Regulations on Non-Profit Internet Services Provision	Feb. 2005	MII	All non-profit Internet information services must be registered in the MII and its local branches.
Regulations on Administrative Protection of Internet Publications	April 2005	MII	Outlining the methods of protection of Internet publications of various categories.
Rules on the Administration of Internet News Information Services	Sept. 2005	The State Council Information Office and MII	Rules to regulate Internet news information services, safeguard national security and public interest, protect legal rights of Internet information services, and promote healthy and orderly development of Internet information services. These new rules include two additional categories of forbidden content compared with previously released regulations: 1) information inciting illegal assemblies, demonstrations, marches, or gatherings to disturb social order; and 2) information released in the name of illegal civil organizations.

SOURCE: Compiled by the author.

traditional media materials. In recent years, the government has passed new rules on Internet information that might be used for collective actions. For example, the Rules on the Administration of Internet News Information Services, passed in September 2005, added two additional categories of forbidden content compared with previously released regulations: 1) information inciting illegal assemblies, demonstrations, marches, or gatherings to disturb public order; and 2) information released in the name of "illegal civil organizations" — those organizations that are not registered with relevant government bodies.[16]

Rules governing operations of the Internet service. The interim provisions on the administration of international wiring of computer information networks established a complex four-tier system for international wiring. The first is the gateway for international wiring. The interim provisions require that all traffic to computer networks outside China be effected through the gateway maintained by public telecommunication networks, that is, the MII.[17] This is reaffirmed by the rules for the administration of international wiring gateway for inbound and outbound computer information.[18] Under the rules, no individual or institution can establish or use other gateways for Internet traffic without prior approval from the government. This requirement facilitates the filtering of information that is offensive to the state. The second is that computer information networks are directly wired through the gateway. It is required that only those approved, interwired networks can directly carry out international wiring through the gateway. The third is that wired networks are defined as computer information networks that carry out international wiring through the interwired networks. The interim provisions require that any entity that intends to connect to the Internet has to file an application with the relevant government agencies for Internet wiring; an entity intending to operate a business on the Internet has to procure a license. Individuals are excluded from the scope of ISPs. The last tier consists of Internet users that are individuals or entities. Individuals and entities engaging in international wiring shall not commit violations or crimes concerning endangering national security or disclosing state secrets and shall refrain from making, checking, copying, and transmitting pornographic information. Also, according to the regulations on the safeguarding of computer information systems, endangering the security of computer networks is punishable by law.

Rules for the users of the Internet services. Individuals and entities intending to log on to the Internet are required to register with the police and relevant government bodies. Failure to register may result in forced "dewiring" by Internet management authorities. Internet users are also not allowed to publish, discuss, or spread any state secrets through the email systems, chat rooms, or electronic bulletin boards.

EXERCISE INTERNET CONTROL

In addition to these formal rules and regulations, the Chinese government has also tried to exercise its political control over cyberspace in order to ensure that it does not become an avenue for disgruntled elements to mount an offensive to undermine the government. Many measures have been taken to achieve this goal.

First of all, the government has frequently tightened Web site management. To a great degree, cyberspace has been managed by the state and other state-regulated agencies. This is especially true in the area of news Web sites. The government has tried to upgrade media organizations that it sponsors, such as the *People's Daily*, the Chinese News Agency, China International Broadcast, *China Daily*, and the News Center of China International Internet, to "national level Web sites." The government realizes that such moves could lead to the formation of several layers of Web site networks, such as national networks, local networks, and foreign embassy networks. Second, the authorities have tried to close so-called illegal Web sites and politically incorrect ones. There are frequent reports on Internet closure, such as the "Field of Ideas" (*Sixiang de jingjie*) and the "New Culture Forum" (*Xin wenming luntan*). The former provided a forum for free academic discussion, and the latter was aimed at promoting democracy in China. Internet closure can be expected to take place during politically sensitive periods. For instance, prior to and during the National People's Congress in March 2005, a leftist Web site ("Revolutionary Marxism") and a liberal Web site were closed because the former provided a forum for criticizing the market-oriented reforms while the latter disseminated liberalism and democracy. Both were regarded as undermining China's social order. Third, the authorities have arrested and even prosecuted Web site owners. For example, in 2000, Huang Qi and his wife Zeng Li, the owners of the Web site "The Heaven" (*Tian wang*), were arrested for "subverting the state." It was reported that a private ISP was prosecuted for allegedly endangering national security by disclosing the email addresses of his clients to an overseas institution identified as an anti-government organization.[19]

Broader measures have been taken to exercise control over Internet users. Among others, blocking and filtering are two widely used methods. The authorities frequently block news sites, especially foreign-based sites such as the *Washington Post* and *New York Times*. The blocking becomes more frequent at times of heightened security such as the anniversary of the 1989 prodemocracy movement and the annual meetings of the National People's Congress and the National Party Congress.

Most international Web sites that are considered to contain politically sen-

sitive information are inaccessible from China. In late August 2002, the popu-   65
lar search engine Google was blocked in China for several weeks. Another
search engine, Altavista, was also blocked.

Filtering has also been widely used. In September 2002, China introduced
new filtering systems based on key words, regardless of site or context. Filtering software is installed on main public access networks in China. According
to a study by the Harvard Law School, carried out between May and November 2002 and updated on December 3, 2002, more than 50,000 of 204,000 Web
sites tested were inaccessible from at least one location in China, although
some were accessible from the United States.[20] Another detailed empirical
study on China's Internet filtering in 2004–2005 by the OpenNet Initiative
(a collaboration between Harvard Law School, University of Toronto Citizen
Lab, and Cambridge Security Program) concluded that China has built the
most sophisticated Internet filtering regime in the world.[21]

In October 2003, the Ministry of Culture announced that by the year 2005,
all of China's 110,000 Internet cafés would need to install standardized surveillance software. The Ministry of Culture also showed its intention to issue
licenses to allow about one hundred companies to manage the majority of Internet cafés. On November 2003, the MII issued rules for approximately thirty
large companies that manage Internet addresses in China. While these regulations were aimed at improving service standards, they also enabled the authorities to strengthen control over sensitive information posted on the Web.

In addition to enforcing direct control, the authorities are using a variety of
means to force Internet firms to take greater responsibility for implementing
the laws and regulations controlling the use of the Internet. In March 2002, the
Internet Society of China issued the Public Pledge on Self-Discipline. The
pledge includes an agreement to refrain from producing, posting, or disseminating pernicious information that might jeopardize state security and disrupt
social stability; contravening laws and regulations; and spreading superstition
and obscenity. By July 2002, the pledge had been signed by over three hundred
signatories.

On December 2003, thirty Internet news and information providers, including Renmin, Xinhua, Sina, Sohu, and Net Ease, signed a new Internet
News Information Service Self-Pledge. All these providers agreed to "obey
government administration and public supervision voluntarily, to resist firmly
the Internet transmission of harmful information such as obscenity, pornography and superstition, and to resist the information that violates the fine culture
traditions and moral codes of the Chinese nation."[22]

In recent years, some foreign companies, including Cisco, Google, Microsoft, and Yahoo!, have been accused of assisting the Chinese government in

66   exercising Internet control. It has been suggested that China's sophisticated Internet infrastructure would not be possible without technology and equipment imported from foreign companies. China's growing Internet is becoming increasingly attractive for foreign investment. In order to gain profit, foreign companies will frequently have to yield to pressure from the Chinese government. For example, in 2005, two U.S. companies, Cisco Systems and Juniper Networks, were granted four out of six contracts to upgrade China's network, CN2. Cisco Systems had previously faced allegations that it assisted China in developing censorship capabilities.[23] In its router contract for CN2, Cisco would provide China with its 12000 Series routers, which are equipped with a filtering capability typically used to prevent Internet attacks (i.e., worms and viruses). This technology can also be used by Chinese authorities to block politically sensitive content. Cisco denied allegations that it had altered its products to suit the objectives of the Chinese government for cyberpolicing. It declared that it did not tailor its products to the Chinese market and that the products it sold in China were the same as those sold in other countries.[24]

In 2002, Yahoo! was condemned by human rights groups for voluntarily signing the Public Pledge on Self-Discipline, which was established based on China's censorship laws. In 2004, Yahoo! came under fire again for giving the personal email address of a Chinese journalist, Shi Tao, to Chinese authorities, which led to his criminal conviction and sentence of ten years in prison. Shi, who was an editor at *Contemporary Business News* based in the Hunan province, attended an editorial meeting at which government officials read an internal document outlining media restrictions before the fifteenth anniversary of the 1989 Tiananmen Square crackdown in June 2004. Shi sent copies of his notes via his personal Yahoo! email account to a pro-democracy organization in the United States. Chinese state security authorities later requested information from Yahoo! that enabled them to identify Shi and use it in his conviction.[25]

In June 2005, Microsoft's blog-hosting service, MSN Spaces, removed words like "democracy" and "human rights" from use in Chinese blog titles and postings.[26] In December 2005, human rights activists criticized Microsoft after it removed the MSN Spaces Web log of a well-known Chinese journalist, Zhao Jing. Zhao, who worked for the Beijing Bureau of the *New York Times*, occasionally broached sensitive political topics on his blog. In January 2006, Microsoft announced a new policy for foreign countries whereby the company would close personal Web logs only when presented with a legally binding order, would inform its users of the reason for the removal, and would continue to make such blogs accessible in other countries.[27]

In 2004, Google decided to omit sources that the Chinese government does not like from its new Google News China edition. In January 2006, Google

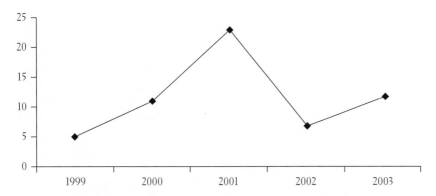

FIGURE 3.3   Internet arrests in China

SOURCE: Adapted from *Amnesty International Journal 2004*, "People's Republic of China: Controls Tighten as Internet Activism Grows," January 17, 2004.

announced that it would launch a search engine in China. Google decided not to offer email or blog services in China in order to avoid the possibility of having to divulge private Internet user information to the Chinese government. Google also stated that it would comply with Chinese laws regarding the censorship of information deemed inappropriate or illegal.

A more coercive move to exercise political control is Internet arrests. Figure 3.3 (also Appendix 3.1) shows a rough picture of Internet arrests in China from 1999 to 2003. These figures are from Amnesty International, which has paid close attention to Internet freedom in China and has collected reported cases of Internet arrests. It is worth noting that while these figures are based on individual arrests, many people were arrested due to their involvement in collective Internet protests (see Appendix 3.1). This is apparent in the cases of Falun Gong after 1999 and the Severe Acute Respiratory Syndrome (SARS) event in 2003.

In March 1998, Lin Hai, a computer engineer from Shanghai, was detained. Lin was considered to be the first person to have been arrested for the use of the Internet in China. He was accused of providing 30,000 email addresses to the VIP Reference, a U.S.-based online pro-democracy magazine. He was charged with subversion and sentenced to two years in prison in June 1999. In 1999, Wang Youcai, one of the founders of the China Democracy Party, was arrested and sentenced to eleven years' imprisonment for subversion. Two of the accusations against him involved sending emails to Chinese dissidents abroad and accepting overseas funds to buy a computer. In June 2000, Huang Qi was arrested after he set up his own Web site, which called for political reforms and helped dissidents trace missing relatives following the 1989 crackdown on the pro-democracy movement.

68   As shown in Appendix 3.1, Internet arrests have continued. Nevertheless, as mentioned in the last chapter, although frequent Internet arrests suggest tightened control over the Internet by the authorities, they also imply that Internet activism is continuing to grow in China. There have been signs of Internet users acting increasingly in solidarity with one another, in particular by expressing support for one another online. As will be seen in later chapters, such solidarity helps to transform individual Internet protests to collective Internet protests.

CONCLUSION

Nevertheless, a very sophisticated Internet control regime does not mean that the Chinese government can always exercise effective control. Many factors can make this control regime less effective. First, Internet users in China are very sophisticated too. The new information technology often enables Chinese Internet users to find ways to get around the censors. Some main methods that Chinese Internet users have employed include 1) short message service, or text messaging via cell phone; 2) tricky passwords such as "elgoog" — Google spelled backward (the search of such words led to the site and allowed free searches until authorities shut it down); 3) overseas servers, which do not adhere to China's regulations and rules, so Chinese Internet users can often find international connections to access banned information; and 4) blogs, which are easily updated to quickly disseminate information and are increasingly becoming a form of mainstream news coverage in China. Moreover, Chinese Internet users have even started an Adopt-a-Blogger program, which seeks international servers to host Chinese blogs and avoid censorship.[28] All these methods associated with the new information technology often empower Chinese Internet users to engage in "guerrilla warfare" with the control regime. Sometimes they win, and sometimes the regime wins.

Second, an effective control regime by design can be ineffective in reality simply because rules and regulations made by the control regime are frequently not enforced. China does not have a tradition of rule of law, and it has not been able to construct an effective infrastructure to enforce laws and regulations. The government makes laws and regulations but often finds it difficult to enforce them. This is also true in the case of the Internet. Certainly, it would be too simplistic to assume that all these Internet regulations and rules have been and will be implemented at the operational level. For example, in recent years, the Chinese government has attempted to implement a system called "accessing the Internet by real identity." The system was designed to enable the police or relevant Internet management authorities to identify Internet users once they connect to the Internet. It required that users purchase an "accessing card" first, for which they have to submit proof of identity. But an official investigation recently concluded that the system has ceased to exist except in name because both Internet users and ISPs have resisted it for various reasons.[29]

A third factor in the difficulty of law enforcement is different interests within the government. As discussed in this chapter, there are conflicting interests between the regulatory regime and the control regime. The highest priority of the regulatory regime is to promote Internet development, while the control regime's priority is to limit the political impact of the Internet. It is not so easy to tell which interest will prevail in reality—the commercial interests of the regulatory regime or the political interests of the control regime. For example, the Chinese government has kept issuing new rules to keep users of both the Internet and mobile phones in line. In early 2006, the government issued new rules to require that people buying prepaid mobile phone cards submit proof of identity. Given the fact that over half of China's mobile-phone accounts are not registered in any name, making it easy for criminals—or dissidents—to use them without being identified by the police, the government had a rationale to design this new system. But when it comes to enforcement, it becomes infeasible due to conflicting interests. As *The Economist* observed,

> Limiting phone-card sales to just a few shops with the ability to process registration requirements would be a blow to mobile-phone companies and huge numbers of private vendors who thrive on such business. It is hard to see how it could be enforced any more rigorously than, say, China's ban on the unauthorized reception of satellite signals. Illegal sales of satellite dishes and cable services offering uncensored foreign satellite channels are big underground businesses in urban China. China's new portals, in their competition for traffic, will continue to test the limits of official tolerance. And in a competitive market few Internet-café operators pay attention to government requirements that users' identities should be registered.

So *The Economist* came to the conclusion that "the market is likely to prevail over restrictions."[30]

The battle over Internet-mediated public space is not only carried out between the control regime and social forces but also between different interests within the government. Apparently, the interaction between different interests within the government has an important impact on the interaction between the state and social forces. The state must be disaggregated when the political impact of the Internet is examined. As emphasized earlier, the frequent occurrence of Internet arrests per se implies that Internet-based collective actions that challenge the state or state organizations have taken place.

So, the questions are as follows: How have some Internet-based collective actions failed while others have succeeded? How does the Internet affect the relations between the state and social forces in China and thus affect political change? The following chapters attempt to answer these questions by examining the interplay between the state and society over the Internet.

APPENDIX 3.1

Reported Internet Arrests in China (1999–2004)

Name	Born	Gender	Detained	Accusation	Date of Trial	Sentence	Province	Occupation	Remarks
Cai Lujun	1969	Male	Feb. 2003	Subversion	Oct. 30, 03	3 years	Hebei	Businessman	Signed an online petition asking for the release of Liu Di
Chen Shaowen	1962	Male	Aug. 02	Subversion	Not known	Not known	Hunan	Writer and former police officer	Posted up to 40 reactionary articles on the Internet
Chi Shouzhu	1960	Male	Apr. 01	Not known	Not known	Not known	Jilin	Student	Printed prodemocracy material from the Internet
Dong Yanhong*	1972	Female	Jan. 01	Publishing subversive information on the Internet	Dec. 13, 01	5 years	Beijing	Qinghua Univ. employee	Downloaded material from the Falun Gong Web sites and disseminated it
Du Daobin	1963	Male	Oct. 03	Incitement to subvert the government	—	—	Hebei	Civil servant	Signed an online petition asking for the release of Liu Di and organized a campaign to support her

Name	Birth year	Gender	Date detained	Charge	Date sentenced	Sentence	Province	Occupation	Activity
Guo Qinghai	1965	Male	Sep. 00	Incitement to subvert the government	Apr. 3, 01	4 years	Hebei	Journalist	Published essays on the Internet on Qi Yanchen's case. Qi was convicted for subversion and disseminating anti-government news via the Internet
He Depu	1956	Male	Nov. 02	Incitement to subvert the government	Oct. 14, 03	8 years	Beijing	Former academic	Published pro-democracy articles on the Internet; member of the China Democracy Party
Huang Kui***	Not known	Male	Nov. 00	Distributing material on the Falun Gong on the Internet	Sep. 01	Verdict not announced	Guangdong	Student	Posted articles opposing the persecution of the Falun Gong on the Internet
Huang Qi	1963	Male	Jun. 00	Incitement to subvert the government	Jan. 01	5 years	Sichuan	Computer engineer	Posted articles on his Web site relating to political and human rights concerns
Huang Qunwei	1978	Male	May 03	Spreading fake or terrorist information	Jun. 11, 03	3 years	Beijing	Unemployed	Posted essays on the SARS on the Internet

(continued)

APPENDIX 3.1
(continued)

Name	Born	Gender	Detained	Accusation	Date of Trial	Sentence	Province	Occupation	Remarks
Jiang Lijun	Not known	Male	Nov. 02	Incitement to subvert the government	Nov. 04, 03	4 years	Liaoning	Not known	Advocated democracy on the Internet and intended to organize a political party
Jiang Yuxia***	Not known	Female	Nov. 02	Distributing material on the Falun Gong on the Internet	Sep. 01	Verdict not announced	Guang-dong	Student	Posted articles opposing the persecution of the Falun Gong on the Internet
Jin Haike**	1976	Male	Mar. 01	Subverting the government	Sep. 28, 01	10 years	Beijing	Geophysicist	Posted articles of political and social concerns on the Internet
Kong Youping	1955	Male	Dec. 03	—	—	—	Liaoning	Worker	Posted articles on a Web site calling for reassessment of the 1989 democracy movement
Li Chunyan***	Not known	Female	Nov. 00	Distributing material on the Falun Gong on the Internet	Sep. 01	Verdict not announced	Guang-dong	Student	Posted articles opposing the persecution of the Falun Gong on the Internet

Name	Year	Gender	Date	Charge	Date	Sentence	Province	Occupation	Activity
Li Dawei	1962	Male	Apr. 01	Subversion	May 01	11 years	Gansu	Former police officer	Downloaded materials from the China Democracy Party Web site
Li Hongmin	Not known	Male	Jun. 01	Subversion	Not known	Not known	Hunan	Not known	Posted articles on the Internet on the 1989 democracy movement
Li Yanfang***	Not known	Female	Nov. 00	Distributing material on the Falun Gong on the Internet	Sep. 01	Verdict not announced	Guangdong	Student	Posted articles opposing persecution of the Falun Gong on the Internet
Li Zhi	1971	Male	Aug. 03	Subversion	Dec. 10, 03	8 years	Sichuan	Civil servant	Communicated with overseas dissident via the Internet
Lin Yang***	Not known	Male	Nov. 00	Distributing material on the Falun Gong on the Internet	Sep. 01	Verdict not announced	Guangdong	Student	Posted article opposing persecution of the Falun Gong on the Internet
Liu Haofeng	1973	Male	Mar. 01	Endangering state security	May 01	3 years	Beijing	Journalist	Wrote articles on the Internet supporting the China Democracy Party
Liu Weifang	Not known	Male	Not known	Incitement to subvert the government	Jun. 01	3 years	Xinjiang	Essayist	Posted essays on the Internet criticizing the government

(continued)

Name	Born	Gender	Detained	Accusation	Date of Trial	Sentence	Province	Occupation	Remarks
Liu Wenyu*	1973	Male	Jan. 01	Publishing subversive information on the Internet	Dec. 13, 01	3 years	Beijing	Graduate student	Downloaded material from the Falun Gong Web site and disseminating it
Lu Xinhua	Not known	Male	Mar. 01	Subversion	Sep. 18, 01	4 years	Hubei	Not known	Posted articles on the Internet on the China Democracy Party
Luo Changfu	1963	Male	Mar. 03	Subversion	Jul. 03	3 years	Chong-qing-	Laid-off worker	Posted articles on the Internet criticizing the government
Luo Yongzhong	1967	Male	Jun. 03	Endangering state security	Oct. 03	3 years	Jilin	Shopkeeper	Posted articles on the Internet critical of government in handling of the SARS
Ma Yan***	Not known	Female	Nov. 00	Distributing material on the Falun Gong on the Internet	Sep. 01	Verdict not announced	Guang-dong	Student	Posted articles opposing persecution of the Falun Gong
Mao Qingxiang****	Not known	Male	Jun. 99	Subversion	Oct. 25, 99	8 years	Zhejiang	Not known	Published articles on the Internet calling for opposition party

Name	Birth year	Sex	Date of detention	Charge	Date of sentence	Sentence	Location	Occupation	Activity
Meng Jun*	1973	Male	Dec. 00	Publishing subversive information on the Internet	Dec. 13, 01	10 years	Beijing	Lecturer	Downloaded material from the Falun Gong Web sites and disseminated it
Mu Chuang-heng	1955	Male	Aug. 01	Incitement to subvert the government	Sep. 10, 02	3 years	Shandong	Writer and lawyer	Published articles on the Internet calling for democracy
Ouyang Yi	1967	Male	Dec. 02	Incitement to subvert the government	Oct. 16, 03	–	Sichuan	Former teacher	Created a pro-democracy Web site and signed a petition
Quan Huicheng	Not known	Male	Oct. 01	Downloading material on the Falun Gong from the Internet	Dec. 01	3 years	Hainan	Not known	Downloaded material from the Falun Gong Web sites and disseminated it
Sang Jiancheng	1942	Male	Nov. 02	Incitement to subvert the government	Nov. 26, 03	3 years	Shanghai	Retired worker	Posted articles on the Internet accusing the government of corruption and signed petition
Tan Qiu	1962	Male	Autumn 02	Not known	Not known	Not known	Guangxi	Hospital worker	Distributed reactionary messages on the Internet

(continued)

Name	Born	Gender	Detained	Accusation	Date of Trial	Sentence	Province	Occupation	Remarks
Tao Haidong	1957	Male	Jul. 02	Incitement to subvert the government	Jan. 8, 03	7 years	Xinjiang	Editor	Wrote and posted books on the Internet critical of the government
Wang Jinbo	1972	Male	May 01	Incitement to subvert the government	Nov. 14, 01	4 years	Shandong	Unemployed	Emailed articles to overseas organizations on the 1989 pro-democracy movement
Wang Sen	Not known	Male	Apr. 01	Subversion	May 30, 02	10 years	Sichuan	Not known	Posted sensitive material on the Internet
Wang Xin*	1977	Male	Not known	Publishing subversive information on the Internet	Dec. 13, 01	9 years	Beijing	Student	Downloaded material from the Falun Gong Web sites and disseminated it
Wang Xuefei*	Not known	Male	Not known	Publishing subversive information on the Internet	Dec. 13, 01	11 years	Shanghai	Student	Downloaded material from the Falun Gong Web sites and disseminated it
Wang Zhenyong	1971	Male	Jun. 01	Downloading articles on the Falun Gong	Not known	Not known	Guangdong-	University professor	Distributed material on the Falun Gong

Name	Birth year	Gender	Date	Charge	Date	Sentence	Province	Occupation	Activity
Wu Yilong****	Not known	Male	Jun. 99	Subversion	Oct. 25, 99	11 years	Zhejiang	Not known	Published a magazine calling for opposition party
Xu Wei**	1974	Male	Mar. 01	Subverting the government	Sep. 28, 01	10 years	Beijing	Reporter	Posted articles of political and social concerns on the Internet
Xu Guang****	Not known	Male	Jun. 99	Subversion	Oct. 25, 99	5 years	Zhejiang	Not known	Published a magazine calling for opposition party
Yan Jun	1973	Male	Apr. 03	Incitement to subvert the government	Oct. 24, 03	2 years	Shaanxi	Biology teacher	Posted material critical of government and the 1989 pro-democracy movement
Yang Zili**	1973	Male	Mar. 01	Subverting the government	Sep. 28, 01	8 years	Beijing	Computer engineer	Posted articles of political and social concerns on the Internet
Yao Yue*	1973	Female	Jan. 01	Publishing subversive information on the Internet	Dec. 13, 01	12 years	Beijing	Graduate student	Downloaded material on the Falun Gong and disseminated it
Zhang Haitao	1972	Male	Jul. 00	Subversion	Not known	Not known	Jilin	Computer engineer	Created a China-based Falun Gong Web site

(continued)

Name	Born	Gender	Detained	Accusation	Date of Trial	Sentence	Province	Occupation	Remarks
Zhang Honghai**	1974	Male	Mar. 01	Subverting the government	Sep. 28, 01	8 years	Beijing	Freelance writer	Posted articles of political and social concerns on the Internet
Zhang Ji	1979	Male	Oct. 99	Disseminating reactionary documents via the Internet	Not known	Not known	Heilong-jiang	Student	Distributed materials on the Falun Gong
Zhang Shengqi	1980	Male	Nov. 03	Leaking state secrets	Not known	10 years	Jilin	Computer firm employee	Posted articles supporting Christian church on the Internet
Zhang Yuhui	1965	Male	Dec. 00	Subversion	Not known	10 years	Guang-dong	Not known	Posted articles on the Falun Gong
Zhang Yuxiang	1965	Male	Mar. 03	Not known	Not known	Not known	Jiangsu	Former armed forces official	Posted sensitive articles on the Internet
Zheng	1986	Female	Mar. 03	Not known	Not known	Not known	Henan	Not known	Posted harmful information on the Internet
Zhu Yufu****	Not known	Male	Mar. 99	Subversion	Oct. 25, 99	7 years	Zhejiang	Not known	Posted harmful information on the Internet

*All six tried together: Dong Yanhong, Liu Wenyu, Meng Jun, Wang Xin, Wang Xuefei, and Yao Yue.
**All four tried together: Jin Haike, Xu Wei, and Zhang Honghai set up a New Youth Study Group in May 2000; Yang Zili joined the group in August same year.
***All six tried together: Huang Kui, Jiang Yuxia, Li Chunyan, Li Yanfang, Lin Yang, and Ma Yan.
****All four tried together: Mao Qingxiang, Wu Yilong, Xu Guang, and Zhu Yufu.

4

The Internet, Political Liberalization, and Political Democratization

INFORMATION TECHNOLOGY AND POLITICAL CHANGES

The linkages between advances in information technology and the development of democracy have become an increasingly important area of research among scholars and policy makers. Most studies are based on the democratic, developed Western countries, and their main concern is whether the information technology revolution is capable of promoting and improving the functioning of the existing democracies. Some optimistic scholars have argued that a positive linkage exists between the development of information technology and democratic improvement. Many new terms such as "digital democracy," "electronic democracy," and "cyberdemocracy," among others, have bound the Internet and democracy closely together and imply that the two have mutually reinforced each other.[1]

In the same vein, scholars have long argued that information technology will help the transition from authoritarianism to democracy.[2] In his study of the third wave of democratization, Samuel Huntington referred to the role of television in producing snowballing or spillover effects in Eastern European transitions.[3] More recently, scholars have argued that the Internet played an important role in bringing down the Suharto regime in Indonesia.[4] In the case of authoritarian China, scholars found that the Internet may pose an insurmountable threat to the regime and that such a threat may arise from Internet use in the mass public, civil society, the economy, and the international community.[5]

On the other hand, some scholars have cautioned that the impact of the Internet on democratic development should not be overstated. In his study of

144 countries, Christopher Kedzie found a statistically significant correlation between network connectivity and political freedom, but he noted that these results cannot conclusively determine causality.[6] Similarly, according to Pippa Norris, there is a significant correlation between democratization and Internet users per capita. Nevertheless, she also pointed out that political change is a determinant of Internet diffusion, not the other way around.[7]

Furthermore, there are pessimistic views of the impact of information technology, especially the Internet, on democratic development in authoritarian states. Scholars have argued that many authoritarian regimes have never failed to exercise political control over newly developed information technology. The Internet is not exceptional. Some scholars have found that authoritarian regimes such as China, Cuba, and Vietnam have translated a long and successful history of control over other information and communication technology into strong control of Internet development within their borders. These authoritarian states have responded to the challenges resulting from the Internet with a variety of reactive measures, including restricting Internet access, filtering content, monitoring online behavior, or even prohibiting Internet use entirely. Moreover, authoritarian regimes often seek to extend control through proactive strategies, guiding the development of the medium to promote their own interests and priorities. Through a combination of reactive and proactive strategies, an authoritarian regime can counter the challenges posed by Internet use and even utilize the Internet to extend its reach and authority.[8] This is especially true in the case of China. While Chinese dissidents within and without China have utilized the Internet to expand their political influence, the communist regime seems to have effectively contained such an influence.[9]

How do we make sense of the two different conclusions? So far I have discussed how the Chinese government has developed information technology as part of its long-term plan to sustain economic growth. To achieve rapid development of information technology, the government has made efforts to establish a regulatory regime to manage this growing sector. But such efforts have also resulted in enormous unexpected consequences, which pose challenges for the communist state. The government has therefore attempted to establish a political control regime to cope with various unexpected political consequences. The establishment and growth of the political control regime has indeed led to various pessimistic conclusions regarding the impact of the Internet on political change in China. Understandably, scholars have argued that the Internet empowers only the state, not the people.

While I have my reservations about the optimistic conclusions, I also believe that the pessimistic view is oversimplistic and that it unduly underestimates the far-reaching impact of the Internet on political change in China.

As in the case of China, while the communist state still exercises tight control   81
over the Internet, social forces have organized successful collective actions
to expand their political influence and even challenge the state. In some
cases, their actions invited the regime's crackdown, such as in the cases of
Falun Gong and the China Democracy Party, while in other cases the state
has had to make concessions with social forces, such as in the case of Severe
Acute Respiratory Syndrome (SARS) and the abrogation of the Measures for
Custody and Repatriation of Vagrants and Beggars in Cities (C&R measures,
hereafter). The Internet has created a very different political environment for
the conduct of politics in China. There are more and more cases in which
social groups have successfully challenged the state and forced it to change its
unpopular policy practice.

From this chapter onward, I shall shift the focus to how information technology has affected political changes in China. In this chapter, I shall first
review the existing literature on how information technology affects politics
and then examine the issue in the case of China. Although most literature in
this regard has been written in the context of developed Western countries, it
is helpful in our understanding of the case of China. To explore whether the
Internet affects Chinese politics is to see what sort of political changes have
taken place, changes that are related to the development of the Internet. So
it is important to define what political changes mean. To do so, I draw on the
existing literature and make some distinctions between political democratization and liberalization. I will attempt to show how information technology,
especially the Internet, has promoted political liberalization, if not political
democratization, in China.

INFORMATION TECHNOLOGY AND CIVIC ENGAGEMENT

In exploring the political impact of the Internet, a key question is whether the
Internet can promote political participation or civic engagement. The impact
of information technology on civic engagement has long interested scholars in
social sciences, especially political science, sociology, and media and communication studies. Yet, no consensus seems to have been reached and disagreements continue. While most debates have focused on experiences in advanced
Western democracies, especially in the trilateral countries (North America,
Western Europe, and Japan), they are quite heuristic in their reflection on
the Internet and civic engagement in authoritarian China. After elaborating
institutional differences between democratic political systems and China's authoritarian one, we will be able to find how information technology can affect
civic engagement in different political settings. The literature on the impact of

82   information technology on civic engagement can be largely divided into two schools, namely, digital empowerment and digital disengagement.

Digital Empowerment

In the modernization theory, which was prevalent in the 1950s and 1960s, information technology was regarded as a precondition for political progress, especially democratic political developments. Scholars in this school believed that democratic development needs certain economic, social, cultural, and technological prerequisites, as developed through economic growth, education, industrialization, and urbanization. The advances in information technology and its spread were regarded as so important in measuring socioeconomic conditions of society that the statistics concerning radios and telephones owned in a country mattered much for determining the occurrence of democracy.[10]

Furthermore, information technology is believed to guarantee the functioning of democratic systems. According to Robert Dahl, a key thinker on modern democracy, the functioning of democracy is threatened more by inequalities associated with information and knowledge than by inequalities in wealth or economic position. Information technology may provide important remedies for political inequality by making political information more universally accessible.[11] Dahl argues that information technology offers several means to reduce political inequality. The evolution of information technology increases accessibility to information about the political agenda, which in turn facilitates public participation. Information technology also expands the means for citizens to contribute to political processes. It makes observation and monitoring of public officials easier for the public at large. As information technology expands the flow of information and communication, it makes governments more transparent, and the more transparent governments are, the smaller the information advantage that elites enjoy with respect to the public at large.

In the same vein, Benjamin Barber contends that the use of information technology can enhance citizen engagement with democratic affairs.[12] Barber made this argument when the revolution in information technology was in its infancy, and he stated his belief in the possibility of telecommunication technology serving as a means for overcoming problems of scale in large democracies and for creating communicative forums such as "town halls," which would not be limited by physical proximity. Such a role of information technology is also emphasized by scholars in the communitarian theory, who claim that technological improvements in the flow of information may both enhance equality and contribute to the construction of stronger communities.[13]

At the empirical level, scholars have found that the modern mass media 83 have a positive role, sustaining and promoting civic engagement. Scholars have demonstrated how newspapers mobilize and reinforce voters[14] and how the news media can contribute to enlightened or reasoned choices among the electorate.[15] Modernization has increased the availability of a diverse range of specialized news media — newspapers, magazines, radio, television, and now the Internet — catering to different markets and providing a rich and dense information environment for citizens in advanced industrialized democracies. The costs of obtaining needed information have been greatly reduced for interested citizens. Modernization has also led to higher levels of literacy and education, which increase the ability of citizens to make use of the information they obtain. All these developments have produced an electorate that is better equipped to participate in and more sophisticated about public affairs.[16]

Since the coming of the Internet age, many scholars have become even more optimistic and believe that the Internet can empower the people in expanding their political participation.[17] Being interactive and reciprocal in its nature of communication, the Internet is said to be able to constrain negative consequences resulting from the old format of one-way communication between politicians and citizens and to make the democratic government more accountable to its people than it would be if citizens depended only on elections and representative mechanisms to exercise their sovereign power. It is believed that the Internet has created a technological condition for the transition from a Schumpeterian elitist democracy to a direct mass democracy.[18] In other words, because the Internet enables political processes to directly and efficiently respond to public opinions and popular demands, it revives the classic essence of democracy by overcoming the two main weaknesses associated with representative democracies, namely, indirect involvement of ordinary citizens in the political processes and, correspondingly, elitism. In this sense, the Internet per se can be regarded as an agent of democratization.

Digital Divide and Civic Disengagement

On the other hand, there are pessimistic views regarding the impact of information technology on civic engagement. For scholars in this school, the progress in information technology does not necessarily mean that there will be improvement in human conditions. Whether information technology can promote civic engagement depends on the political–institutional context in which information technology operates. Among others, two concerns have stood out in the presentation of such pessimistic reviews.

84   First, some scholars have argued that new information technology, especially the Internet, is not able to change inequalities of power and wealth,
which were regarded as major barriers to civic engagement. They contend
that new information technology has unleashed new inequalities of power
and wealth and thus has reinforced deeper divisions between the information
rich and the information poor and between the activists and the disengaged.
The widening of the global and social divides means that Internet politics
disproportionately benefits the elite. Second, many other scholars have questioned the nature of Internet-based human interaction. Instead of promoting
civic engagement, they believe that Internet-based human interactions tend
to discourage civic engagement.

Digital Divide and Inequalities

The Internet operates in the political–institutional context. Whether the
Internet can promote civic engagement depends more on who uses it than
on its technological nature. Before the coming of the information age, the
interest group school had already highlighted how information technology
(e.g., broadcasting, television, etc.) could facilitate political participation. For
instance, David Truman wrote that "the revolution in the means of communication" is a precondition to the development of the interest group system.[19]
Truman went so far as to remark that "the revolution in communications has
indeed largely rendered obsolete . . . Madison's confidence in the dispersion
of the population as an obstacle to the formation of interest groups."[20] Today,
scholars have continued to stress how organized interests can overcome politically decentralizing capacities of information technology. While traditional
advocacy organizations and parties are moving to extend their dominance to
the new realm of information technology, traditional media firms will successfully colonize new technology, preserving patterns of power established in the
era of broadcasting.[21]

Organized interests can reassert their control in the virtual political sphere
and establish their predominance through designing the Internet. According
to Anthony Wilhelm, "design" refers to "the architecture of a network, including whether a network is interactive, moderated, secure, and uncensored, with
sufficient capacity reserved for noncommercial purposes."[22] The architecture of the network can facilitate or inhibit public communication. The fact
is that much of today's means of communication are owned and controlled
by private, transnational conglomerates. Because corporate giants tend to be
interested in deploying services primarily to large businesses and to affluent
residential customers, the decentralization of the Internet can be easily cir-

cumvented. Despite a rapid development of commercially viable networks, the cost of advanced services to the home continues to be high, including online services, cable or satellite connections, digital broadcasting, digital subscriber lines, and others. There are substantial costs attached to subscribing to an ISP, cable television, or direct-broadcast satellite. Furthermore, the government as a highly organized interest can also design the Internet to its own advantage. Scholars such as Lawrence Lessig have long argued that governments can most certainly regulate the Internet, both by controlling its underlying code and by shaping the legal environment in which it operates.[23] All such institutional factors can easily diminish the political and civic potential of the Internet.

Furthermore, the digital divide between the information rich and the information poor also disables effective civic engagement. Because information technology such as email, Usenet, and the Internet is unequally distributed, misused, and designed to reify asymmetrical power relations, it poses formidable obstacles to achieving a more just and humane social order instead of promoting a robust public sphere.[24]

To effectively engage in political participation, one must possess some antecedent resources, such as the skills and capacities that enable a person to participate in the virtual political public sphere. But the reality is that the barriers to entering a digitally mediated public sphere are high, including the cost of accessing or purchasing capital-intensive hardware, the universal literacy needed to manipulate and navigate new media environments, and the higher-order learning—communicative skills and critical thinking—required to participate effectively in public-sphere discussion and debate. Consequently, many among the underclass are unable to engage in public communication and political activities to voice their concerns and needs in their own language.[25]

The digital divide also makes the digitally mediated public sphere exclusive rather than inclusive. Ideally, democratic participation must be inclusive: everyone affected by a certain policy has the opportunity to access and use essential digital media to express his or her preferences and influence policies. The development of information technology enables those who have access to digital media to amplify their voices on public matters and might simultaneously further marginalize those who do not have that access.

The Nature of Internet-Facilitated Human Interaction

A second major source of the pessimistic view regarding the impact of information technology on civic engagement relates to the nature of Internet-facilitated human interaction. In this regard, scholars are concerned with the potential undermining of the methodical pace of democratic deliberation due to digital

86   rhythms and speeds unparalleled in human history.[26] For some scholars, intensive use of information technology may diminish social capital, counteracting whatever gains in participatory equality might flow from it. The information revolution may advance the speed of politics, thus undermining deliberation and consolidating the trend toward government by public opinion poll.[27]

In his study of the impact of television on U.S. politics, Robert Putnam demonstrated that the people who watched the most television were the least socially trusting and the most reluctant to become engaged in community life. Citizens raised in a TV cultural environment were less likely than their parents to trust others, join voluntary associations, and vote. Television may displace other leisure activities and community involvement outside the home; watching prime-time television entertainment, with its emphasis on violence and crime, may produce a "mean world" syndrome; and television may have a particularly strong effect on childhood aggression.[28]

The rapid development of information technology seems to have worsened this situation. For instance, Benjamin Barber later revised his earlier optimistic view of the Internet and asserted that contemporary information technology may undermine the quality of political deliberation and the nature of social interaction.[29] Cass Sunstein contends that the revolution of information technology has led to the decline of the "general interest intermediary," the failure of the public commons, and the replacement of these by a political communication system that fosters fragmentation and polarization.[30]

Effective political deliberation requires a sound civic society, which, according to Jean Cohen and Andrew Arato, comprises structures of socialization and association as well as organized forms of communication in the real world.[31] In this sense, the political public sphere represents the vital channel in civil society in which individuals and groups can become informed about issues, discuss and debate these issues autonomously, and ultimately have an impact on policy agendas. Within such a public sphere, concerned people could talk to one another as equals and could persuade others of the best course of action in the realm of public affairs. But information technology seems to have undermined traditional, face-to-face human interaction. According to Barber, the nascent forms of virtual community are abstract and amorphous, lacking the specificity, context, and tangibility of face-to-face interactions. He states, "There may be a new form of community developing among the myriad solitaries perched in front of their screens and connected only by their fingertips to the new web defined by the Internet. But the politics of that 'community' has yet to be invented."[32]

The digitally mediated human interaction can hardly lead to democratic deliberation. In democratic deliberation, according to Wilhelm, interlocutors in

a political debate need to provide reasons to support their arguments, and these
reasons can be validated intersubjectively in a public space. Deliberation entails debates, discussion, and persuasion in the public sphere. Private thoughts
or isolated activities do not meet the threshold of publicness because they are
not exposed to the scrutiny of others. Furthermore, deliberative participation
in a public forum, face-to-face or virtual, means that those participating ought
to spend time reflecting on the merit of alternative arguments and positions
rather than just responding or voicing their own preferences unreflectively.

All these functions cannot be performed in Internet-mediated human interaction. The Internet is said to be an uncivil environment in which online
communication resembles more the sound-byte culture of television than the
sedate and respectful discussions said to predominate in small-town assemblies
or group meetings. In a digital public sphere, individuals are interested mainly
in vocalizing their individual or private interests and care little for adapting the
position of another through persuasion, negotiation, and compromise.

INFORMATION, COLLECTIVE ACTION, AND POLITICAL LIBERALIZATION

As discussed earlier, both optimistic and pessimistic views are reflected in the
studies of the political impact of the Internet on authoritarian political systems
in general and in China in particular. New information technology has provided a new political arena where the state and society compete for power. It
is too early to declare who is the winner and who is the loser in this battle. The
state, corporations, and other organized interests undoubtedly take advantage
of the Internet to empower themselves. Nevertheless, there are cases in which
less organized social groups and disorganized underclasses have succeeded in
organizing collective actions to challenge the power of organized interests,
especially the state. In these cases, information technology enables marginalized groups to overcome resource limitations and other more serious barriers
to gain political power.

Therefore, a more important question is how social groups, especially those
among underclasses, have succeeded in organizing such collective challenges
to the state. The linkage between the Internet and civic engagement provides
a good angle for us to explore the impact of the Internet on politics.

Liberalization vs. Democratization

To explore the impact of the Internet on Chinese politics, it is useful to make a
distinction between political liberalization and political democratization. The

88   definition given by Guillermo O'Donnell and Philippe Schmitter becomes relevant here. According to them, political liberalization can be defined as "the process of making effective certain rights that protect both individuals and social groups from arbitrary or illegal acts committed by the state or third parties."[33] It is a process and a movement that depart from the usual practice of authoritarian regimes. Such a movement has the effect of lowering the costs (real or anticipated) of individual expression and collective action. Once some actors have dared to exercise those rights publicly and have not been sanctioned for doing so, as they were at the zenith of the authoritarian regime, others are increasingly likely to dare to do the same. On the other hand, political democratization "refers to the processes whereby the rules and procedures of citizenship are either applied to political institutions previously governed by other principles, or expanded to include persons not previously enjoying such rights and obligations, or extended to cover issues and institutions not previously subject to citizen participation."[34]

While the process of moving from political liberalization to democratization can be regarded as a continuous one, the two can also be viewed as two separate processes for the sake of analysis. Although it is difficult to identify a clear-cut demarcation between liberalization and democratization, O'Donnell and Schmitter implicitly suggested a difference of qualitative nature between the two; that is, democratization requires a structural change, but liberalization does not. Liberalization can take place within the existing political framework. As they point out,

> Authoritarian rulers may tolerate or even promote liberalization in belief that by opening up certain spaces for individual and group action, they can relieve various pressures and obtain needed information and support without altering the structure of authority, that is, without becoming accountable to the citizenry for their actions or subjecting their claim to rule to fair and competitive elections.[35]

Liberalization can exist without democratization, and when it does, a situation that O'Donnell and Schmitter called "liberalized authoritarianism" appears. Although China's regime remains authoritarian, political liberalization has taken place from time to time due to the rise of different factors such as a reformist leadership, new social forces, and power struggles within the regime.[36] In this context, I argue that information technology, especially the Internet, has provided new opportunities for political liberalization. Some particular types of liberalization such as regime openness, transparency, and political accountability would be unlikely without the presence of new information technology such as the Internet.

The impact of information technology on political liberalization can be explored in different ways. This investigation attempts to focus on how infor-

mation technology has made different forms of collective actions possible, in- 89
cluding those aimed at challenging the existing regime and forcing the regime
to respond to its challengers by initiating some sort of political liberalization.

INFORMATION TECHNOLOGY AND COLLECTIVE ACTION

Despite growing scholarly interest in the impact of the Internet on political
liberalization, political science scholarship in this area is still underdeveloped.
Because my focus is on how information technology has made collective challenges to the existing regime possible, I attempt to bring the social movement
literature into my investigation. More concretely, this study tries to explore
how the Internet enables the organizers of collective actions to transform a
challenge from an idea into an action and thus pose an actual challenge to
the regime.

To challenge the regime, the organizers of social movements have to make
what Mark Beissinger called "events," or challenges to the regime.[37] To explore
the impact of the Internet on political liberalization is therefore to examine
not only how the Internet makes new types of collective action possible but
also how it has formed a "sustained interaction" with the regime or a chain of
events that challenges the regime.

According to Beissinger, the organizers of social movements everywhere
face different sets of constraints. There are preexisting structural constraints
(conditions) such as the accumulated resources, established patterns of behavior, or norm-delineated conditions that facilitate or impede action through
their presence. There are also institutional constraints that "define the ways
in which agents pursue their interests through their power to instill regularity
and predictability in social affairs and to preclude alternative ways of acting."[38]
Institutions mean regularity and predictability and instill a sense of "normal-
ity" and belief in the impossibility of alternatives by rewarding those who work
within the rules and punishing those who do not.

To challenge the existing regime is to break institutionalized regularity and predictability. The creation of "events" becomes important in this
regard. Events can be understood as contentious and potentially subversive
acts that challenge normalized practices, modes of causation, or systems of
authority.[39] Hannah Arendt defined "events" as "occurrences that interrupt
routine processes and routine procedures."[40] So, events are "purposeful forms
of action whose perpetrators aim to transform rather than to reproduce, to
overturn or alter that which, in the absence of the event, others would take
for granted."[41]

Any organizer of social movements in China will have to face all the above-
mentioned constraints. To explore how the Internet facilitates collective action

90   in China is to see how it helps the organizers of collective action to overcome different sets of constraints and thus create events that challenge the regime. Four hypotheses can be formed in exploring the issue.

> Hypothesis 1: *Information technology provides new sources of information space, enables individuals to form communities in a digitally mediated public sphere, and empowers these communities to participate in politics.*

Scholars have long emphasized the significance of information for the government. Robert Dahl understands the historical development of modern political institutions as driven by information problems embedded in demands for policy. For him, a central feature of modern polyarchy was the creation of "new institutions in order to adapt democracy to the growing need for the mobilization of specialized knowledge." [42] According to him, a central dynamic of the modern state is that the development and exercise of power is associated with asymmetrically distributed information and that the organization of democratic power in response to public as well as elite demands for public policy is regulated by the need for information. The state in this sense can be regarded as more than an allocator of services and values; it is an apparatus for assembling and managing the political information associated with the expression of public will and with public policy. [43]

The question in democracies is how the state shares information with its citizens in order to realize the latter's political rights. By its design, democracy as a system in which political elites compete for power requires a relatively free flow of information; otherwise, the system will not function. [44] In authoritarian China, the question becomes how the government could monopolize information in order to effectively control its citizens. If information is free to flow, then total control becomes unlikely.

In the pre-reform era, China's political system was characterized by totalitarianism. According to Carl Friedrich, totalitarian regimes are characterized by a totalist ideology, a single party committed to this ideology, a fully developed secret police, and the monopoly of mass communications, operational weapons, and all organizations. [45] Furthermore, the Communist party defines "ideology" as what Karl Marx called the "second side" of the superstructure, namely, the ideas and convictions that support the existence of the system. This ideology broadly encompasses such elements as public opinion, morality, theoretical thought, political ideas, philosophy, religion, art, and literature. [46] As Stuart Schram has observed, "In China, as well as in the Soviet Union, ideology means the idea, theory or hypothesis recognized by the leaders." [47]

The communist state led the development of the mass communications system in order to mobilize mass support to the regime. According to Alan

Liu, mass media is the communists' organizational approach to social mobilization. To make an organization effective, its members have to be dedicated
to the goals of the organization and competent in their professional skills. The
media must disseminate ideology and educational matter in order to transform its population into efficient and dedicated members of the communist
society.[48] The monopoly of information is also intended to cultivate a "new
people," uniquely imbued with "socialist morality," who act spontaneously
and habitually in accordance with socialist values.[49]

In this sense, the monopoly of information ultimately empowers the state
by enabling it to exercise both "formal" and "informal" control, using Norbert
Elias and Michel Foucault's terms. According to Elias and Foucault, the early
modern state imposed control formally to encourage certain behaviors and
threatened draconian punishments for their violation. In contrast, the modern
state enlists its subjects as participants in their own governance. In the process,
it shifts the locus of control internally.[50] It is hardly true that in China, citizens are allowed to take part in politics. As a matter of fact, the state instructs,
commands, and punishes on one hand and educates, informs, persuades, and
discourages on the other hand.

The monopoly of information flow has an important impact on the relations between the state and society, as well as on individuals. There is little
space for the existence of civil activities. After the Communist party took over
power in 1949, the state adopted measures to reshape the sphere of intermediary organizations in the light of reordering class relations, restructuring the
economy, and legitimizing power. All organizations regarded or even sus-
pected to be "counter-revolutionary" by the government were banned. On
the other hand, in order to mobilize millions of people to implement public
policies and to achieve the party's and even Mao Zedong's personal political
purposes, enormous mass civilian bodies, or "administered mass organizations," were created by the party-state. Party cadres and governmental officials
used such organizations to organize youths, workers, women, and other social
groups into bodies resembling a "conscription society."[51]

In terms of interpersonal relations, China in the pre-reform era was characterized by social atomization—the obliteration of social ties that are not
directly harnessed to the party's aims. The state recognized no legitimate distinction between private and public spheres. Allegiances not subordinated to
the party were regarded as subversive to its aims. Consequently, as William
Kornhauser pointed out, an "atomized society" is formed, "a situation in which
an aggregate of individuals are related to one another only by way of their rela-
tion to a common authority in a variety of independent groups."[52] The reason
is simple. A totalitarian regime requires "atomized masses" not only to keep

92 power, by preventing alternative loyalties independent of the regime, but also to ensure that there are no obstacles to inhibit the total mobilization of the population.[53] In such a situation, "alienation," "anomie," and "loneliness" are normal characteristics of the structure of social relations.[54]

Information technology, especially the Internet, has drastically changed this situation. It has undermined "social atomization" imposed by the regime and enabled individuals to form communities in a digitally mediated public sphere and thus has empowered these communities to participate in politics.

As discussed in Chapter Two, China has achieved a rapid development of the Internet. Due to the size of the Chinese population, the absolute number of Internet users is huge, and an Internet society is rapidly evolving, although the proportion of Internet users in the total population remains small.

The rapid development of the Internet has led to the fast expansion of information space, thus providing Internet users with more alternative sources of information than ever before. In this sense, the Internet has expanded freedom of information access in China as in democratic countries. But there are differences between Chinese users' online behavior and that of their counterparts in democratic political institutions. Table 4.1 shows the results of the China Internet Network Information Center's (CNNIC) surveys regarding Internet users' main purposes for accessing the Internet. It is worth noting that the categories in Table 4.1 are not mutually exclusive. Still, this table indicates that most users go online to obtain information. It is remarkable that there has been no major change in the categories despite a dramatic increase in the number of online users.

Table 4.2 shows what kind of information Chinese Internet users search for.

TABLE 4.1

Most important reasons for going online in China (%), 2002–2004

	Jan-02	Jul-02	Jan-03	Jul-03	Jan-04
Get information	46.1	47.6	53.1	46.9	46.2
Education	4.3	6.6	4.8	7.2	7.9
For work / business needs	6.2	1.6	2.0	0.8	0.8
Entertainment	31.1	18.9	24.6	28.6	32.2
Get free Internet resources	3.3	1.2	1.9	1.7	1.8
Communication	4.9	4.4	3.8	3.2	2.7
Stock trading	2.5	0.9	1.1	2.1	1.5
Online shopping	0.4	0.3	0.1	0.2	0.1
Bandwagoning	0.6	0.3	0.3	0.6	0.3
Making friends	—	16.1	8.1	7.6	5.2
Others	0.6	2.1	0.2	1.1	1.3

SOURCE: *Survey Report on the Development of China's Internet*, China Internet Network Information Center (CNNIC), various years.

TABLE 4.2

Information searched for by Internet users in China (%), 2002–2004

	Jan—02	Jul—02	Jan—03	Jul—03	Jan—04
News	74.0	75.8	78.0	76.9	70.9
Software & hardware	55.6	60.3	53.4	47.6	44.7
Entertainment	46.5	41.3	44.6	44.9	41.7
Living services	27.8	24.9	27.8	32.1	34.1
Cultural activities	20.4	14.8	17.9	19.0	18.2
E—book	37.4	35.6	32.6	31.5	28.8
Education & technology	31.8	28.8	30.1	28.2	41.8
Military	—	—	—	—	8.1
Sports	—	21.2	20.4	16.9	12.8
Finance, insurance & real estate	16.4	15.7	15.6	15.1	12.1
Auto	—	8.4	8.0	9.6	20.5
Job	22.2	19.0	22.1	20.3	8.4
Trading	9.9	6.7	7.5	7.5	9.1
Enterprises	—	5.3	6.5	6.9	7.5
Weather forecast	—	5.0	7.2	7.5	—
Travel & transportation	11.4	7.3	7.6	6.7	5.7
Advertisement	6.4	5.1	5.8	5.6	3.8
Health care	7.7	4.9	4.9	5.6	5.7
Making friends	4.5	2.8	2.9	2.6	1.9
Laws, regulations & policies	13.7	8.3	8.5	8.2	7.7
E—government	—	2.5	3.1	3.5	3.6
Games or prizes	—	—	—	—	17.6
Others	1.6	0.8	0.7	0.8	0.8

SOURCE: *Survey Report on the Development of China's Internet*, China Internet Network Information Center (CNNIC), various years.

It is very clear that Chinese users go online mainly to read news, followed by obtaining computer hardware and software knowledge. Why is gaining information, particularly from reading news, the highest priority for Chinese users? One explanation lies in China's political setting. In a political arrangement in which the state controls the media, free flow of information is difficult, and readers are not able to access the necessary information and news through traditional media such as newspapers and broadcasts, which are still tightly controlled by the state. Although great changes have been made to China's mass communications system since the reform and open door policy in the 1970s, information pluralization in traditional media still remains unchanged.[55] Within such a political setting, cross-nation Web sites have enormous advantages over China's mass communications system in providing alternative information and news sources. The Chinese users can gain information and news that they cannot get from traditional media or prohibited public access. The existence of alternative sources of information and news is an important prerequisite for a free society. In this sense, the development and expansion of

94 the Internet in China have contributed to an increase in information access, even though the political system still remains authoritarian.

Needless to say, the Chinese government is highly vigilant regarding possible negative political influence arising from the rapid Internet development. As discussed in Chapter Three, it has paid much attention to political control over the development of the Internet, as well as to its technological progress and administrative regulations. Tight political control over the Internet, however, does not mean that collective action becomes an impossible enterprise for social groups. State control certainly makes collective action more difficult, but it does not eliminate its possibility. While information technology enables the authorities to filter and block the flow of information, it also enables the Internet users to counteract the efforts by the authorities. When Chinese users exchange information on how to work with information technology, a common interest is "proxy" technologies used to overcome the firewalls established by the regime. As Table 4.3 shows, "search engine" and "downloading and uploading software" are among the most demanded services among Chinese Internet users. A significant portion of the users have learned to circumvent official blockages to access overseas Web sites. Such technological capabilities do not exist among users in a free society because they do not need them. The Internet technology has created a new game altogether in that the government is unable to use traditional methods to control information access.

Furthermore, it is not in the interest of the state to have total control over Internet activities. The operation of the new socioeconomic system requires free flow of information. The state's arbitrary intervention of information flow often causes serious damage to the existing system. A market economy in a globalization age is based on free flow of information. Crude methods used by the regime such as shutting down search engines only cause greater internal and external dissatisfaction. As Marcus Franda observed, "With more than 200,000 different routes around the major nodes of the Internet, attempts by Chinese authorities to program blockages in large numbers of routes would render Internet service almost unusable."[56] This observation remains valid and becomes even more relevant today due to faster development of the Internet in recent years. Indeed, the government has had great difficulties achieving the twin goals — a free flow of information and a tight control over sensitive political information.

When total control becomes counterproductive, the government has to turn to other strategies. It has appealed to more realistic and feasible measures to govern cyberspace. What Russell Hardin called "coordination" strategy becomes valuable for the government.[57] According to Hardin, the state does not need to be a "gunman" state in order to solicit social obedience. An Orwellian vision of society does not necessarily mean effective and efficient governance.

TABLE 4.3

Services that were used most frequently (multiple choices, %), 2002–2004

	Jan-02	Jul-02	Jan-03	Jul-03	Jan-04
Email	92.2	92.9	92.6	91.8	88.4
News	—	20.4	21.3	20.7	59.2
Search engine	62.7	63.8	68.3	70.0	61.6
Software downloading and uploading	55.3	51.0	45.3	43.0	38.7
Information acquiring	46.7	40.3	42.2	37.8	47.2
Online chatting, pager	59.6	45.5	45.4	45.4	39.1
BBS services, newsgroup	23.2	18.9	18.9	22.6	18.8
Free personal/Web site hosting	11.8	8.6	6.8	6.2	5.0
E-government	—	1.4	1.9	2.1	2.0
Online game	17.1	18.6	18.1	18.2	14.7
Stock trading	7.4	7.1	5.5	5.4	3.7
Online shopping and trading	7.8	10.3	11.5	11.7	7.3
Short message	8.0	8.8	8.8	7.8	3.8
Online education	11.8	8.9	8.9	8.9	6.2
E-journal	—	11.2	9.5	8.2	3.9
IP telephone	1.7	1.0	1.0	1.0	0.8
Internet banking	2.1	2.8	3.6	4.3	4.5
Online hospital	—	0.8	0.7	0.8	0.5
Online auction	—	0.7	0.9	1.1	0.8
Online meeting	0.6	0.3	0.3	0.5	0.4
Ticket and hotel reservation	—	0.7	0.8	0.5	0.4
Multimedia entertainment	22.1	29.3	22.6	22.0	13.5
Telnet	—	—	1.1	1.2	0.6
Information broadcasting	—	—	3.3	3.5	2.0
Online selling	—	—	2.1	2.2	2.1
Information system (ERP, CRM, SCM)	—	—	1.2	1.1	0.8
Online recruiting	—	—	—	—	4.7
Online database	—	—	—	—	0.9
Online alumni	—	—	—	—	15.7
Other services	0.4	0.2	0.1	0.2	0.2

SOURCE: *Survey Report on the Development of China's Internet*, China Internet Network Information Center (CNNIC), various years.

The state can keep its citizens under control without going to Orwellian extremes by developing "conventions" to keep citizens from transgressing the boundaries and punishing those who attempt to do so. This is the strategy that the Chinese government has adopted in governing cyberspace. Two tactics have been used. First, the government exercises only selective control over information flow; that is, it blocks only information with political sensitivity that can undermine regime legitimacy and is perceived as violating national security. Second, the government also uses selective penal measures to constrain those who have attempted to transgress the boundaries that the government has established for Internet users. The government allows limited information liberalization, but once Internet users break that limit, governmental inter-

96   vention will come to "correct" online behavior. Indeed, once Internet users transgress the boundaries, the nature of the interactions between the government and Internet users changes. It tends to become what Hardin called a "conflict interaction," in which "one party gains only if another loses."[58] As will be discussed later, in such a situation, what strategies social groups use in their interaction with the regime becomes important in deciding whether they can succeed or not.

> Hypothesis 2: *Information technology reduces the organizational cost for potential challengers while increasing the cost of crackdown on information-based social movements on the part of the regime.*

There are always potential challengers inside China even with tight political control by the communist regime. The absence of formal opposition in China does not mean that there is no challenge to the communist regime. Even since the reform and open door policy of the late 1970s, social movements often suddenly arise to challenge the regime, such as the Democracy Wall movement in the late 1970s, the pro-democracy movement in 1989, and the democratic party movement in 1998. Whether a given challenge can succeed is another matter. Unfortunately, most challenges fail. Once the regime feels challenged and threatened, it will initiate a crackdown. Given the nature of China's authoritarian regime, any social movement that challenges the regime involves huge political risks. Hence, any social movement organizers face an uphill task. Organizing a social movement takes time and is a long process. Intervention from the regime can occur at any time, and so can a crackdown. Most social movements have failed during the process of their formation. It is extremely difficult for social movements to produce any practical result.

Information technology, especially the Internet, has changed this situation dramatically. The Internet helps reduce organizational costs and mobilize potential supporters. First, it is more difficult, if not impossible, for the regime to find out who the organizers are. In organizing conventional forms of social movements, the physical presence of organizers is important; but with the Internet, the presence of organizers is no longer that crucial. Second, the Internet helps spread information to potential challengers more efficiently than conventional means of communications allow. Because information diffusion per se is a part of organizing a social movement, it can invite intervention from the regime. Information technology often enables organizers to avoid such a governmental intervention. Third, the Internet also helps neutralize those who are more sympathetic to challengers. Information monopoly had been an important means for the communist regime to maintain its rule. Information control, filtering, and manufacturing and misleading interpretations are common prac-

tices in all authoritarian regimes.[59] Information technology breaks the governmental monopoly on information, and potential participants are able to access
more original information and then make their own rational judgments.

Furthermore, in some cases, the Internet per se can play the role of the
movement organizer, overcoming organizational impossibility. This is to say
that the Internet transforms the organizing of social movements from an enterprise of the impossible to reality. This is quite apparent in the recent occurrence involving "flash mobs," a phenomenon where people gather at a pre-
determined point, conduct certain acts, and then disperse as quickly as they
gathered. When participants in a flash mob were asked who the organizer was,
they answered that they were also trying to find out how it was "organized."
Certainly, in such cases, a piece of information on the Internet becomes the
organizer. Participants here identify an idea and associate themselves with
such an idea. Participants get together at a particular place at a particular time
to materialize such a particular idea. To a degree, the siege of Zhongnanhai by
Falun Gong resembles a flash mob gathering. In other words, the Internet can
become a forum to gather social forces with similar political orientations.

Meanwhile, information technology increases the cost of the regime's
crackdown on collective action. This is due to a number of factors. First is
the decentralized nature of information technology. Despite the existence of
the "digital divide" in China, the Internet's use has increasingly widened. It
has reached most urban families and some parts of rural areas. As shown in
Chapter Two, as the development of information technology is an integral part
of nation-state building, the regime has thus made enormous efforts to expand
the reach of the new technology. The Internet has been widely used even in
low-income social groups. The existence of a digital divide does not mean that
social groups cannot engage in political participation via the Internet. With
such developments, national mobilization on the part of the regime is still
possible, but its cost increases drastically. The Internet enables the organizer
of a collective action to initiate national mobilization to challenge the regime.
When challengers can be mobilized nationwide, the cost of the regime's crackdown is likely to increase. It is one national mobilization against another.

Second, a crackdown by the regime often generates huge external pressure.
The Internet is a means of globalization, linking domestic affairs to international affairs and transforming local issues to global issues and vice versa. Globalization and the consequent interdependence impose serious constraints on
any sovereign state. This is especially true on the issue of democracy and human rights, which are of great concern to the international community. Globalization enables the international community to exercise its influence over
China's domestic affairs. International trade and foreign investment require the

98   free flow of information. When an economy becomes increasingly knowledge-based, it becomes unlikely for the regime to control information flow. The communist regime finds it increasingly difficult to prevent China's domestic political issues from being internationalized. Once a local human rights violation can be internationalized, the cost of such a violation increases.

Third, traditional coercive methods of cracking down on information-based social movements are becoming more and more unproductive for the regime. The daily functioning of the new socioeconomic system requires the free flow of information. The regime's arbitrary intervention of information flow often causes great domestic dissatisfaction not only among potential challengers but also among ordinary citizens. Excessive coercive measures on the part of the regime can transform the "observers" of collective action into its agents. Information-induced social movements are based more on reasoning than on emotional factors. Not only do the participants of collective action know what is going on, "observers" know too. Any unreasonable and unjustified crackdown on the part of the regime is likely to invite an alienation of itself from the majority of the population.

> Hypothesis 3: *Information technology provides a channel for reformist leaders within the regime to gain support from social forces, makes the regime fragmented, and thus creates a chance for political liberalization.*

As emphasized earlier, the state must be disaggregated in an examination of the political impact of the Internet in China. In Chapter Three, I disaggregated the state at the bureaucratic level—namely, between the regulatory regime and the control regime—and argued that conflicting interests between the two bodies often make the enforcement of Internet control less effective on the part of the state. Such a disaggregated perspective can also be applied at the leadership level. Despite its insistence on so-called collective leadership, the communist regime is not monolithic but rather consists of different political fragments from which opportunities for liberalization often arise.[60] O'Donnell and Schmitter's concepts of "hard-liners" and "soft-liners" become relevant here. According to O'Donnell and Schmitter, the hard-liners are those who believe that the perpetuation of authoritarian rule is possible and desirable, while the soft-liners are aware that the regime they helped to implant, and in which they usually occupy important positions, will have to make use of some degree or some form of "electoral legitimation."[61] One can argue further that political liberalization becomes possible not necessarily because the soft-liners are willing to pursue electoral legitimization, but as long as they are willing to explore new sources of political legitimacy, liberalization remains possible.

Within the Chinese communist regime, power competition between hard-

liners and soft-liners is a norm, and power struggles have not disappeared since
the formation of the Communist party in the 1920s. Mao Zedong used to sum-
marize the history of the party as a history of political struggles between the
two different lines within the party. Therefore, despite its authoritarian nature,
the political dynamism for liberalization exists within the system. Political liberalization more often than not is a consequence of unstated cooperation between reformist leaders and liberal social forces. But it is not easy for such cooperation to succeed within the communist regime. Intensive internal power
struggles often "kill" liberal elements, not facilitate them. Conflicting interests
are often set against each other without being known outside. Frequently,
liberal forces are contained and eliminated before they are able to reach the
outside world. Moreover, high political risk is involved when liberal forces
within the regime try to join forces with the general public. Take the case of
Zhao Ziyang during the 1989 pro-democracy movement as an example. Zhao's
liberal stand toward the student movement was confronted by strong conservative forces within the party. When Zhao attempted to reach out to social forces
that supported him, conservatives in the party quickly rallied together and
eventually ousted Zhao.

The Internet is changing situations like this. It helps political mobilization
on the part of reformist leaders. In the case of Zhao, his physical presence (at
Tiananmen Square) was important for political mobilization. But in mobilization via the Internet, reformist leaders do not need to make such physical efforts to reach out. Social forces that favor political changes can show their support quickly via the Internet. Furthermore, mobilization via physical presence
is often local and regional, but mobilization via the Internet is nationwide.
As we will see later, this is true in the case of the SARS event. Once political
support is mobilized nationwide, the conservatives have to consider the cost if
they openly confront the reformists. In this case, Internet mobilization poses
a political deterrent to the conservatives. With the successful presence of unstated cooperation between reformist leaders and liberal social forces, policy
adjustment becomes possible for the reformist leaders. This is likely to lead to
the beginning of the process of political liberalization.

> Hypothesis 4: *The Internet has made it possible to form a "sustained interaction"
> between the challengers and the regime, that is, an event or a chain of events, and
> therefore to push consistently for political liberalization.*

As O'Donnell and Schmitter have observed, a distinctive characteristic of
the early stage of political liberalization is its precariousness and dependence
upon governmental power. A challenge is likely to invite a reaction from a
still arbitrary and capricious regime, so whether that challenge can sustain or

100   encourage another challenge depends on the reaction from the regime. Here, whether liberalization could take off and then become sustainable depends on the interaction between challengers and the regime. If an initial challenge was not sanctioned by the authoritarian regime, it would likely encourage other challenges to follow. Furthermore, one can argue that what governmental reaction a given challenge could invite also depends on the nature of the challenge. O'Donnell and Schmitter observed that if initial liberalized practices are not too immediately and obviously threatening to the regime, they tend to accumulate, become institutionalized, and thereby raise the effective and perceived costs of their eventual annulment. This trend is likely to lead to political democratization. On the other hand, when a given challenge poses an immediate threat to the regime, the latter is likely to take coercive measures against that challenge and even eliminate it in order to prevent it from inviting any new challenges. In this case, political liberalization becomes impossible.

The Internet has made sustained collective action possible even when the organizers continue to face an arbitrary and capricious regime. Since its inception, the Internet has not only created individual events of social movements, but it has also provided the dynamics of an "eventful" development of social movements. As shown in Table 3-3 and Appendix 3.1, frequent Internet arrests imply the frequent rise of Internet protests in China.

This is possible because of different factors I discussed above, such as the decentralized nature of the Internet, lower organizing costs, speedy flow of information among potential challengers, and the capability of national mobilization on the part of challengers. A case in point is the Falun Gong. Even though the regime cracked down on the movement, Falun Gong followers continue to initiate waves of public protests, despite their small scale, against the regime. The materialization of these acts totally depended on continuous effective communications among Falun Gong followers via information technology. Members of the Falun Gong have used the Internet and email to circulate information about repression against the group. The Internet, email, and bulletin board services are also widely used by other groups such as dissidents and Tibetan exiles to circulate information or protest against repression, publicize their cause, or draw support for online petitions and open letters. Email and the Internet have provided an effective means of communication within China and with various Chinese dissident communities abroad. Sustained Internet activism was observed by Amnesty International. According to its 2004 report, such Internet activities include "signing online petitions, calling for reform and an end to corruption, planning to set up a pro-democracy party, publishing 'rumors about the SARS,' communicating with groups abroad, opposing the persecution of the Falun Gong and calling for a review of the 1989 crackdown on the democracy protests."[62]

Sustained action is more apparent when the challenges are perceived by the regime as helpful, not threatening. Such a situation is likely to lead to unstated cooperation between reformist leaders within the regime and liberal social forces without. Such cooperation is likely to be institutionalized, if initially perceived "helpful" challenges turned out to actually be helpful. The regime is likely to begin to adjust its policies to allow previously constrained social members to exercise their rights. The case of the SARS serves as an excellent example. During the spread of the SARS, social groups exercised enormous pressure on the leadership and eventually forced it to change its previous policy practice. Although a number of people were detained for disseminating information about the spread of the SARS, political pressures from both inside and outside the regime remained. Such positive interplays between the regime and social forces are more likely to lead to political liberalization.

CONCLUSION

While examples will be provided to support these hypotheses in the chapters that follow, some tentative conclusions can be reached here. First, information technology has made it possible for social groups to initiate novel forms of collective action. Political entrepreneurs or protest organizers are able to overcome resource barriers by using comparatively inexpensive information technology. We will see that, without information technology, challengers would not have been able to organize nationwide collective actions such as the Falun Gong siege, the China Democracy Party petition, and the chain of events that eventually led to the abolition of the C&R measures.

Second, information technology promotes political liberalization by providing the organizers of collective action with the means to create events, to make an event eventful, or to use one event to create another. Sociologist Larry Griffin once noted that events are "imbued with sociological import because it is in and through their unfolding that we see the collision of social structure and social action."[63] Events affect China's political liberalization in very different ways. Not all events have equal political impacts. Some events pose a direct challenge to the communist regime, while other events do not. So, different events have different political consequences.

Third, Internet-based collective actions have their limitations in China. Put simply, such collective actions are able to promote political liberalization, but so far they have not been able to trigger political democratization.

102   This is because democratization requires a structural change to the existing regime, but liberalization does not. With democratization taking off, the existing regime is likely to be replaced by a new one, and current power holders are likely to lose power. Furthermore, democratization requires that rulers become increasingly rule bound and that no one can control the free flow of information arbitrarily. Such a structural change is apparently not happening in China, as many studies of the Internet have proved.

    Internet-based collective actions can promote political openness, transparency, and accountability to a great degree. These developments are important parts of political liberalization. Compared with the situation before the information age, Chinese leaders are now more accountable to citizens and are willing to change old policies and political practices as long as the existence of the regime is not threatened. Such a change is partly due to the existence of new forms of collective actions that enable social forces to exert pressure over the regime.

5

THE INTERNET, CIVIC ENGAGEMENT, AND PUBLIC DISTRUST

CIVIC ENGAGEMENT AND COLLECTIVE ACTION

In the last chapter, I formed some hypotheses on how information technology can provide new dynamics for political changes in China. The Internet provides new sources of information and a condition for civic engagement, and thus introduces changes into the interaction between the state and society. The linkage between the Internet and civic engagement gives us a good angle to explore the impact of the Internet on politics. In this chapter, I shall first discuss how information technology can actually affect civic engagement and then use some empirical cases to elaborate on how Internet-based civic engagement has affected Chinese politics.

Academic interest in the impact of information technology on civic engagement is growing. Many scholars have emphasized the social–political domains where advances in information technology serve as a powerful stimulant to the formation of civil society and the public sphere. The formation of civil society was regarded as an independent variable favorable to liberalization and democratization, particularly in explaining the East European transitions from communism.[1] Some scholars have argued that information technology substantially promotes the formation, development, and growth of civil society and thus makes the genuine democratic performance of political institutions possible.[2] Following Jurgen Habermas,[3] some scholars have emphasized the importance of the public sphere, especially communication, on civil society and believe that modern information technology has constituted the most effective means of communication in today's world.[4] In short, the spontaneity and plurality of modern information technology has given rise to the electronic public sphere and consequent independent, pluralistic, and active civil society; and such a civil society will undoubtedly create a socially favorable setting that encourages modern democracy to overcome its somehow formalistic feature and to become embedded in people's political consciousness and their daily social practice.

Exploring the impact of the Internet on politics involves examining how civic engagement takes place in the electronic public sphere. Of course, it is important to place the Internet in China's authoritarian, political–institutional context. Like elsewhere, looking at the Internet as a new form of technology alone does not inform us on how it affects civic engagement. The Internet operates in a given political–institutional context, and how the Internet affects civic engagement depends on the interplay between the Internet and the existing political–institutional setting.

As discussed in the last chapter, in advanced democracies the Internet is believed to have led to a decline of social capital and civic engagement. The situation in China is apparently different, where the Internet has enabled social groups to develop social capital and thus has promoted civic engagement. But interestingly, while the Internet in advanced democracies has led to a decrease in public confidence in the government, it has had a similar function in China; specifically, it has had a negative, even destructive, impact on public trust in public institutions.

According to Robert Putnam, "civic engagement" refers to active participation in public affairs.[5] Michael Walzer also points out that "interest in public issues and devotion to public causes are the key signs of civic virtue."[6] In authoritarian China, citizens can hardly participate in public affairs in a way that their counterparts in democratic countries do. But this does not mean that there is no civic engagement in China. Over the years, citizens in China have developed their own forms of political participation.[7] After China entered the information age, civic engagement also began to take place over the digitally mediated public sphere. When major events occurred, intensive Web site discussions would suddenly follow and this would exert high political pressure on the authorities. The Chinese official media has recognized the political significance of digitally mediated civic engagement. According to an official report, without intensive civic engagement over the Internet, the government would not have initiated many policy changes in the past years.[8]

The question to ask is how Internet-mediated civic engagement takes place in China. More specifically, two questions have to be addressed. First, how does information technology enable individuals or netizens to engage in civic

engagement? And second, how do individuals overcome the problem of collective action given that civic engagement is a form of collective action?

In rational choice theory, the relations between information and individual engagement are instrumental. Changes in the cost and variety of sources of information directly affect levels of political participation. As information becomes less costly and is provided by a greater variety of sources over which individuals have control, more citizens are likely to become engaged in politics. Information is central to behavior, and uncertainty provides the drive for such information. Because uncertainty is a basic force in human affairs, the acquisition and use of information to reduce uncertainty is an elemental feature of all human activity. So, Anthony Downs argues that "coping with uncertainty is a major function of nearly every significant institution in society" as well as a major activity of the political individual. According to Downs, "most uncertainty is removable through the acquisition of information."[9] If information is a prerequisite to active participation, then those with more information are more likely to have the capacity to participate in politics.

In this sense, contemporary information technology matters for collective action. Information technology differs in important ways from traditional print and broadcast mass media. According to Bruce Bimber, information technology offers a vastly greater volume of information than other media, often at comparably lower costs, from a virtually limitless number of competing sources. More important, it provides a higher degree of purposiveness and selectivity by permitting citizens to control what information they acquire and where and when they acquire it. The evolution of information abundance has created the most potentially important change in citizens' information environment so far by reducing the cost of information, multiplying channels, and providing possibilities for greater purposive control and selection.[10]

Politics is "public" by its very nature. There is a huge gap between the free flow of information promoted by advances in information technology and the shaping of public discussions on political issues. The act of obtaining information is individualistic in nature. It is considered "private action" rather than "collective action." In both conception and reality, there is a process of transition from the private sphere to the public one.[11] Though the Internet promotes the free flow of information in the private sphere, the question remains: Can the Internet further promote the transition from the private action of information acquisition to the collective action of political participation? If collective action is to take place, the collective action problem has to be overcome first.

As collective actions take place frequently, the collective action problem

106   must be dealt with. There are different strategies to overcome the collective action problem, such as conditional cooperation, convention, selective incentives, the state, the community, political entrepreneurs, property rights, and norms. While scholars in different schools emphasize different factors, some have found that forming identity politics, or class consciousness if using the Marxist term, could become an effective and efficient strategy in overcoming the collective action problem.

In recent social science literature, scholars have put much emphasis on "social capital" or "trust" to explain how individuals overcome the collective action problem.[12] "Social capital" is usually defined as "features of social organization, such as trust, norms, and networks, that can improve the efficiency of society by facilitating coordinated action."[13] Social capital facilitates spontaneous cooperation among individuals, and it is a "soft" solution to the collective action problem. As Robert Bates notes, "In a world in which there are prisoner's dilemmas, cooperation communities will enable rational individuals to transcend collective dilemmas."[14] This view is also shared by Sidney Tarrow, who has written on collective actions (social movements) for decades. According to Tarrow, overcoming collective action problems requires "shared understandings and identities" because these are the foundation of trust and cooperation.[15] Building such identities and understandings works best in face-to-face communities and networks, but in the absence of physical proximity, communication systems that bring people into contact with the circumstances and plights of others can on occasion serve as a viable alternative.

Furthermore, networks and communities can be built in different ways. As Putnam points out, any society is characterized by networks of interpersonal communication and exchange. While some of these networks are primarily "horizontal," bringing together agents of equivalent status and power, others are primarily "vertical," linking unequal agents in asymmetric relations of hierarchy and dependence.[16] Networks of civic engagement are to "represent intense horizontal interaction" and are an essential form of social capital. "The denser such networks in a community are, the more likely that its citizens will be able to cooperate for mutual benefit."[17]

Apparently, the digitally mediated public sphere is highly decentralized. Participants interact with one another horizontally, and coercive coordination is virtually absent. While low information cost matters in providing incentives for participants, social capital, or what Tarrow called "shared understanding and identities," is even more important in coordinating collective actions. With such shared understanding and identities, collective actions tend to be motivated by what Dennis Chong called the "public spirit." It is reasonable to assume that the public spirit directed against the authoritarian regime exists

in China. As will be analyzed later, the Internet helps reinforce such a public
spirit on one hand and provides an effective forum for participants to express
this public spirit collectively on the other.

DIGITAL DIVIDE, SOCIAL ACCEPTANCE, AND CIVIC ENGAGEMENT

It is important to address the issue related to digital divide and social acceptance of the Internet before I explore how civic engagement takes place in
the Internet-mediated public sphere. As discussed in earlier chapters, scholars
have debated whether digital divide obstructs political participation. Also important is social acceptance of the Internet. It is difficult to say that information
technology per se creates the dynamics for political changes. People induce
political changes. Social acceptance matters. If social members do not accept
the Internet, they will hardly use it to pursue their own political courses.

Does digital divide obstruct civic engagement? As discussed in Chapter
Two, like in many other countries, digital divide exists in China. Digital divide does matter. Table 5.1 shows that financial and educational factors have
restricted the people's access to the Internet. It is true that digital divide empowers some social groups and not others. But this does not mean that digital
divide weakens social groups in their engagement of political participation.
One can argue that digital divide affects the degree of political participation.
But it can hardly be argued that digital divide has a significant impact on social
groups due to the fact that modern information technology is increasingly
becoming affordable for most of them.

Also, digital divide is less serious in urban China than in the country as a
whole. What Table 5.1 presents is an overall situation in China. A 2003 survey
among non-users by the Chinese Academy of Social Sciences (CASS survey,

TABLE 5.1

Reasons for not using the Internet in China (percentage, 2003)

1. No knowledge on computer/Internet	37.7
2. No facilities to access the Internet	21.3
3. Do not feel it is useful to access the Internet and do not want to do so	14.8
4. No time to access the Internet	14.3
5. Too old or too young to access the Internet	6.8
6. Too expensive to access the Internet	5.6
7. No interest in the Internet	4.5
8. Afraid that children will be hurt or be affected negatively	1.7
9. Other reasons	5.1
10. Don't know / without any reasons	11.5

SOURCE: *Survey Report on China's Internet Development*, CNNIC, January 2004. http://www.cnnic.net.cn.

TABLE 5.2

Reasons for not using the Internet in urban areas (percentage, N: 1,382)

Don't think that the Internet is useful	46%
Economic (e.g., no computer at home, not affordable)	27%
Technical (e.g., no skills)	23%
Oppose using the Internet	4%

SOURCE: The Center for Social Development of the Chinese Academy of Social Sciences, 2003nian hulianwang baogao (*The 2003 Report on the Internet*), Beijing, 2003. The survey was conducted among citizens in China's twelve major cities.

hereafter) found that various factors have led to the digital divide in urban China and that the financial factor played a less important role in discouraging people from accessing the Internet. As indicated in Table 5.2, 27 percent of urban Chinese were not able to access the Internet because of economic factors and 23 percent because of a lack of skills to access the Internet. The majority (46 percent) did not access the Internet because they did not believe that the Internet was useful to them. In this sense, the same report argued that the Chinese non-users did not access the Internet not because of digital divide but because of "digital choice," meaning that they chose not to access the Internet for whatever reasons.

Despite the digital divide, the nature of decentralization of Internet technology has an important impact on the formation of social capital among Internet users. Journalist Thomas Friedman has observed how the decentralization of the Internet affects relations among individuals and between the state and society. According to Friedman, information is increasingly being democratized thanks to advances in modern digital technology, and the Internet is the pinnacle of the democratization of information. A situation of decentralization follows where "no one owns the Internet, it is totally decentralized, no one can turn it off, it can potentially reach into every home in the world and many of its key advances were done by collaboration among individuals—many who have never met each other—who worked together over the network, contributing their ideas for free." [18]

The decentralization of the Internet also has an impact on the relations between the state and society. According to Friedman, "The days when governments could isolate their people from understanding what life was like beyond their borders or even beyond their villages are over. Life outside can't be trashed and made to look worse than it is. And life inside can't be propagandized and made to look better than it is. Thanks to the democratization of information, we all increasingly know how one another live—no matter how

isolated you think a country might be. The minute you think you have devised 109
a new higher, thicker wall to hide behind, you discover that technology has
found a way to lower it. And the minute you think you have drawn a new line
in the sand to protect you, technology finds a way to erase it." [19]

After comparing the Internet with traditional media such as newspapers
and TV in China, Joseph Chan also pointed to the nature of decentralization
of the Internet. According to Chan, the Internet radically differs from the traditional mass media in its interactivity, huge channel capacity, networking potential, and capability for both massive and personalized communication. The
decentralized mode of network structure has resulted in global interconnect-
edness. Boundaries such as national, provincial, and metropolitan borders can
be more easily evaded. Chan reached a cautious conclusion that "the Internet
does not operate in a social vacuum. However, it is relatively more fluid and
malleable than traditional mass media such as newspapers and television." [20]

Also important is that rapid commercialization has led to intensive competition among different media forms. Now, major TV stations and newspapers
have established their own Web sites. As Chan observed, "To break news and to
reproduce news reported elsewhere have become part of websites' instincts. . . .
No webpage has a monopoly over information for long in cyberspace." [21]
Consequently, Web pages do not need to wait for the Xinhua News Agency's
official version of some issues and can take the lead to make news. Such decentralizing effects create a favorable condition for social acceptance and civic
engagement.

How does the Internet affect human relationships among its users? By the
end of 2003, the number of Internet users in China was already the second
largest in the world, next to that of the United States, meaning that China had
developed a sizable Internet society. [22]

The 2003 CASS survey found that 52 percent of urban Chinese users regarded the Internet as a "library," 46 percent as a place for entertainment,
and 44 percent as a place for gathering among known and unknown friends.
The same survey also revealed that only 26 percent regarded the Internet as a
marketing place and 6 percent as a banking place. [23]

The China Internet Network Information Center (CNNIC) survey in 2003
found that social acceptance of the Internet was high among both users and
non-users. The attitudes toward the Internet were not much different between
users and non-users. Figure 5.1 reveals that 31.9 + 54.8 = 86.7 percent of Internet users in 2003 believed that using the Internet would enable them to work
more efficiently. The figure among non-users was even higher — 87.5 percent.
As discussed in Chapter Two, a *Far Eastern Economic Review* survey in 2002

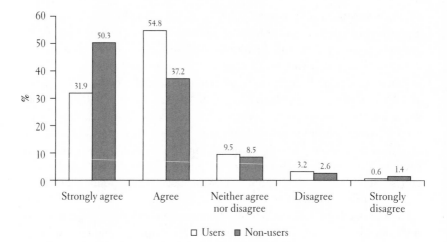

FIGURE 5.1   "Using the Internet will enable people to work more efficiently"
SOURCE: *Survey Report on China's Internet Development*, CNNIC, January 2004. http://www.cnnic.net.cn.

found that business elites in China have also used the Internet both at work and at home. The same survey also indicated that the Internet helps business elites keep abreast of world developments (see Figure 5.2), which is crucial for more and more firms in China to make their businesses successful given the fact that China has been closely integrated with the rest of the world.

A positive acceptance is also reflected in Chinese perceptions of the negative impact of the Internet. While there are news and analyses that indicate that privacy in the age of information is becoming an impossible enterprise, the majority of Chinese are not troubled by such a development. Figure 5.3 shows that nearly 61 percent of Internet users do not believe that using the Internet will invade their privacy, while 60 percent of non-users have the same perception.

Figures 5.4 and 5.5 further confirm Chinese citizens' positive attitudes toward the Internet. In Figure 5.4, we can see that 59 percent of users do not believe that using the Internet will enable one to befriend bad company, while the figure among non-users is 52.7 percent. Figure 5.5 shows that those who do not believe that using the Internet will subject one to bad influence are more than those who believe the contrary. More interesting is that the non-users (50 percent) are more optimistic than the users (43.8 percent). This is largely because the perceptions of the users are based on their actual experience of using the Internet, while the non-users' perceptions are not based on experience.

Logically, high social acceptance of the Internet should lead to a similar high level of trust. Figure 5.6 confirms this association. It reveals an overall level of trust of the Internet among users and non-users. While 55.8 percent of users trust the Internet, 56.5 percent of non-users have such trust. The level of distrust is extremely low among both users and non-users.

The CASS survey (2003) shows that the level of trust in Internet-provided information is slightly higher among the users than the non-users. As shown in Table 5.3, nearly 48 percent of non-users trust information available on the Internet, while the figure among Internet users is 57 percent. The same survey also found that about 51 percent of Internet users responded that, based on their own experiences, the Internet can benefit human relations, while this figure was 42 percent among non-users. Also, the longer users used the Internet, the more positive their attitudes toward the Internet were.[24]

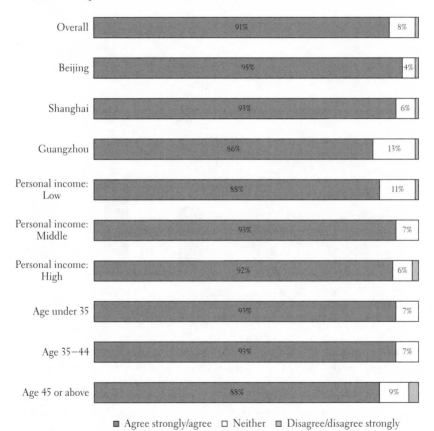

■ Agree strongly/agree   □ Neither   ■ Disagree/disagree strongly

FIGURE 5.2   "The Internet keeps me up to date with world developments"

SOURCE: Adapted from Far Eastern Economic Review, China's Elite 5: A Study of Affluent and Influential People in China (Hong Kong, 2003).

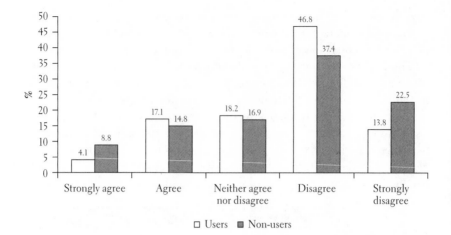

FIGURE 5.3 "Using the Internet will invade one's privacy"
SOURCE: *Survey Report on China's Internet Development*, CNNIC, January 2004. http://www.cnnic.net.cn.

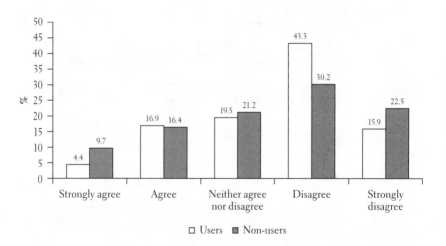

FIGURE 5.4 "Using the Internet will enable one to befriend bad company"
SOURCE: *Survey Report on China's Internet Development*, CNNIC, January 2004. http://www.cnnic.net.cn.

It is worthwhile to point out that the level of trust is also dependent on the sources of information. Nearly 30 percent of urban Chinese believe that information from emails is most reliable, followed by Internet forums (24 percent), Internet advertisements (18.5 percent), and chat rooms (13.7 percent).[25]

The Internet helps to form a group identity among Internet users. As shown

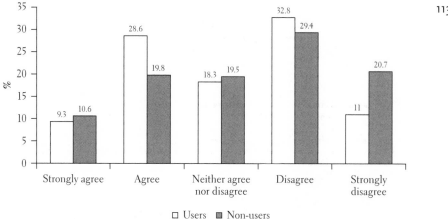

FIGURE 5.5   "Using the Internet will subject one to bad influence"
SOURCE: *Survey Report on China's Internet Development*, CNNIC, January 2004. http://www.cnnic.net.cn.

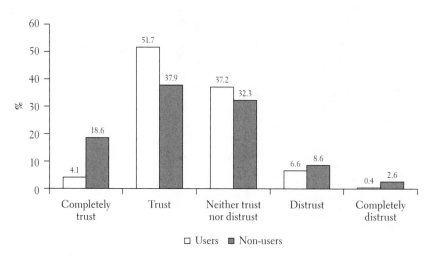

FIGURE 5.6   The level of trust of the Internet
SOURCE: *Survey Report on China's Internet Development*, CNNIC, January 2004. http://www.cnnic.net.cn.

in Figure 5.7, the overwhelming majority of people do not think that the use of the Internet has a negative impact on their contact with other people. On the contrary, more than 47 percent of the respondents believe that the use of the Internet has increased their contact with people who share their hobbies and recreational activities, and 31 percent believe that it has increased their

TABLE 5.3

Trust of information available on the Internet among Internet users
and non-users in urban China (by percentage)

	Users	Non-users
All information from the Internet is reliable	0.8	1.1
Most information from the Internet is reliable	56.7	47.8
Half of the information from the Internet is reliable	34.8	39.7
Most information from the Internet is not reliable	7.5	10.5
All information from the Internet is not reliable	0.1	1.0

SOURCE: The Center for Social Development of the Chinese Academy of Social Sciences, *2003nian hulianwang baogao* (*The 2003 Report on the Internet*), Beijing, 2003. The survey was conducted among citizens in China's twelve major cities.

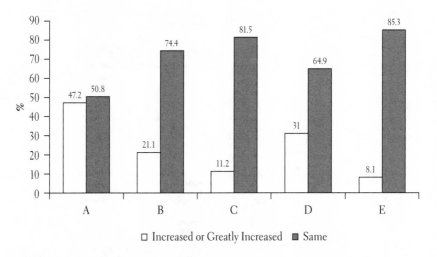

□ Increased or Greatly Increased   ■ Same

FIGURE 5.7   The Internet and interpersonal interaction in China, 2003

NOTE: A, B, C, D, and E stand for the following five questions:

A: Has the use of the Internet increased or greatly decreased your contact with people who share your hobbies/recreational activities?

B: Has the use of the Internet increased or greatly decreased your contact with people who share your political interests?

C: Has the use of the Internet increased or greatly decreased your contact with people who share your religion?

D: Has the use of the Internet increased or greatly decreased your contact with people who share your profession?

E: Has the use of the Internet increased or greatly decreased your contact with your family and friends?

SOURCES: Adapted from UCLA Center for Communication Policy and the Chinese Academy of Social Sciences, *The World Internet Project*, Beijing: The Chinese Academy of Social Sciences, 2003.

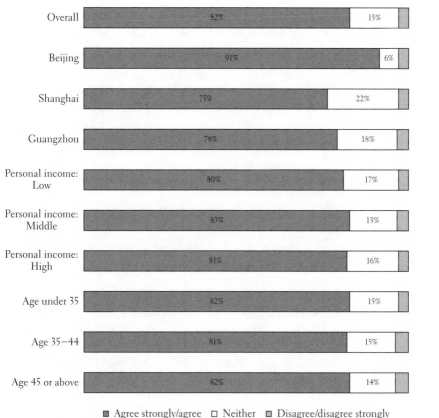

■ Agree strongly/agree   □ Neither   ▣ Disagree/disagree strongly

FIGURE 5.8   "The Internet is a good way to keep in touch with people"
SOURCE: Adapted from *Far Eastern Economic Review, China's Elite 5: A Study of Affluent and Influential People in China* (Hong Kong, 2003).

contact with people who share their professions. The same survey also shows that the average number of online friends met in person is two, but the average number of online friends never met in person is seven.[26] This simply implies that Internet users do engage in social interaction and that, on average, the Internet-based community is larger in size than the face-to-face community. A similar trend is also found among business elites in China. As shown in Figure 5.8, an overwhelming majority of business elites believed that the Internet is a good way to keep in touch with people.

The Internet has facilitated the forming of group identities, increasing trust

TABLE 5.4

Public opinions of the Internet and politics in urban China (percentage, 2003)

	Strongly agree and agree (among users)	Strongly agree and agree (among non-users)
1. More opportunities are available to express one's political opinions by using the Internet	71.8	69.1
2. More opportunities are available to have a say on what the government does by using the Internet	60.8	61.5
3. One can better understand politics by using the Internet	79.2	77.4
4. Government officials can better understand popular opinions	72.3	73.3

SOURCE: The survey was conducted by the Center for Social Development of the Chinese Academy of Social Sciences in 2003. The figures collected here are from Yang Taoyuan, Han Bingjie, and Miao Junjie, "*Suzao daguo wangmin*" ("Molding Internet Users in a Great Nation"), *Liao Wang* (*Outlook Weekly*), February 23, 2004, p. 26.

among Internet users. More importantly, it has also provided citizens a new tool to engage in political participation. As shown in Table 5.4, most Internet users believe that the Internet enables them to have more opportunities to express their political views, to have a say in what the government does, and to better understand politics. The Internet also enables government officials to understand the citizens' political opinions better. Interestingly, similar opinions also exist among non-users, implying that Chinese non-users are also very positive toward the Internet even though they do not have experience in using it.

THE INTERNET AS THE PUBLIC SPHERE

As discussed above, the technological nature of the Internet makes it very difficult for an authoritarian state to intervene and control the free flow of information. It is also true that the Chinese state has encountered increasingly greater difficulties in controlling cyberspace discussions that promote public consciousness and consequently collective action. The Internet has indeed constituted a public space for free discussions in many ways. Moreover, a high degree of social acceptance of the Internet makes this new technology an efficient tool for civic engagement.

In China, more and more Web sites have developed independently of the government, such as the "Field of Ideas" and the "New Culture Forum." The efforts by the state to close such Web sites are not the end of the story. The decentralized effects of Internet development mean that the battle between

the state and society is an enduring one. When existing Web sites are closed,   117
new ones are likely to emerge. This cyberspace "guerrilla warfare" is similar
to what happened to the relationship between the nationalist government and
liberal intellectuals in China in the 1930s. While dissident intellectuals in the
1930s relied on printed materials to voice their grievances and thoughts, now
those individuals have progressed to using information technology. Needless
to say, the Internet provides enormous advantages for intellectuals who use it
as a platform for public discussions that the government dislikes and provides a
way to work around the government's tight control, which aims to completely
eliminate such free discussion space. It is fair to say that the development of
the Internet has at least provided a new "public field" for social groups to jostle
for space vis-à-vis the authoritarian state.

New strategies have also been developed to conduct public discussions.
Many liberal social groups have used non-political Web sites, which normally
focus on non-political public issues, to conduct public or political discussions. Some Web sites, such as "Jin Yong Martial Arts Novels," are "private,"
non-political, or based on a common hobby. They have gradually expanded
their scope to cover almost all kinds of political topics, including democratic
elections in Taiwan and the 1989 pro-democracy movement.

Another method the social groups have frequently used to discuss public
issues online is utilizing Web sites run by the governmental authorities. This
is exemplified by the "Strong Nation Forum" (*qiangguo luntan*) in the *People's
Net*, a Web site managed by the Communist party's central organ, *People's
Daily*. It is found that the forum frequently tends to be more liberal in content than *People's Daily*, as more liberal political discussions are allowed in
the electronic forum than in its parent newspaper. This can be attributed to
"the nature of freedom of the Internet, its spontaneity and its unlimited-ness,
which decide jointly its popularity and capability to resist control."[27] Another
important factor is the liberal orientation of the forum editors. Since the reform and open door policy, Chinese democratic elites have been searching
for every opportunity to voice their opinions and exchange ideas freely. This
is especially true for the newspaper editors of more prominent newspapers
such as *People's Daily* and *Guangming Daily*. In the 1980s, liberal newspaper
editors played an important role in promoting the so-called bourgeois liberalization,[28] the legacy of which continues today. These editors were able to turn
their liberal views into reality by allowing and encouraging liberal political
discussions via the Internet.

Cyber discussions have had an important impact on people's perceptions
of politics in China. As discussed in the previous chapter, whether informa-

118   tion technology encourages civic engagement in a democratic political setting is a controversial issue, and some researchers indeed have found that
information technology tends to encourage individuals to isolate themselves
from society. The spread of information technology, especially the Internet,
more often than not creates barriers for civic engagement; instead of encouraging collective action, the Internet is more likely to make it difficult to take
place.

Nonetheless, survey data from China presents a rather different picture.
It confirms a positive relationship between the use of the Internet and group
identity. The Internet seems to have made a more substantial political impact
in China than in some democratic countries. For example, in China, nearly
80 percent of the people think that by using the Internet they can better understand politics, compared with 43 percent in the United States, 31 percent
in Japan, and 48 percent in South Korea (Figure 5.9).

Also, nearly 61 percent of Internet users in China think that by using the
Internet, they can have more say about what the government does, compared
with 20 percent in the United States, 24 percent in Japan, and 26 percent in
South Korea (Figure 5.10). This is largely due to the fact that in democratic
countries, besides the Internet, people have other channels to express their
opinions and to participate in politics, while in China the Internet is perhaps

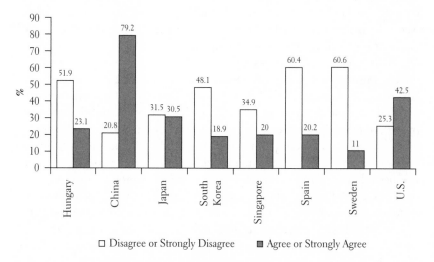

□ Disagree or Strongly Disagree   ■ Agree or Strongly Agree

FIGURE 5.9   "Do you think by using the Internet people like you can better understand politics?" (all respondents, 18 and above), 2003

SOURCES: Adapted from UCLA Center for Communication Policy and the Chinese Academy of Social
Sciences, *The World Internet Project*, Beijing: The Chinese Academy of Social Sciences, 2003.

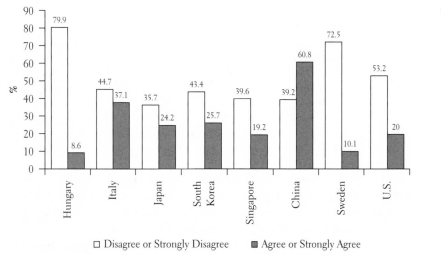

□ Disagree or Strongly Disagree   ■ Agree or Strongly Agree

FIGURE 5.10   "Do you think by using the Internet people like you can have more say about what the government does?" (all respondents, 18 and above), 2003

SOURCES: Adapted from UCLA Center for Communication Policy and the Chinese Academy of Social Sciences, *The World Internet Project*, Beijing: The Chinese Academy of Social Sciences, 2003.

the single most important avenue for people to criticize government policies and to participate in politics.

POPULAR DISTRUST OF PUBLIC INSTITUTIONS

This chapter has so far discussed how the Internet has facilitated the formation of social capital among Internet users in China. The Internet enables its users to access information and communicate with other people despite the often tight control on the part of the government. Social members can no longer be atomized by the government but are able to form voluntary groups. Data also shows that the Internet helps users understand politics better and have a say in what the government does. As discussed earlier, in many Western democracies, modern information technology has actually reduced the level of popular confidence in public institutions. Some questions can be raised related to China in this context: How does the Internet affect popular confidence in public institutions in China? Does the Internet affect popular confidence the way it does in the West? How does China's authoritarian political setting affect popular confidence in public institutions?

Although it is difficult to conduct public opinion surveys regarding public

TABLE 5.5

Public opinions on corruption in China:
Five areas where people believe corruption is most serious (multiple choice, percentage)

1. Government projects and public constructions	38.54
2. Public security organs, procuratorial organs, and people's courts	38.53
3. Medical and health care sector	29.24
4. Education sector	26.13
5. Organization and personnel departments	21.20

SOURCE: The Xinhua News Agency, January 26, 2004; *Ming Pao* (Hong Kong), January 27, 2004; *Lianhe Zaobao* (Singapore), January 27, 2004.

institutions in China, all available information points to a serious crisis of public confidence in government institutions. Among other reasons, the most important is corruption among party cadres and government officials. Corruption has prevailed even since the reform and open door policy in the late 1970s. Despite great efforts by the leadership to contain corruption, the situation continues to worsen. Rampant corruption often leads to collective action against the regime. In 1989, popular sentiments against corruption eventually led to the pro-democracy movement. Needless to say, corruption has undermined public trust in the government.

Table 5.5 demonstrates public perceptions on corruption in China. The survey presented in Table 5.5 was conducted by the Central Commission for Discipline Inspection (CCDI) of the Chinese Communist Party in ten of China's provinces. One can question whether the CCDI has underestimated popular perceptions, but the survey does contain useful information on public opinions. Except for the first area, the areas represent the most important public institutions in China. The medical and health care sector is closely associated with people's daily lives. Because of rapid commercialization, it has become extremely expensive for people to use the services in this sector. More and more people dare not visit doctors, and they are not able to afford skyrocketing insurance fees. Furthermore, it is education that most people, especially rural Chinese, depend on for a better future. Nevertheless, corruption has also rendered the services in this sector unaffordable for many Chinese. An investigation conducted by the State Commission for Development and Reform in 63,484 educational institutions (universities, colleges, middle and high schools, and primary schools) revealed that in 2003 alone, these institutions collected 2.1 billion *yuan* of illegitimate fees.[29] Education has become an extremely profitable industry that the Chinese call the "nouveau riche," much akin to the newly rising IT industries.

Politically more significant is corruption in government institutions. For example, in most countries, citizens rely on the judicial system to uphold justice. But in China, the judicial system — which includes the public security organs, procuratorial organs, and people's court — is perceived as the most corrupt. In the pre-reform era, these institutions were the tools for the communist regime to exert its coercive rule. Today, these institutions are not mechanisms to guarantee justice but tools to make profits. According to an investigation by the China Auditing Administration, in 2003 public security organs in twenty-six provinces collected 16.5 billion *yuan* of illegitimate fees.[30]

Because China does not have democracy, almost all government officials are selected by organizational and personnel departments at different levels. Ideally, government officials should be selected based on their performance and merits. Unfortunately, every government position now has a price. Corruption in this sector has not only undermined public confidence in the government but has also weakened its legitimacy and effectiveness. In 1990, China began to implement the Administrative Procedural Law. Within thirteen years (until 2003), there were 800,000 cases in which citizens suited governmental organs or government officials. In 2003 alone, there were more than 100,000 such cases.[31]

The Chinese leadership has made increasingly greater efforts to cope with corruption in the public sector. The 1989 pro-democracy movement almost toppled the regime. Since the early 1990s, every Chinese administration has placed anti-corruption efforts as its highest priority. Waves of anti-corruption campaigns have been initiated. For instance, in 2003, the government prosecuted several high-ranking former government officials at the governor–minister level, including Guizhou governor Liu Fangren, Yunnan governor Li Jiating, Hebei party secretary Chen Weigao, Minister of Land and Resources Tian Fengshan, and China Construction Bank Chairman Wang Xuebing.[32] Also in 2003 alone, 972 government officials (e.g., state attorneys and judges) were prosecuted in the people's court system alone.[33]

As shown in Figure 5.11, public opinions of the anti-corruption drives on the part of the government are actually quite favorable. The survey was conducted by the CCDI. One can cast a reasonable doubt on these figures: for the purpose of propaganda, the commission might have overestimated the level of public satisfaction. But given the great efforts made by the top leadership in curbing corruption, one can assume that the level of public satisfaction has increased over the years. A more interesting and important question is, Why is there still a serious crisis of public confidence in public institutions given the increasingly greater efforts to fight corruption on the part of the regime?

The Internet has played a unique role in undermining public confidence

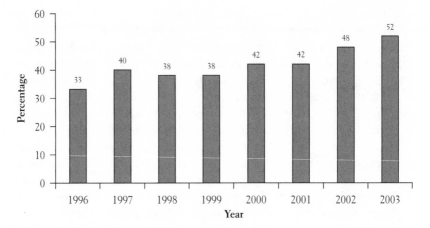

FIGURE 5.11   Approval rate of the government's anti-corruption performance
SOURCE: Lianhe Zaobao, Singapore, January 27, 2004.

in public institutions. China's traditional media, such as newspapers, TV, and broadcasting, all of which are still under tight control by the regime, have focused on releasing information publicizing the government's achievements in curbing corruption. By contrast, the Internet is full of information on how serious corruption is in the public sector. Chat rooms, emails, and forums often bring cases and stories of corruption to Internet users, who in turn spread such information to non-users. Unlike government-controlled traditional media, the Internet enables informants to describe their cases and stories vividly. It is questionable whether all their stories are true, but they can certainly affect popular perceptions of public institutions. Once a major incident of corruption is "discovered" by an informant, enormous numbers of Internet users will express their opinions on it and soon form a forum—an Internet-based collective action against corruption. Some cases are discussed below in order to highlight how such Internet-facilitated events can undermine popular trust in the government and exert pressure on it.

THE INTERNET AS A TOOL FOR PUBLIC EXPRESSION: CASES

The linkages between pubic distrust and the Internet can be examined in two ways. On one hand, public discussions of public institutions in the Internet-mediated public sphere inform the public of the performance of public institutions and help the public form its perceptions of public institutions. The veracity of such information is less important as participants tend to believe

the information available in these public discussions given the high degree of
social acceptance of the Internet.

On the other hand, the disgruntled public continuously searches for ways to express its distrust of public institutions, and once a major event takes place, the Internet becomes the most important channel for it. Needless to say, the importance of the Internet increases due to the lack of other channels of expression such as newspapers, TV, and radio. In other words, the Internet is an effective tool for social groups to create "events" that enable them to realize self-expression. Here, the "event" becomes a form of civic engagement and exerts public pressure on the regime.

With the rapid development of the Internet, Internet discussion has increasingly become an eventful event for social groups in China. The following four cases show how such events could become powerful in producing instant pressure for the regime.

The Retrial of Liu Yong

Liu Yong was a local organized crime boss even before he started investing in legitimate businesses. In 1995, he founded the Jiayang Group in Shenyang, the capital city of the Liaoning province in Northeast China. The Jiayang Group—which had interests in clothing, entertainment, and real estate—was believed to serve as a cover for Liu's illegal activities. He was accused of amassing some 600 million yuan in illegally gained assets. Through the commercial activities of the Jiayang Group, Liu allegedly bought off more than 500 government, judicial, and police officials to run huge rackets in Shenyang's real estate and tobacco markets. Liu was once regarded as a very successful businessman by local governments. As a result of his wide network of local governments, Liu was selected as a delegate to the Shenyang People's Congress. But Liu did not hesitate to resort to violence to solve problems. Court documents revealed that post-1995 activities by his mob led to forty-two people being injured, sixteen of them seriously, while one eventually died of fatal wounds.[34]

In July 2000, Liu Yong was detained in a local crackdown that led to corruption convictions of numerous Shenyang officials. The Tieling Intermediate People's Court, which handled Liu's case in the first instance, tried Liu in thirty-two different cases, involving the death of one person and crimes including racketeering, bribery, property damage, gun possession, and interference in law enforcement. He was sentenced to death and fined 15 million *yuan* in April 2002. The ruling immediately received wide popular support among local residents in Shenyang.

Nevertheless, a few months later, in August 2002, the Liaoning Higher

People's Court gave Liu a two-year reprieve on the death penalty.[35] While the charges against him remained virtually the same, the court made a significant change: the new ruling effectively saved his life. The new ruling was deemed just and fair when read out at Liu's earlier appeal, with judges citing the confession by police that Liu was brutally tortured while in custody. According to China's law, evidence collected from forced confessions is inadmissible, but the new ruling suggested that the court felt there was enough additional evidence to warrant Liu's execution in accordance with the first ruling.

The new ruling immediately resulted in massive public response, decrying the higher court's reprieve of Liu's death penalty. While local state media did report angry popular sentiments, it was the Internet that helped local residents reach out and transfer the case from the local to the national level. As all kinds of previously unreleased reports on the case were posted on different Web sites, the Internet became an effective tool for people from different parts of the country to express their opinions on the new ruling. Popular sentiments rapidly built up and soon created tremendous pressure for the central government to act. On October 8, 2003, the Supreme People's Court in Beijing took over the case, marking the first time since the 1949 Communist revolution that China's highest court would hear a common criminal case. On December 22, the Supreme People's Court upheld the death sentence, which allowed an immediate execution of Liu Yong.

Deep distrust of the Liaoning Higher Court among the public was not without sound reasons. The ruling by the Liaoning Higher Court was believed to be influenced by "external forces." A popular perception in the Internet community was that Liu Yong had such financial and political clout that even when he was in jail, "powerful people" in the local government were protecting him. While this accusation is difficult to independently verify, Liu's defense counsel did organize a panel of top-tier legal professors whose opinions were made public.

Judicial independence in China has been very problematic. Influential senior officials can make persuasive calls to judges. In this case, it was believed that the Liu Yong defense team used experts' opinions to influence the court's ruling. Tian Wenchang, Liu's defense lawyer, wrote many letters appealing to various government agencies to intervene on behalf of his client. Tian was quoted as saying, "I'm against administrative intervention and call for judicial independence. Everyone knows that intervention is bad for justice. But when one runs out of other forms of recourse, one has to rely on it. This is a vicious circle and it is sad."[36] Tian was able to receive the opinions from fourteen of the country's top legal experts. In a six-page affidavit, they expressed the unanimous view that the original verdict against Liu had been heavy-handed.

The opinions of these legal experts should not have been admitted as evi-   125
dence and should not have affected the outcome of the case. These experts
were not witnesses, nor were they involved in the case in any capacity. Nevertheless, such a technical interference apparently worked to influence the
court's ruling. Interestingly enough, these experts were commissioned by Liu's
attorney and were expected to deliver an opinion favorable to Liu. This was
a widespread view among those who followed the event closely. Indeed, Tian
admitted that these experts were paid.

Another important source of public distrust of the judicial system is judicial
regionalism. Because local courts are financed by the local government, it is
impossible for these courts to be independent from the local government.
Due to Liu Yong's wide range of connections in the local government, he was
believed to have used his financial power to buy over all these powerful figures
to help him.

The retrial by the Supreme People's Court was also controversial. The decision to carry out the retrial was regarded as political in China's legal circles.
It was believed that the Communist party's Committee of Politics and Law,
which runs the country's security services, ordered the top court to issue a new
verdict and sentence Liu to death. Zhou Yongkang, the second-ranking member of the committee, insisted on a death sentence because he did not want a
precedent set allowing confessions to be thrown out of court. Senior members
of the Political Bureau also agreed that Liu should be executed because public opinion seemed to be in favor of it.[37] This retrial apparently enabled the
government to appease popular sentiment. Popular support of the retrial and
of the new ruling was very strong in both traditional media and the Internet.
In this sense, one can argue that the retrial served a useful political purpose
but was legally destructive.

The Arrest of University Student Liu Di

On November 7, 2002, twenty-two-year-old Liu Di, a fourth-year psychol-
ogy student at Beijing Normal University, was taken away by Beijing security
agents from the home she shared with her eighty-year-old grandmother, Liu
Heng, who was once arrested as a "rightist" in 1957.

Like her peers in colleges, Liu Di usually spent her spare time surfing the
Internet and posting her thoughts in online forums. In 2001, Liu started her
own chat room, "A Life Likes Fire," after police closed down the one she pre-
ferred. Liu published several articles on the Xici online bulletin board. Using
the online name Stainless Steel Mouse (*bu xiu gang laoshu*), she earned a
reputation as a sharp-witted member of a burgeoning online community in

126   China, where participants found a rare space to publicly express their opinions about social and political issues.[38]

For months after her arrest, nothing was heard from her. Her family did not know where she was; she had no access to legal counsel. The authorities refused to tell her family what she had done to warrant her arrest; the school merely said the young Liu was involved with an "illegal organization." Later, the authorities searched the family home, removing her computer, notebooks, and floppy disks. They also took three banned books, including the prison letters of leading Chinese dissident Wei Jingsheng and a book on the Tiananmen protests. After these actions, the Beijing branch of the State Secrecy Bureau notified Liu's family that she was being held on charges of "being detrimental to state security."

All her friends knew that the arrest was politically motivated. In some essays, Liu outlined a fantasy world in which people's souls and minds could exist inside cyberspace while their physical bodies remained in the real world. She questioned, "When most of human life is lived inside the cyber world, the Communist party will still exert repressive control over the real world, but what meaning will it have?"

But what made the authorities intolerant of Liu were her attacks on the arrest of Huang Qi more than one year prior. Huang Qi was jailed in June 2000 for setting up a Web site called "*Tian wang*" that opposed the government's verdict on the 1989 Tiananmen democracy protests that were brutally crushed by the military. Liu Di urged Internet users opposed to China's draconian Internet rules to spread "reactionary" ideas on the Web and then give themselves up to the police at an appointed time as a sign of protest and solidarity with Huang Qi. In one essay posted on the Internet, Liu called on her readers to ignore government propaganda and live freely. She wrote, "As long as you feel you are completely free to make your own decision, then even if you are living in a Nazi camp . . . you are still free." Liu continued, "Even though the Chinese Communist Party in reality has power over us, but if we can't feel it, pretend and live as if it doesn't exist, . . . we have made this power ineffective in our lives . . . then it would be as if it doesn't exist and we are free people." So, she suggested that people should stop going to political study sessions, stop watching the news on TV or reading the party mouthpiece *People's Daily*, and only read "reactionary" material.[39]

What the authorities did not expect was that the arrest of Liu Di could form an Internet-based social movement. The arrest of Liu immediately generated unusual responses in cyberspace. Soon after the news of her arrest spread through the online forums where Liu had been a regular, her virtual network of friends sprung into action, launching a global movement for her release.

A Web site was set up in Malaysia to post updates about her situation, articles she had written, and a petition demanding her release. The petition included thousands of signatures, many of which were individuals inside China who courageously used their real names. Prominent Beijing academics and writers, including Yu Jie and Liu Xiaobo, took up the cause and wrote essays supporting Liu. Sympathizers began to add the prefix "Stainless Steel" to their online monikers in a sign of solidarity and defiance.

Most of the millions of Internet users in China are, like Liu, young, educated, and living in cities. As journalist Sophie Beach observed, many of the opinions Liu expressed were shared by members of her online community. Therefore, when Liu disappeared, some in China were aware that they could be next. Instead of being cowered into silence by that possibility, they were empowered to speak out.[40] On Liu's twenty-third birthday (October 9, 2003), her supporters launched a month-long protest, ending on the one-year anniversary of her arrest. They pledged to spend one day in a darkened house to symbolically join Liu in prison.

Despite more arrests being made during the process of this Internet-based social movement, the movement generated enormous pressure for the Chinese government. In November 2003, Liu was granted bail, meaning that she was free without trial. The decision was made by the newly established leadership under Hu Jintao. Hu succeeded Jiang Zemin as general secretary of the Communist party at the Sixteenth Party Congress in November 2002 and became state president in March 2003. By the time Liu Di was released, the period of political sensitivity was over. Another important fact is that newly appointed premier Wen Jiabao visited the United States a few days after Liu's release. Apparently, the United States, which has been very critical of China's human rights record, also played an important role in leading to the release of Liu.[41]

Needless to say, Liu Di was arrested for political reasons, and she was released for political reasons as well. Although the government played a political game, popular confidence in China's judicial system was seriously undermined. As one observer pointed out, Liu's case is unremarkable in a country where many other journalists are in prison for their writing and a sophisticated security apparatus monitors what citizens read and write online. Due process was completely ignored in Liu's case, as it had been in many of the cases of the other imprisoned journalists. Authorities' failure to put Liu on trial or release her after a year violated the Criminal Procedure Law, which sets a two-month time limit for a suspect to be detained during investigation. However, loopholes in the law allow for an extended detention period under vaguely defined special circumstances. As a result, detainees in political cases are routinely held for months or even years before being convicted.[42]

The Trial of Shanghai Lawyer Zheng Enchong

On October 28, 2003, the Shanghai Second Intermediate People's Court sentenced lawyer Zheng Enchong to three years in prison on charges of "illegally providing state secrets to entities outside of China."[43]

Zheng was a lawyer with Shanghai's Siwei Law Firm. His license was revoked in 2001 after he stated that it was necessary to amend Article 10 of China's constitution, which stipulates the right of the state to own the land in cities and towns and the right "to expropriate the land in the country in public interests" from collective owners. Zheng's troubles with the Shanghai authorities stemmed from his long-standing practice of assisting families displaced in Shanghai's urban redevelopment projects. Even after his license was revoked, he continued to provide legal advice in redevelopment cases, and by the time of his arrest in June 2003, he was reported to have assisted families in more than 500 cases.[44]

Although Zheng had provoked the Shanghai authorities over a certain period of time, the trigger for his arrest stemmed from his assistance to families involved in a lawsuit alleging official collusion with a wealthy property developer, Zhou Zhengyi. Zhou's case had raised much attention in China's and Hong Kong's media due to Zhou's close relationship with several officials in the central government as well as with key political figures in the Shanghai government.

On May 28, 2003, the Jing'an District People's Court in Shanghai began hearing a lawsuit by six homeowners representing 2,159 original residents of a property on West Beijing Road. The defendants alleged that a company controlled by Zhou Zhengyi had, with the connivance of local officials, evaded requirements to provide appropriate housing to displaced families in return for the waiving of payment for a seventy-year lease on the property, valued at 300 million *yuan*. A few days after Zhou Zhengyi's trial commenced, Zheng Enchong was arrested. Police searched Zheng's home and removed a large number of documents.

The arrest of Zheng immediately triggered a new wave of Internet protest. The redevelopment issue had become increasingly problematic in China. The authorities often fail to provide either public consultation with affected inhabitants in planning the redevelopment of portions of the city or disregard a fair assessment procedure for determining compensation. Residents are often offered insufficient compensation to allow them to obtain other housing in the city or are moved to remote districts that have poor transportation links. Such actions on the part of the government often lead to protests among affected residents. Moreover, when their complaints are not heard locally and their problems not solved by local authorities, affected residents often travel to Beijing individually and collectively, seeking help from the central government. During the period from Zheng's arrest to his trial, the Internet within and without China was full of discussions. People from different parts of China posted their stories and their complaints on the Internet.

In July 2003, Jiang Meili, Zheng's wife, sent an open letter to Chinese president Hu Jintao and Premier Wen Jiabao calling for the central authorities to take over the Zhou Zhengyi case. Outside China, the Geneva-based International Commission of Jurists issued a letter to the Chinese government condemning Zheng's arbitrary arrest and detention and the unlawful revocation of his license in 2001. Many other international organizations also issued similar open letters to China's leaders. However, official proceedings continued against Zheng, with the Shanghai procuratorate referring Zheng's case to the courts in early August 2003. When Zheng was on trial, more than 200 police officers were deployed around the courthouse because more than 200 protesters, most of whom Zheng had helped, turned up to protest his prosecution.

After Hu and Wen came to power, the new leadership tried to establish a pro-people image. Wen stressed that the new administration was determined to solve the problems resulting from city redevelopment. But unlike in Liu Di's case, both Hu and Wen were silent in the Zheng case. Inside China, people seemed to understand Hu and Wen. They had just come to power not long before and had not consolidated their power base. Jiang Zemin continued to be powerful because his faction was dominant in the top leadership—the Political Bureau and its Standing Committee. As many of Jiang's people were believed to be involved in the case of Zhou Zhengyi, it would have been politically unwise for Hu and Wen to take over Zheng's case.

Despite such a political rationale, it was a bad move for China's judicial system. Zheng was guilty of stealing state secrets because he passed on an internal Xinhua News Agency document to a human rights group in New York. The document, considered to be a "state secret" by the Shanghai State Secrecy Bureau, referred to the surrounding by 500 policemen of more than 500 workers who went on strike on May 9, 2003, following the announcement that three-quarters of Shanghai Yimin Food Product No. 1 Factory's workers would be laid off. Although this strike was little known outside, it had been known in Shanghai. Nevertheless, the Shanghai state secrecy bureau judged that this internal report was a state secret. Knowledgeable Chinese know that such a charge is commonly used by Chinese authorities to silence anyone

130   who opposes government policies. For most Chinese, the main message from Zheng's case is that politics continues to be in command and that China is not yet a country under rule of law.

The BMW Case

On October 16, 2003, Dai Yiquan, accompanied by his wife Liu Zhongxia, drove a quadricycle filled with green Chinese onions in Harbin's Daoli District and accidentally scratched the side mirror of Su Xiuwen's BMW. Su got out of the car and began to beat Dai. Dai did not hit back. Surrounding residents then advised Su to back her car up a little to see how seriously her mirror was damaged. Then an astonishing thing happened: the BMW suddenly rushed onto Liu Zhongxia, who stood about 30 centimeters in front of the vehicle. Liu was killed immediately. Su continued to drive the car for 10-odd meters, knocking down another dozen people, and was stopped by a tree on the roadside. The last person to be knocked down was sandwiched between the car and the tree.

On October 18, police detained Su Xiuwen for a traffic violation and issued a statement that Su was absentminded while driving and was totally at fault. The case was transferred to the Daoli District in Harbin City, where Su was ordered to pay 21,505 *yuan* to Liu's family and was sentenced to two years in prison with a third year reprieve. Later, however, the police issued a statement that Su did not hit the villagers on purpose and that, because she was unable to sleep in the prison, she was released and given medical treatment.[45]

Such a result immediately angered millions of people in China. Initially, local media in Harbin kept silent. Then the story appeared online. China's Internet users were infuriated by the "BMW driver" case, distributing pictures of the scene with comments on many Chinese bulletin board sites and Web sites. People started posting the story in Internet forums. Emotions snowballed into a rage. The mainstream press then picked it up, and almost all national and local news media were soon involved.

The volume of Internet chatter on the topic exceeded even the number of comments posted during the outbreak of SARS one year before. On one Web site, 110,000 people responded to an online poll. Among some 70,000 comments on the news on Sina, a famous Chinese web portal, most netizens said the court judgment was unfair to the victims, especially the woman who was killed by Su's BMW, also forty-five years old. Chat rooms were rife with rumors. Amid rumors of judicial corruption and the driver's high-level political connections, the incident became the hottest topic on Internet chat rooms and in newspapers.[46] The case touched some of the sorest points in China today—nepotism, corrupt courts, and the widening chasm between the bottom rungs of society and the top.

The initial allegation was that Su Xiuwen was the daughter-in-law of Han Guizhi, an alternate member of the Fifteenth Communist Party Central Committee, president of the Party School of Heilongjiang Provincial Communist Party, vice-secretary of Heilongjiang Provincial Committee, chairman of the Provincial Political Consultative Conference, and secretary of the Party Leadership Group. To many people, that meant that her family had used its connections to get her off lightly. The rumor swirled for quite a while before Su's family and the official mentioned came out to publicly refute such a connection.

Others wondered whether Su killed Liu intentionally. An anonymous netizen who used the same model vehicle as Su's—a BMW X5 3.0—listed eight reasons online to prove Su intentionally rushed into the crowd to murder. Many focused on whether Su indeed spoke the words "Do you not believe that I will knock you dead?" before getting into the car. Dai Qingjiang, nephew of Dai Yiquan, said a person at the scene told him that Su uttered that phrase before knocking thirteen people down. But nobody indicated that in court. Sixteen-year-old Dai Mengyao, daughter of Liu Zhongxia, was quoted in a Shenyang newspaper: "My mother was 45 years old when she was killed by the BMW and Su Xiuwen is 45 years old as well. But their fate is different. Su drives an expensive BMW and my mother can't even sell onions now."[47]

It was reported that Su paid Dai Yiquan more than 90,000 *yuan* in compensation and that the other twelve injured were paid about 180,000 *yuan* in total. It was also reported that Su signed a deal with Dai, requiring Dai not to pursue the case any further, including speaking to the news media.[48]

Resentment of the rich and sympathy for the poor were the main driving forces in this discussion. Many people hate the *nouveau riche*. More importantly, the percolating resentment is aimed at Chinese who have profited unlawfully from the opportunities opened up by economic reforms. Many of the wealthy are government officials or politically connected businessmen who use their ties to secure land, contracts, and real estate, amassing huge private wealth from state assets.[49]

China's economic reforms have produced a growing income gap. While the newly rich enjoy ostentatious displays of wealth—villas located behind high fences, imported cars, and private schooling—most of the population is poor, sometimes earning only a few hundred dollars a year. Still worse is the sense of insecurity, with wave after wave of layoffs at state-run factories and only a small percentage of the population covered by health insurance. The newly rich publicly show little sense of charity or social conscience. Some

132   have spirited ill-gotten wealth abroad, leaving behind bankrupt companies and destitute workers.

Corruption in China's legal system also irked the public. Media investigators uncovered many instances that demonstrated that the local legal system went out of its way to make things easier for Su. Besides preventing unfavorable depositions from being read out in court, they sent Su out of detention on parole with the excuse that she had a headache — not one of the illnesses that make one eligible for parole. Suffice it to say that many had the suspicion that Su's family had probably pulled a few strings, although nobody could produce any evidence.

The intense reaction sparked concern at the highest levels of the Communist party, and officials reopened the investigation. Central authorities demanded a complete review of the case, including a reinvestigation of Su's family background. Meanwhile, Chinese Internet police deleted most of the postings. Some Internet users urged them not to delete the postings. Needless to say, such calls did not prevail, and Internet discussions disappeared completely within a few days inside China.

On March 29, 2004, a special judicial panel in northeastern China ruled out corruption, upheld a previous court ruling in the BMW case, and closed it. It was reported that allegations of corruption and influence peddling were "groundless." The panel also determined that Su did not intend to kill Liu but was instead a bad driver.[50]

Never before has the Internet played such an important role for ordinary Chinese to take part in an event. The Internet allowed members of the public to vent their opinions and frustrations outside the entirely state-controlled press and ineffectual government complaint offices. Furthermore, the government would never have felt the pressure to order a review without the weight of public opinion carried online.

The case also shows that Internet-mediated social movements can quickly undermine popular confidence in China's legal system. The overwhelming criticism eventually led to tighter control of online discussions on the part of the government. For the government, if public anger could not be stabilized, public confidence of the legal system and, eventually, of the whole system would be "destroyed" by the Internet. Because no discussions are allowed, the impact of the new ruling resulting from the new round of investigations is unknown to the public.

In all these cases, the Internet enabled organizers of collective action (events) to accumulate a critical mass in a relatively short period of time. The immediate nationwide mobilization empowered these events to generate enormous pressure for the government. These events seriously undermined popular confidence in the government. In a positive sense, these events could also be used by the government as tools to regain popular support. For instance, in the case of Liu Yong, the retrial helped the government win back popular support. Nevertheless, it is still questionable that by so doing the government is able to win back popular trust in China's judicial system. Indeed, all these cases show that to solve legal issues by taking political action will further undermine public confidence in the judicial system.

CONCLUSION

This chapter demonstrates that new information technology, especially the Internet, has changed the interaction between the state and society in different ways. First, it has undermined the monopoly of information on the part of the communist regime and has thus provided possibilities for the formation of digitally mediated civic society. Individuals are no longer atomized by the regime, and they are able to form their own collectivity. Second, like other forms of civic society, the formation of digitally mediated civic society has significant political consequences. It provides a public space for citizens to engage in politics. Third, civic engagement in China, instead of increasing popular trust in public institutions, has led to public distrust.

The digital divide, a gap between those "online" and "offline," exists in China. This phenomenon is not so different from elsewhere in the world. But digital divide does not exacerbate traditional political inequalities. Despite digital divide, the Internet has provided a platform for an increasingly large number of individuals to take part in politics in China. This might be due to two factors. The first is the nature of decentralization of the Internet. As explained earlier, the nature of decentralization makes governmental control difficult on one hand and provides space for citizens to engage in politics on the other. The second factor is unique to China; that is, voluntary and autonomous political participation can hardly exist in other areas. The Internet serves as an effective tool for individuals to overcome tight political control, and thus voluntary participation becomes a possible enterprise.

The evidence shows that the level of social acceptance of the Internet is high in China. High social acceptance leads to high levels of digital trust. Such digital trust helps form social capital among individuals. The formation of social capital in turn helps individuals overcome the atomization imposed by the authoritarian regime and provides means for collective action. The presence of digitally mediated collective action is also a result of the democratizing effects of the Internet. As information costs fall and information sources multiply, more and more people are able to access the Internet. As surveys show, the acquisition of new information makes citizens better informed on politics.

What are the consequences of digitally mediated civic engagement? In the West, some scholars have contended that information technology has led to civic disengagement—that is, individuals tend to "bowl alone." The case of China does not seem to fit that trend. In China, the impact of the Internet on civic engagement is very positive. While traditional media is still tightly controlled by the government, the Internet has rendered government control extremely difficult, if not impossible. When information monopoly becomes impossible, individuals can communicate with one another and form a group identity. Indeed, the fact that digitally mediated collective action frequently takes place implies that individuals in China do not bowl alone; instead, they bowl together.

Interestingly, the impact of civic engagement on popular trust in China is quite similar to that in the West. Researchers have found that new information technology has led to low levels of public trust in political institutions in advanced democracies like the United States and Japan, despite their different nature. In China, as this chapter shows, civic engagement has led to a popular distrust of public institutions. In an authoritarian political setting, public institutions are usually established and imposed from above. Individuals do not have rights to take part in the process of institutional formation. But the Internet undermines the monopoly of information by the government. While existing public institutions are subject to public discussions, the formation of new public institutions is to be contested among citizens. Public distrust of public institutions is also a result of the fact that China is still not a country under the rule of law. Frequent political interventions in legal or bureaucratic affairs often further undermine popular perceptions of public institutions.

Digitally mediated civic engagement is significant for political liberalization in China. The Internet helps build a civic foundation for liberalization. It helps form a digitally based civic society and civic engagement. Moreover, digitally based collective actions and social movements can also generate enormous political pressure on the communist regime. Once the monopoly of information becomes impossible, the regime has to adjust its old policy and political practice in accordance with changing social reality. Such are the driving forces for political progress in China.

6

Interaction Strategies, Collective Action, and Political Consequences

FAILURE AND SUCCESS OF COLLECTIVE ACTION

So far, I have demonstrated the impossibility of a total control of information flow over the Internet by the government. I have also examined how civic engagement takes place in the Internet-mediated public sphere and its impact on public trust in public institutions. While the impossibility of complete Internet control creates possibilities for collective actions, civic engagement helps promote collective actions. Nevertheless, there is a gap between information acquisition and collective action. With the development of information technology, people now have, despite authoritarian control, more opportunities to access alternative sources of information than before. But if an individual's private action cannot be transformed into collective action aimed at public political participation, political liberalization and then democratization will find it difficult to take off. Thus the central questions are how collective actions actually take place and how changes in policy practices follow on the part of the regime.

As discussed in the previous chapters, scholars have debated the political impact of information technology, especially the Internet. While many argue that the Internet empowers society, others have contended that it empowers the state. At the empirical level, evidence exists to support both arguments. The Internet empowers the state in certain areas, in some other areas it empowers society, and in still other areas the state and society are mutually empowered over the Internet-mediated public space. As I argued earlier, the interaction between the state and society over the Internet-mediated public sphere is not necessarily a zero-sum game, and when conditions are "right," it could be a win-win game.

It is not a question of whether Internet-based collective action is possible because such collective actions tend to become increasingly popular in China. As described in the last chapter, since its inception, the Internet has not only created individual events of social movements but has also provided the dynamics of an "eventful" development of social movements. The question is whether Internet-based collective action can succeed in challenging the state. As already discussed, the Chinese state can be utterly ruthless in dealing with those Internet users who pose a direct challenge to the state and has cracked down on many Internet-based collective challenges. But, in recent years, there have been many Internet-based collective actions that succeeded in challenging the state. When major events occur, very intensive and extensive Web site discussions suddenly arise, put high political pressure on the authorities, and push the latter to change existing policy practices.

The Internet has played an important role in the processes of Internet-based collective action. Without the Internet, it would be impossible for social forces to bring their influence to bear in such a short period of time. The Internet has enabled social forces to react to events more quickly and effectively. So, the question is why some collective actions have failed while others have succeeded.

I argue that interaction strategies matter. Due to the authoritarian nature of the Chinese political system, whether a given Internet-based social movement will succeed or not is largely dependent on how the state views that social movement. If a given collective action is perceived as undermining the legitimacy of or posing a threat to the state, it is likely to invite a crackdown by the state. On the other hand, if a given collective action is perceived to be constructive to the state, it is likely to succeed. I have argued earlier that it is important to disaggregate the state when one looks at the political impact of the Internet. In Chapter Three, I attempted to disaggregate the state at the bureaucratic level and showed that conflicting interests between different bureaucratic organizations have an impact on the effectiveness of Internet control on the part of the state. Further, the state can be disaggregated at the leadership level. Whether a given Internet-based social movement is "destructive" or "constructive" is judged subjectively by major Chinese leaders. But different leaders have different perceptions. Therefore, how social forces interact with Chinese leaders matters in deciding the success or failure of a given Internet-based social movement. In this chapter, I shall first discuss why interaction strategies between the state and society matter and then present several empirical cases to explain why some collective actions have failed while others have succeeded.

INTERACTION STRATEGIES

I have argued in early chapters that the nature of a particular challenge affects how the state will respond and thus whether that challenge will likely lead to political liberalization. So, to examine the impact of the Internet on political liberalization, one needs to identify Internet-based challenges (online activities) with different natures. Following Albert Hirschman's analysis, three main categories of Internet activities can be identified: "exit," "voice," and "loyalty."[1]

Loyalty

According to Hirschman, loyalty refers to "special attachment to an organization."[2] The "loyalty" type of Internet activities includes those online activities that show their loyalty to the state. In China, such activities are no different from traditionally government-controlled media such as newspapers, broadcasting, TV, and others. In this sense, the Internet has empowered the state. The Chinese state has used the Internet widely for various purposes, such as promoting and publicizing its ideologies and policies. At the societal level, "Internet nationalism," which has gained popularity in China,[3] can be regarded as a loyalty type of Internet activity. To a great degree, Internet nationalism is mutually empowering to the state and social forces. While it can enhance the legitimacy of the state, it also provides (nationalistic) social forces a channel to influence the government's policy orientations, if not policy per se.

Loyalty does not mean in any sense irrationality because loyalty can encompass different kinds of interests. Hirschman observed, "A member with a considerable attachment to a product or organization will often search for ways to make himself influential, especially when the organization moves in what he believes is the wrong direction; conversely, a member who wields (or thinks he wields) considerable power in an organization and is therefore convinced that he can get it 'back on the track' is likely to develop a strong affection for the organization in which he is powerful."[4] So, even the most loyal member can exit because loyalty is often an important part of his bargaining power vis-à-vis the organization.[5]

For whatever reasons, as long as individual members are loyal to their organizations, they are unlikely to openly challenge those organizations. The loyalty type of Internet activities are not the main focus of this analysis because they do not directly set themselves up against the state. My discussion thus focuses on the other two types of activities, namely, "exit" and "voice."

Exit

"Exit" activities refer to those Internet-facilitated collective actions that directly challenge the state. According to Hirschman, when "some customers stop buying the firm's products or some members leave the organization: this is the *exit option*."[6] Given the fact that formal opposition ("exit") is not allowed to exist in China's political system, the exit option is highly risky, and it is thus a choice of "no choice" for those who engage in this sort of Internet-based collective action. The decision whether to exit is often made in light of the prospects for the effective use of "voice." If people are convinced that voice will be effective, they will not exit or will postpone their exit. But more frequently, users will turn to the exit option only when the voice option fails because once people choose the exit option, they lose the opportunity to use voice, but not vice versa.[7]

Moreover, once the exit option is chosen, the nature of the interaction between the collective action and the state changes. According to Hirschman, "Exit has a destructive rather than salutary effect."[8] So, the exit option means that a given collective action begins to challenge the existing state. From the perspective of the Chinese state, such an act should be regarded as aiming at "overthrowing" the government. Such a perception often justifies the excessive measures taken by the state against Internet-based collective actions. In other words, the choice of the exit option means that challenges will inevitably be an affront to the state, and more often than not, a crackdown by the state also becomes inevitable.

Despite China's tight political control, the Internet has made the exit option available. While people are not allowed to criticize the state via traditional media such as newspaper, broadcasting, and TV, they can complain via the Internet. The frequent crackdowns on the Internet-based collective actions do not mean that the state is able to eliminate use of the exit option by challengers. As examined in Chapter Three, exit activities tend to become "eventful" in forming a chain of consistent challenges to the state. In other words, more arrests are likely to lead to more protests. This is partly because of the low organizational costs of Internet-based actions and partly because of the unlimited potential of Internet technology, as discussed earlier.

Michael Chase and James Mulvenon have described Internet-based dissent activities among Chinese dissidents in detail.[9] Apparently, almost all such activities are outside China. But it is important to note that many actions were first organized within China, such as the Falun Gong and the China Democracy Party, and only after they were crushed inside China, they "exited."

Although the exit option often leads to a crackdown by the state, its impact

on political liberalization cannot be underestimated. The existence of the
exit option can actually exercise high pressure on the state. The fear of the
exit option often forces the state to appreciate voice, which is often regarded
as constructive to the state. The state cannot afford to alienate all social forces.
The fear of total alienation makes the state willing to make compromises regarding voice activities.

Voice

"Voice" activities are those Internet-facilitated collective actions that do not
pose a direct challenge to the state but that promote gradual political liberalization. According to Hirschman, when the organization's members express
their dissatisfaction directly to some authority or through general protest addressed to anyone who cares to listen, they have chosen a voice option. As a
result, relevant authorities once again engage in a search for the causes of and
possible cures for members' dissatisfaction.[10] For a member, to resort to voice,
rather than exit, is to make an attempt at changing the practices, policies, and
outputs of the organization to which the member belongs. Voice is to change,
not escape from, an objectionable state of affairs, whether through individual
or collective petition to the authority directly in charge, through appeal to a
higher authority with the intention of forcing a change in practice, or through
various types of actions and protests, including those that are meant to mobilize public opinion.[11]

The voice option has become the most efficient means for any organizers of
Internet-based collective actions to change political practices in China. This
is due to two main factors. On one hand, as Hirschman pointed out, the voice
option is the only way in which dissatisfied members can react whenever the
exit option is unavailable.[12] As mentioned earlier, formal opposition forces
do not exist in China. Even though the Internet has provided some form of
exit, the exit option contains high political risks. Once challengers choose the
exit option or are identified as an opposition to the state, the confrontation
between them and the state becomes inevitable. As discussed above, protesters
are frequently arrested, detained, and punished. On the other hand, given the
fact that the Internet has created new forms of exit, the state is likely to allow
voice to exist and even to play a role in reducing the opportunities for exit.
The voice option is not a direct challenge because challengers do not identify
themselves as opposition to the state. In most cases, such collective actions are
targeted at specific policy or issue areas.

Given the fact that the voice option is not a confrontational approach, the
state is more likely to tolerate such an option in some instances and, in other

140   instances, to use popular voice to change old political practices and improve the state's performance. The voice option is especially useful when there is unstated cooperation between reformist leaders inside the state and social forces outside the state. The nature of China's political system is such that it is not an easy task for any reformist leaders to undertake reform initiatives within the system. In most cases, they have to rely on initiatives from local governments or social forces. This is especially true when a generation of technocrats has replaced revolutionaries in the top leadership positions and much emphasis has been placed on so-called collective leadership in the post-Deng era. Great leaders like Mao Zedong and Deng Xiaoping were often able to take reform initiatives, but technocrats are less able to do so. Under the principle of collective leadership, reform initiatives often involve striking some balance among the conflicting interests of leaders. When there is a deadlock between the soft-liners and hard-liners, voice outside the state becomes important to break such a deadlock. The soft-liners or reformist leaders are likely to form an implicit cooperation with the voice people to make changes to policies or practices.

INTERACTION STRATEGIES MATTER

The above brief discussion already implies how different strategies can lead to different political consequences. The importance of interaction strategies can further be perceived from a game theory point of view, which incorporates strategic behavior into the neoclassical model of rational choice.

Rational choice places much emphasis on the strategic structures of social relations. According to Russell Hardin, to speak about "strategic structures is to focus on the way in which outcomes are determined by the interactions of choices by several or many actors, each trying to achieve certain results that may differ substantially from the outcomes of their interactions."[13] Hardin identified three categories of strategic interaction—namely, conflict, coordination, and cooperation. In a pure conflict interaction, one party can gain only if another loses. A coordination interaction is the virtual opposite of this. In such an interaction, each party can gain only if others also gain. A cooperation interaction involves elements of both conflict and coordination. As Hardin explains, "I have something you want and you have something I want. I'd rather have what you have than what I have and you'd rather have what I have. We can both benefit by exchanging. There is conflict because each of us has to give up something in order for the other to gain. And there is coordination because we can both be made better off at once by exchanging."[14]

What Hirschman referred to as voice is certainly embedded in Hardin's coordination and cooperation strategies. While Hirschman provided a perspective from the viewpoints of participants (society), Hardin's perspective is more helpful in understanding state behavior. By combining the two perspectives, we can have a better understanding of how different interaction strategies lead to different consequences.

In Hirschman's terms, the voice stands between loyalty and exit. Social groups can use the voice option in a positive way to gain something from the state. They can be constructive. For example, social groups can engage in online activities to push changes to existing policy practices on the part of the state. By doing so, they do not aim at "overthrowing" the state but at improving its performance. On the part of the state, the leadership also benefits from such a voice option to provide a dynamic for changes and therefore to improve its governance. In this sense, one can argue that there is an implicit strategy of coordination between social groups and the reformist leadership, as discussed in the previous chapters.

Nevertheless, social groups can also use the voice option in a "negative" sense. In this case, social groups aim at exchanging what they have or what they can do for certain actions on the part of the state. For example, they can restrain themselves from using the exit option in exchange for benefits on the part of the state. In other words, social groups exercise pressure on the state but do not openly oppose it or challenge its legitimacy in their online activities. In return, the state is likely to change or liberalize its policy practice in the favor of social groups.

On the other hand, Hardin seems to put much emphasis on how the state can use different strategies in its interaction with social forces. His interest is to see how power can be exercised more efficiently via different strategies. It seems to him that "power and cooperation are heavily intertwined in the organization of society and government; they are mutually reinforcing in the sense that power is based in cooperation and it also enables cooperation."[15]

Successful social coordination, whether intended or unintended, can create extraordinary power. The state does not always need to appeal to coercive means to rule; instead, it can use other strategies such as coordination and cooperation. For example, obedience to law is based on the threat of sanction. If people are made to obey the law by threat of force, the state will be unable to mount adequate mechanisms of enforcement. No state could possibly compel people to obey all its rules at gunpoint. According to Hardin, a moderately organized state can typically keep its citizens under control without going to such extremes. Most individuals cannot expect to benefit from seriously transgressing the law because the police, as weak as they may be, can be expected to apprehend a significant proportion of transgressors. The state need not compel everyone at gunpoint; it needs merely to make it in virtually everyone's clear interest individually to comply with the law.[16] Coordination can work more efficiently than coercive measures. The coordinated powerful group can do many things at far less cost than doing these things would otherwise have involved. Coordination not only creates power; it also reduces the need to use power.[17]

Back to Hirschman's term. One can argue that the exit option on the part of social groups is likely to invite a conflicting strategy on the part of the state. Furthermore, while the voice option is likely to invite the coordination strategy on the part of the state, such a strategy can in turn induce cooperation on the part of social groups. It provides social groups with incentives to be loyal to the state (in a positive sense) and to be cooperative with the state (in a negative sense).

THE RISE AND FALL OF INTERNET-MEDIATED COLLECTIVE ACTIONS

In the following sections, I present five cases of Internet-facilitated collective action. The first two cases—the Falun Gong siege of Zhongnanhai and the China Democracy Party—fall into the exit category, while the last three cases—the Severe Acute Respiratory Syndrome (SARS) event, the death of Sun Zhigang, and the Sun Dawu events—fall into the voice category. One can see how different interaction strategies on the part of social forces lead to different types of collective action, which affect China's policy outcomes differently. Needless to say, interaction strategies are not a given, and they are formed and subject to changes during the process of the interaction between the state and social forces.

The Falun Gong Siege of Zhongnanhai

On April 25, 1999, just weeks before the tenth anniversary of the Tiananmen crackdown, as many as 11,000 Falun Gong (FLG) followers from North and Northeast China grabbed the headlines of the world's news media by "laying siege" to the communist leadership compound, Zhongnanhai, and staging an eighteen-hour "sit-in." Their representatives made a number of requests to the government. Among others, these included a recognition of the organization, a clarification that it is not an "opposition organization," the release of its forty-five followers arrested a week earlier by the Tianjin Public Security Department, and assurance that the government would not take action against those involved in the gathering. The demonstration was peaceful and orderly. No banners were displayed and no slogans were chanted. Protesters cooperated with police, dispersed peacefully at nightfall, and even collected their own garbage.

Nevertheless, the top leadership was unnerved for various reasons. First, the FLG was equipped with effective organizational methods and modern information technologies. The demonstration had caught China's public security services by surprise. The leadership soon found out that the FLG was not a simple organization but a highly structured one based on modern information technologies such as email, the Internet, and mobile phones. The leadership was alarmed by the FLG's tight, secret-society–type organization, which bore some resemblance to the underground Communist party in the 1930s and 1940s.[18] For instance, at the grassroots level, members were grouped into loosely constituted "cells," with Master Li Hongzhi being able to remotely guide and issue directions to 39 teaching centers, 1,900 instruction centers, and 28,000 practice sites throughout China through electronic communications.[19] Second, the FLG seemed to have mobilized support from many Communist party members. For years, the FLG was able to win over many party members. Although there are no estimates, a number of party members were involved in FLG activities. For example, among the 50,000 FLG followers rounded up by police in a week (in July 1999), 1,200 of them were party cadres. More seriously, party members more often than not played a leading role in the FLG. For example, according to an internal report, 7 percent of regular members and 46 percent of the leading organizers of the FLG movement in the Shandong province in the 1990s were party members.[20] This is confirmed by the fact that all five representatives negotiating with the government during the Zhongnanhai siege were cadres from some of the core organizations of the Chinese Communist Party (CCP) itself. They were variously from the Supervisory Department, the Railway Department, the Second Headquarters of the General Staff, the Public Security Department, and Beijing University. This immediately caused an official of the Political-Legal Committee to claim, "The Falun Gong has pierced into the stomach of our party."[21]

The regime reacted to the FLG challenge forcefully. On July 22, 2002, three months after the April 25 siege, the government made a national announcement that the FLG was an "illegal organization that disseminated heretical beliefs." It outlawed the Study Society of Falun Beliefs and arrested some core members of the FLG and put them away on long prison terms. While the regime mobilized a nationwide crackdown, the FLG put up strong resistance. Throughout 1999 and 2000, FLG followers staged demonstrations in Beijing and other cities through holding street sit-ins, distributing leaflets, disseminating messages across the Internet, and even using some radical methods to challenge the authority of the government. All these caused the government to further declare the FLG an "evil cult" and to mobilize all the necessary resources to suppress it. The crackdown continued for many years, and the regime was finally able to bring the situation under control inside China. While the FLG continues to be proactive outside China, its activities inside China have undoubtedly been seriously constrained by ruthless policies on the part of the state.

In its initial stages, the FLG was extremely successful in mobilizing its followers via modern information technology. Nevertheless, the siege of Zhongnanhai changed Chinese leaders' perceptions of the FLG, especially Jiang Zemin, the then–state president and party secretary in general. For many FLG followers, the siege of Zhongnanhai only meant the use of the voice option, and many had hoped that their voice could "correct" the state's de facto policy practices that were not favorable to the FLG. But on the part of state, the siege was regarded as an open challenge and thus an exit option. The perceived exit option on the part of the FLG led to the state's immediate adoption of the conflict strategy against the FLG. The state carried out a concerted effort nationwide to crackdown on the FLG. Once the interaction between the FLG and the state became a zero-sum game, the FLG was forced to choose the exit option and began to challenge the state openly in exile.

However, using the strategy of conflict does not enable the state to become the winner. Due to the FLG's capability to mobilize, conflicts between millions of FLG followers and the state have not come to an end. The FLG followers all over the world continue to incite activities to show their displeasure with the state. Communication among its followers within and especially without China is still very much active. When opportunities arise, FLG followers can quickly initiate a protest movement. For instance, when the SARS hit China badly from March to June 2003, the FLG became very active in North China, especially Hebei, an area with a history of peasant rebellions.[22] Since the CCP attained power in 1949, China had never witnessed such a massive and sustained nationwide opposition movement. Modern information technology has undoubtedly played an important role in sustaining FLG mobilization. Needless to say, the state continues to face mounting international pressure over various human rights issues related to the FLG. It is reasonable to say that a conflict strategy has dramatically increased costs for both the state and the FLG in their interaction.

The China Democracy Party

In June 1998, a number of grassroots dissidents in China attempted to found the China Democracy Party (CDP),[23] triggering a political storm that spanned

eleven provinces and lasted as long as six months.[24] Information technology   145
played an important role in facilitating the CDP movement in two ways. First,
it provided effective communications among China's democracy activists in
different regions and thus helped them form a concerted collective action.
Second, the Internet provided a political forum in which activists could make
attempts to form their party identity, despite its eventual failure.

A number of factors encouraged Chinese democratic activists to initiate
such a collective action. First, the CCP held its Fifteenth National Congress
in 1997, signifying the consolidation of Jiang Zemin's power in the ruling
party. After the party congress, political control began to loosen gradually.
This provided a favorable political setting for the CDP. Second, the CCP
had earlier on declared that it would sign the United Nations' International
Covenant on Civil and Political Rights in 1998. Third, American president
Bill Clinton was scheduled to visit China in June 1998 for the first time since
the June Fourth Incident in 1989. Democratic activists believed that all these
factors should restrain Beijing from taking action against them.

On June 25, 1998, dissidents in Zhejiang—Wang Youcai, Wang Donghai,
and Lin Hui—submitted to the Zhejiang Bureau of Civil Affairs "An Open
Announcement of the Founding of the Zhejiang Preparatory Committee of
the China Democratic Party" and an application for the founding of the party.
They claimed that the objective was to "realize direct democratic elections,
construct a constitutional democratic state and power-sharing mechanism." It
was the first time in the history of the People's Republic that democratic activists made an open application to establish an opposition party and politically
challenge the current regime.

The relevant authorities did not take any action against the collective action during the China–U.S. summit. It was not until July 10, after Clinton left
China, that Wang Youcai was arrested. The arrest led to criticism against the
state among democratic activists within and outside of China. Fifty days after
the arrest, on August 30, Wang Youcai was released.

The initial act in Zhejiang province was soon followed by another attempt
in Shandong province. On September 5, before a visit to China by Madame
Robinson, a senior official of the Commission of Human Rights Affairs in
the United Nations, three dissidents in Shandong—Xie Wanjun, Liu Lianjun, and Jiang Fuzhen—declared the founding of the Shandong Preparatory
Committee of the CDP. They sent by post the declaration of the founding
of the party and the application for the founding to the Shandong Bureau of
Civil Affairs.

Surprisingly, the response from the Shandong Bureau of Civil Affairs was
so moderate that it was beyond the activists' expectations. Five days after Xie

Wangjun sent out the letter, two officials of the Shandong Bureau of Civil Affairs formally received the activists. The two officials explained that, according to the laws of social organizations, founding an organization required the satisfaction of four conditions: 1) having 50,000 *yuan* in registration capital; 2) declaring an office site; 3) providing background information of the assistant secretary of the party and members above that level; and 4) declaring that the organization had more than fifty members. The activists in Shandong quickly disseminated through the Internet this news with headlines such as "A Major Breakthrough! The Chinese Government Lifted the Party Ban!" and "A Better Turn for the Party Founding Attempt in Shandong!"

However, this optimism soon proved to be premature. Not long afterward, the local public security department arrested Liu Lianjun and Xie Wangjun for allegedly "distorting social order." Ten days later, they were released. Also, by mid October, all the thirteen activists in Shandong were released.

News of what happened in Shandong immediately spread all over the country through the Internet. In a short period of time, one democratic activist after another in eleven provinces founded their own provincial-level preparatory committees of the CDP. A number of the overseas activists also established overseas offices. The movement was soon "radicalized" by Xu Wenli, an old activist in Beijing. Xu was an activist in the democratic movement in Beijing from 1978 to 1979. On November 6, 1998, Xu declared the founding of the "Preparatory Work Team for National Congress of the CDP." In addition, he founded a branch in the Beijing and Tianjin areas, trying to show that this was a "formal organization" that, unlike other preparatory committees elsewhere, needed no approval from the government. He even successfully persuaded Qin Yongmin, an activist in Hubei, to establish formally the "Hubei Branch of the CDP."

In the proclamation of the Preparatory Work Team for National Congress of the CDP, Xu announced that the CDP would gradually establish its own national and religious institutions and its own Taiwan policy, as well as research institutes on the national defense strategies. Also, the proclamation openly welcomed the return of the democratic activists currently in exile overseas to become the leaders and advisors of the preparatory committee.

Xu's radical steps provoked Chinese leaders, who had changed the way they handled democratic activists for some years. The regime had practiced a model of arrest and release, then arrest and release again. With the perceived "radicalization" of the CDP movement, the regime now decided to take a hard-line approach. On November 21, 1998, the Xinhua News Agency published Li Peng's conversation in an interview by foreign reporters. Li Peng, then chairman of the National People's Congress (NPC), asserted that "an

opposition party was completely not allowed." On December 18, Jiang Zemin   147
officially announced a new policy that "the government has to be fully vigilant
of the interventionist as well as the subversive and separatist activities of the
rival forces within and outside the country, and have to resolutely annihilate
them right from their embryonic stage."

By late December 1998, the movement was largely suppressed by the regime, and some main organizers, including Wang Youcai, Xu Wenli, and Qin
Yongmin, were imprisoned for periods that lasted from ten to thirteen years.
Despite the regime's crackdown, many CDP members remain active on the
mainland, waiting for another opportunity to rise. In addition, the CDP has
also developed an "organization in exile" in the United States.

In the CDP case, the Internet apparently played a contradictory role. On
one hand, it helped the CDP mobilize its supporters nationwide and even beyond China's national boundary. The Internet served as an effective forum for
CDP followers to communicate with one another and discuss various issues.
On the other hand, the Internet seemed to have facilitated the radicalization
of the movement. Over the Internet, CDP followers interacted horizontally
and without a hierarchy, meaning that they could compete with one another
freely without any institutional constraints. Well-informed individual CDP
leaders attempted to maximize their own interests in the event at the expense
of the nascent political party.

On the part of the state, initially the Jiang Zemin leadership seemed to be
tolerant of the CDP in the face of the international community. Even though
there were no signs to indicate that the leadership was ready to allow an opposition party to arise, different approaches to the CDP in different provinces
and cities implied that there was space for such political forces. If the state
perceived such efforts as "loyal," it would likely have been tolerant. Once the
movement radicalized and its leaders began to mobilize nationwide support
for its course, it was perceived to have transformed itself from a loyalty option
to an exit one and therefore invited a conflict strategy on the part of the state.
The consequence of the conflict strategy in this case is not much different
from that of the FLG.

The Death of Sun Zhigang and the Abolition
of the "C&R" System

On March 20, 2003, Sun Zhigang, a twenty-seven-year-old man, was beaten
to death by eight inmates in the infirmary of a custody and repatriation center
in Guangzhou. After the news was spread through the Internet, the whole
country was stirred up and enormous pressure was placed on the Chinese gov-

148   ernment. On June 20, Primer Wen Jiabao declared that the "Measures for the Custody and Repatriation of Urban Vagrants and Beggars" (C&R, hereafter), which led to the death of Sun, were to be abolished from August 1, 2003, and would be replaced by the "Measures of Management of Urban Vagrant Beggars." It was the first time in the People's Republic of China's history that one civilian death caused a state regulation to be revoked. The abolition of the C&R is an important improvement of the human rights situation in China and thus an important step toward the country's political liberalization. Sun's case shows how Internet-facilitated collective action can provide an effective channel for civilian political participation and thus affect policy outcomes. It also shows how Internet-based social protests can provide reformist leaders in Beijing with an opportunity to change existing policy practices.

Sun Zhigang, a graduate from Wuhan University of Science and Technology in the Hubei province, first found a job in Shenzhen and then went to Guangzhou in early 2003 to work at a garment company. On the night of March 17, Sun left home as usual and went to an Internet bar. On the way, local police in Guangzhou detained him for failing to show a temporary residence permit and sent him to a C&R center. Over the next three days, he was directed to three different places: a Guangzhou police station, a municipal C&R center, and the center's infirmary. On March 20, Sun died in the infirmary.

Sun's parents in Hubei traveled to Guangdong to seek the true cause of Sun's death. After a month of efforts, they were not able to clear their doubts because the local government agencies were not cooperative. So, they took their story to the *Nanfang dushi bao* (*Southern Metropolitan News*), a rather liberal major newspaper in Guangdong. In early 2003, the newspaper reported the first two cases of the SARS and thus provoked local authorities. Though several journalists were criticized and even punished, they received overwhelming public support through the Internet. The newspaper continued to speak for the people. The journalists made their own investigation into Sun's death and then published a full account on April 25. Other local and national newspapers then picked up the story, and it quickly became a national issue. It is particularly important to note that the Internet played a key role in encouraging these journalists to stay their course. Before the story was published by the newspaper, a great amount of discussion had already taken place on the Internet.

The disclosure of Sun's case immediately triggered a major debate in China. Three questions become the foci, including 1) the process of criminal investigation into a case such as this; 2) the prevalence of police abuse; and 3) the constitutionality of the C&R system.

After the media publicized Sun's story, the central government ordered the

relevant authorities to investigate the case and punish the perpetrators as seri-   149
ously and as quickly as possible. This is a usual practice of the Chinese state.
The state believed that a quick solution could prevent the negative impact of
Sun's case (criticisms against the state) from spreading to the whole country.
On June 27, twelve people found guilty of beating Sun to death received death
penalties or terms of imprisonment ranging from three years to life. Another
six civil servants in Guangzhou were also sentenced to two to three years in
prison for their malpractices that were partly to blame for the tragedy.[25]

Nonetheless, people were already mobilized by modern information technologies. While the progress of the criminal investigation was closely watched,
people put a great deal of emphasis on how to improve China's existing practices and measures related to human rights violations. The C&R system naturally became an immediate target of attack.

The C&R system can be traced back to a 1961 party directive titled "Forbidding Free Movement of the Population," which aimed to restrain the rural
population from entering cities. In 1982 the State Council added "Measures for
the Custody and Repatriation of Urban Beggars," aimed at providing shelter for
homeless people in cities. Nevertheless, the C&R measure was actually meant
to strengthen the Household Registration System (i.e., *hukou zhidu*) in order to
exercise tight political control over the population. The C&R system provided
the legal basis for internment and deportation of vagrants by public security
authorities. It requires urban vagrants and beggars to be properly housed and
eventually deported to their hometowns and for the local governments to make
proper arrangements for them. In theory, the day-to-day oversight of C&R centers falls under the Ministry of Civil Affairs' responsibilities, but in practice, the
public security apparatus, especially local police, runs the system.

Since the early 1990s, with the rapid development of the market economy,
China had seen millions of migrants moving within the country and seeking
job opportunities. The C&R system became a means for local governments
to protect their own populations against outsiders (i.e., migrants from other
localities). Millions of people were detained, including the poor, migrant
workers, women who were kidnapped for sale on an underground market,
and petitioners who sought justice from the government.

The C&R system was dominated by extortion practices for more than a
decade. It allowed local government officials and police to abuse human
rights in various ways, including arbitrary detention, physical abuse, and ex-
tralegal ransom. The most vulnerable citizens were the so-called three nos —
those with no ID card, no temporary resident permit, and no work permit.
The conditions in C&R centers were appalling. Food and sanitary conditions
were abominable. Detainees were routinely subjected to beatings by police,

150   sometimes resulting in death. Police even used the C&R system to kidnap the powerless and demand ransom from their families or friends. Indeed, ransom collection strongly motivated police to detain as many people as possible, leading to gross violations of human rights.

The Chinese government went along with the practice of such human rights violations because it served so-called sociopolitical stability, the highest priority of the Chinese state since the reform and open door policy in the late 1970s. The C&R system was especially useful in high political seasons such as during a Party Congress, a People's Congress, a visit by a foreign dignitary, or a bid to host the Olympics. In advance of such events, the C&R system was used to "clean up" the cities. Even though human rights violations in C&R centers were widely known, the state did not have any incentive to change this practice.

The death of Sun Zhigang stirred up people's sense of outrage against the C&R system. People from different parts of the country posted their stories on the Internet or circulated their views to one another via email, telling about their nightmare experiences in C&R centers. But more importantly, educated citizens began to question the constitutionality of the C&R system. It became the hottest topic among students as well as professors in all major universities. Since the pro-democracy movement in 1989, no event had involved so many universities and had so aroused people's great interest in discussing China's legal reform. On May 16, three Ph.D. candidates for doctorates of law in Beijing's universities submitted (via fax) a petition to the Standing Committee of the NPC to reexamine the constitutionality of the 1982 "Measure for the Custody and Repatriation of Urban Vagrant Beggars." Meanwhile, they also posted the letter on the Internet.[26]

Their petition held that under the PRC's Administrative Punishment Act and its Legislature Act, citizens could be deprived of their freedom only by laws and that such laws must be passed by the NPC or its Standing Committee. In other words, the State Council and the various provincial governments have no power to make regulations that in effect deprive citizens of their personal freedom, and therefore, the C&R, arising from party and State Council directives, is unlawful. The petition immediately spread to the whole country, and popular support was overwhelming. Later, five prominent legal scholars stood up to support the three doctoral students by calling for a special investigation into the case and into the status quo of the C&R system itself and its implementation.[27]

Obviously, the petition drew attention to the fact that China's rulers, especially at local levels, had violated the Constitution for decades with impunity and that ordinary citizens had paid an onerous price for violating local regulations. "Voice" generated by the death of an ordinary citizen was so overwhelmingly strong that the leadership had to make an effective response. What happened inside Zhongnanhai is still unknown, but what the world saw was that reformist leaders, especially new premier Wen Jiabao, put their weight on the side of popular sentiments and against human rights abuses. As mentioned earlier, on June 20, the State Council declared the abolition of the C&R system. Sun Zhigang was regarded as a political martyr because his death led to the demise of an "evil" regulation and created a condition for ordinary citizens to use, for the first time in the history of the People's Republic of China, the Constitution to constrain the power of state organs.

The "Release" of Private Entrepreneur Sun Dawu

Sun Dawu was a very prestigious Chinese private entrepreneur in Hebei. In 1989, Sun formally registered his Dawu Farming and Husbandry Group. By 1995, it was ranked at 344 among the top 500 private corporations in China. One year later, the Xushui county, where the company was located, declared the Dawu group a key township enterprise and recognized it as an economic engine of the region. The company employed nearly 2,000 workers.

But Sun Dawu was also active politically. He was very critical of government policies, especially those that discriminated against private enterprises, and even of China's political system. He associated himself with Chinese liberals such as Li Shenzhi, former deputy president of the Chinese Academy of Social Sciences (CASS); Tu Runsheng, advisor to former party secretary Zhao Ziyang; and Wu Jinlian, a Beijing-based liberal economist. Sun spoke at major Chinese universities such as Beijing and Qinghua. He also established his own Web site, circulating his papers and speeches via the Internet. He struggled for farmers' rights. He believed that farmers should stand up and speak for themselves and that they should have their own organizations and demands. He claimed that the problems of rural poverty stemmed not only from unjust policies but also from the political calcification of the country. When he spoke at Beijing University, he asked the students, "How can there be farmers' rebellions unless there is government oppression? What is the situation now? Farmers cannot see any hope; the countryside is a land of desperation. That is why I have said farmers need a third liberation."

In many articles on his Web site, Sun called for China's political reform, which, he believed, should aim at establishing a multiparty system, a free media, and popular political participation. In one article, he questioned the viability of the Communist party, a taboo subject in what remains an authoritarian state, and suggested that multiparty democracy was the only solution for

152   China's rural population. He criticized Maoist coercive policies, saying, "Mao Zedong was a great proletarian revolutionary who made the country's people stand up. Chairman was also a great feudal sentry who made the country's people kneel." He even lambasted the central government by telling Beijing students, "The government should be blamed for the bad credibility of our country. . . . The masses have begun to understand democracy and the rule of law, and they have a common yearning for democracy." [28] According to Sun, it is the government, not people, that does not want democracy.

Disappointed by China's policy practices, Sun began to challenge them. Although the Chinese government began to legalize the private sector in the early 1990s, private enterprises were often denied loans from state banks. Frustrated by this policy, Sun established what was, in essence, a financial cooperative that operated much like a small private bank. It took deposits from residents, issued loans for a fixed period, and paid interest rates two or three times higher than those offered by state-owned banks.

On May 27, 2003, Sun was detained by a local bureau of public security on an allegation that the Dawu Group illegally absorbed more than 10 million yuan of public funds over a three-year period.[29]

Like the death of Sun Zhigang, the arrest of Sun Dawu immediately stirred up national sentiments against the relevant authorities. Chinese intellectuals and private entrepreneurs showed their strong support of Sun. Extensive discussions were carried out via the Internet. The attack was directed at the government regulations that prohibited private enterprises from getting loans from state banks. Liberal legal scholars argued that Sun should not have been detained but that the relevant government regulations should have been abolished. Discussion forums were also initiated by liberal economists in Beijing. The local government did not expect that the arrest of Sun would lead to such a nationwide reaction.

Pressure mounted on the central government. In August, central leaders got involved in the case. On October 30, 2003, Sun was sentenced to three years in prison with a four-year reprieve.[30] After his release, Sun decided not to appeal the decision to a higher court, as such a move was believed to be unrealistic. A few months later, in January 2004, the Hebei provincial government issued a new policy to liberalize the previously rigid regulations of prohibiting loan access to private entrepreneurs. The new policy also stated that the government would not examine how private entrepreneurs accumulated their initial capital. So far, their "illegal" methods of capital accumulation could be regarded as "criminal." The issue of legality of initial capital accumulation was exempted from the new policy. Like the death of Sun Zhigang,

the Sun Dawu event led to a major policy concession on the part of the Hebei   153
provincial government.

Why was the Sun Dawu event able to bring about positive results? This is mainly due to the fact that the "voice" from this event was in accordance with the efforts of the leadership in legitimating capitalism in China since the early 1990s. Capitalism, and thus capitalists, did not have a legitimate base in China's constitution. According to the 1954 Constitution, China's political system was based on the working class as its leading class and the worker-peasant alliance as its foundation (Article 1). With regard to the economic system, the constitution said that the state would aim at eliminating the exploitative system and building a socialist system.

After Deng Xiaoping returned to power, the CCP leadership passed a new constitution, the 1982 Constitution. Though the 1982 Constitution still emphasized that the state sector had to be dominant in China's economy, it recognized that individually engaged economic activities in both rural and urban areas were complementary to the state sector (Article 11). What was later called the private enterprise — made up of companies that employed more than eight workers — was not legalized.

In 1988, the first constitutional amendment was made, making two significant changes related to China's economic system. First, one paragraph was added to Article 11 that stated, "The state allows the private economy to exist and develop within the legal boundary. The private economy is complementary to the socialist public economy. The state protects legal rights and interests of the private economy, provides it with leadership, supervision and management" (Article 11, paragraph 3). Second, paragraph 4 of Article 10 was revised: The state recognized that "land use right can be transferred in accordance with legal regulations." This change was significant because it meant that the state legalized employment, capital accumulation, land commercialization, and other newly rising economic activities. Five years later, in 1993, the second constitutional amendment was made. The 1993 amendment gave up the planned economic system and formally declared that a socialist market economy was to be established.

The official confirmation of the market economy led the leftists, both old and new, to levy serious criticisms against capitalistic development in the middle 1990s. Despite all the controversy, the leadership decided to press ahead. The Fifteenth Party Congress in 1997 further pointed to how a market economy could take root in China and declared a program of partial privatization of state-owned enterprises. Further, based on the 1993 amendment, the Second Session of the Ninth NPC in 1999 made a constitutional amendment

154   that, for the first time since the establishment of the People's Republic, provides constitutional protection for the private economy.

While it will take a long time for the CCP to establish an interest-based political order, all these constitutional changes in the 1990s show that the party leadership has made great efforts to adjust China's political system not only to promote further economic development but also to accommodate capitalist economic institutions. In February 2000, Jiang Zemin raised a new concept of *san ge dai biao* (literally, "three represents"). According to this concept, the CCP represents the "most advanced mode of productive force, the most advanced culture, and the interests of the majority of the population."[31] The "three represents" theory is undoubtedly the CCP's affirmation of the non-state sector in the economy. More importantly, it also shows that the CCP has begun to consider how the interests of newly rising classes or social groups can be represented. At the Sixteenth Party Congress in 2002, the CCP leadership further legitimized party membership of private entrepreneurs.[32]

Despite all these changes at the central level, policy implementation continues to be problematic at all levels. Many policy practices are against the private sector and thus private entrepreneurs.[33] What local governments in Hebei province did to Sun Dawu was a reflection of such policy practices. The Sun Dawu event gave rise to popular voice to oppose discriminatory policy practices against the private sector. This in turn created an opportunity for the central government to correct such policy practices. One can assume that without approval or a tacit nod from the central government, local governments in Hebei would not have been able to change their old policy practices.

The SARS Event

On March 12, 2003, the World Health Organization (WHO) issued a global alert on the outbreak of a new form of pneumonia-like disease with symptoms that are similar to those of the common flu.[34] This illness, officially known as the Severe Acute Respiratory Syndrome (SARS), was first found in the Guang-dong province in China in November 2003 and then was spread to many parts of the world in a matter of a few weeks. When it was found in China, related Chinese authorities lied to the whole world about the situation in the country. Consequently, when the SARS spread to different parts of world, people, especially in Asia, were angry with China's initial lackluster reaction. The Chinese government faced the greatest international pressure since its crackdown on the pro-democracy movement in 1989. Fortunately, China's new leadership adopted forceful and effective measures to contain this disease in the next few months, and it succeeded.

The SARS case deserves mention because it shows how social groups can   155
make use of the Internet to break tight information control on the part of
the state and force the latter to promote China's political transparency and
accountability—important steps toward political liberalization. The SARS
case also demonstrates that political liberalization does not necessarily weaken
the state; instead, many measures of liberalization such as political transparency and responsibility can strengthen it in one way or another.

How did information technology nullify the state's tight control of information flow in the SARS case? To answer this question, it is worth noting some
important characteristics of China's political system, including political priority, political correctness, non-transparency, and political fragmentation. All
these factors prevented China's political system from responding to the SARS
quickly and effectively, and information technology came in to remedy some
serious shortcomings of the system.

In China, whether a matter is considered political or not is usually decided
at the very top with almost no input from below. Not everything is regarded as
political, and not every issue is resolved politically. In democratic countries,
whether a given event is political or not is usually decided by a confluence of
factors such as public opinion, public pressure, and politicians' perceptions.
This is because the public is an essential part of politics via political participation. When a given social event happens, the public can immediately contribute its part to politics. In China, the boundary of politics has to be perceived
and defined by top leaders, collectively or individually. Of course, the public
can express their views by engaging in popular demonstrations or protests, but
it is very risky to do so. Furthermore, only after a social event enters the boundary of politics and becomes political will top leaders begin to pay attention to
it. A non-political issue, even if it is serious, can be dealt with by local governments or central bureaucracies, and top leaders are unlikely to be involved in
the first place. This is what happened to the Falun Gong. Initially, the FLG
was regarded as a non-political issue. Before its siege of Zhongnanhai, the FLG
had been active for many years, and in some locations there were small-scale
conflicts with public security forces. But even public security agencies did not
think it was serious, and they did not report all these events to the top leadership. In 1997, FLG followers protested against the Beijing city government in
front of the Beijing TV station building. It was a well-known case, but no top
leader paid serious attention to the FLG. Only when the FLG succeeded in
grabbing the headlines of the international news media by "laying siege" to the
communist leadership compound in 1999 did the top leadership formally define the FLG as a serious political issue. In the next few years, the regime mobilized every possible national resource to consistently crack down on the FLG.

156   This is also true in the case of the SARS. The first two SARS cases were found in Guangdong in November 2002 and were defined as "unidentifiable" pneumonia. Although the early spread of the SARS did cause local public panic, neither Guangdong nor Beijing officials perceived the matter as serious. In February and early March, when the SARS spread to different parts of Guangdong and Hong Kong, it was still regarded as a medical issue, *not* a political one. Needless to say, a medical issue should be handled by local governments and at most by relevant central bureaucracies such as the Ministry of Health. At that time, those who were affected began to die, but the SARS had not entered China's political domain. Only when the SARS went beyond China's territorial boundary and reached Taiwan, Singapore, Canada, and other parts of the world and generated mounting international pressure did the top leadership begin to regard the SARS as a political issue and thus mobilize national resources to combat the disease.

A second characteristic of China's political system is the practice of political correctness. A usually dominant political practice is that good things can be exaggerated but bad things are not supposed to be publicized. The SARS spread because it was not accorded sufficient attention in the first place. Several local newspapers in Guangdong did report SARS cases, but all the reports were suppressed and journalists were criticized and even fired. Among many factors, the most important was that from October 2002 to March 2003 was the highest season of China's politics. In October 2002, the CCP held its Sixteenth National Congress, the most important event every five years. The Sixteenth Party Congress handled the leadership succession from the third generation to the fourth generation. Then in March 2003, China held the Tenth NPC, during which a new government was formed.

Neither party leaders nor government officials are democratically elected. In order to justify the legitimacy of new leaders, a good "environment" has to be created. Prior to the party congress, the party propaganda machine drummed up political support to usher in a new set of leaders in a solemn environment. After the party congress, another campaign followed to promote the party's new policies. This was also true before and after the Tenth NPC in March 2003. All official newspapers devoted much attention to the new leaders and their policies. Indeed, during the Tenth NPC, one candidate from Guangdong formally raised the issue of the SARS, but no top leader paid serious attention to it. Of course, no newspaper was allowed to report the SARS during such a period of time. Actually, if the SARS had been widely reported, popular awareness would have been created and preventive measures taken. It was unfortunate that the SARS came to China during a season of high politics.

A third characteristic of China's political system is its non-transparency.

China's system is not representative, and leaders are not chosen by Chinese   157
people. There are no effective mechanisms for people to take part in the political process. Because of the lack of mechanisms between the regime and the
people, the process of decision making and policy implementation occurs in
a lockbox. It is difficult for those on the outside to find out what is happening
inside the regime. In the case of the SARS, when the regime was accused of
withholding SARS information from the public and the international community, the world was told that the Chinese government had already begun
to take measures against the spread of the SARS. For the regime, news about
the tenacious spread of the SARS was detrimental to social stability. As mentioned above, when the SARS spread to different parts of Guangdong, there
was some panic. The government seemed to believe that if the SARS could be
controlled silently, then social stability would not be disturbed. Furthermore,
in order to ensure social stability, which is vital for economic development,
releasing half-truths to or withholding information from the public can also
be justified. With non-transparency, the regime does not need to be sensitive
to outside pressure (neither domestic nor international) unless the matter becomes a political issue.

A fourth characteristic of China's political system is political fragmentation and thus a lack of policy coordination. There are tensions between the
center and the provinces. In the case of the SARS, there were conflicting interests between Guangdong provincial officials and top leaders, and between
the Gaungdong provincial government and the Ministry of Health (MOH)
in Beijing. Why did the Guangdong provincial government suppress reports
on the SARS? Guangdong did not have any incentive to publicize the SARS
outbreak partly because of its economic rationale and partly because of its
political rationale. As the largest trading province in China, Guangdong is
highly dependent on foreign investments and tourism (from Hong Kong and
Macao). Provincial officials were afraid that the publicity of the SARS would
cause chaos and social instability and thus affect foreign investments and local
economic performance. Politically, from late 2002 to early 2003, Guangdong
was also experiencing a local power succession. Guangdong party secretary
Li Changchun was appointed a member of the Standing Committee of the
Political Bureau in Beijing. That meant that Li would leave Guangdong soon
to take up this appointment. Within a month or so, Zhang Dejiang, who
was previously party secretary of Zhejiang, was appointed to take over Li's
position. When Zhang Dejiang came to Guangdong, the SARS had already
spread. Guangdong local officials did not want the SARS to "welcome" the
new party secretary. Needless to say, Zhang also did not want the SARS to
bring chaos to Guangdong, the new territory under his charge. Thus, local
reports about the SARS were suppressed. Neither the central government nor

158   the public in Guangdong was able to get enough information on this new virus.

Tensions between the MOH and Guangdong were also obvious. The two units were of the same administrative rank, and there was a lack of coordination between them. While the Guangdong Bureau of Health was obliged to report to the MOH, no issue would be given priority as long as the MOH did not accord due attention to it. In the case of the SARS, it was rational for the MOH to want to bring the issue under control. If an issue cannot be solved within the MOH, the ministry can ask higher-level government units to intervene, meaning that the issue would go beyond the boundary of a medical problem and become political in nature. Nevertheless, the MOH from the very beginning regarded the SARS as a medical issue. Even when the international community began to criticize China, the MOH viewed all kinds of critiques as politicizing a medical issue. No doubt, as long as the SARS was regarded as a medical issue, top leaders were unlikely to get involved. Both the MOH and the Guangdong provincial government can report directly to the Political Bureau or the State Council, especially given the fact that Zhang Dejiang is a member of the Political Bureau. Information is not available regarding whether the MOH and the Guangdong provincial government reported the SARS situation to the top leadership, but it can reasonably be assumed that even if they did, they did not provide enough information for the top leadership to realize the political significance of the SARS outbreak.

There was also bureaucratic fragmentation. Self-interested bureaucratic behavior played a role in China's delayed reaction to controlling the spread of the SARS. In this case, fragmentation happened between the party's Department of Propaganda (DOP) and the MOH not only because their interests conflicted but also because they belonged to different lines of political authority, such as the CCP and the State Council, respectively. The DOP is the party's mouthpiece in charge of justifying the party's rule. Understandably, the interest of the DOP is not to report news that could bring a negative impact to the party. In this regard, there is no difference between the Guangdong provincial DOP and the central DOP in Beijing. The DOP seriously constrained the flow of information and disabled both relevant government departments and the public from obtaining enough information on the SARS. Apparently, like the MOH, the DOP should share the responsibility for the spread of the SARS.

More seriously, there was a conflict between the civilian government and the military sector. This conflict is worse than the lack of coordination between the MOH and the DOP. The military is virtually an independent kingdom in Chinese politics, and the civilian government always has difficulty in bringing

TABLE 6.1

Popular concerns about the SARS in five Chinese cities on May 24, 2003 (percentage)

	Beijing	Shanghai	Guangzhou	Chongqing	Nanjing	Total
Very much concerned	49.3	43.8	33.2	37.4	40.6	40.8
Concerned	42.4	46.3	47.1	53.6	46.4	47.2
Do not care	6.8	6.9	14.4	5.7	8.7	8.5
Less concerned	1.5	2.5	4.8	2.4	3.9	3.0
No concern	0.0	0.5	0.5	0.9	0.5	0.5
Sample number	205	203	208	211	207	1,034

SOURCE: Adapted from Zhou Xiaohong, "SARS *liuxing qijian de shehui chuanyan yu gongzhong yulun diaocha*" ("An Investigation of Social Rumors and Public Opinions during the SARS"), in Ru Xing, Lu Xueyi, and Li Peilin, eds., *Shehui lanpishu: Zhongguo shehui xingshi fenxi yu yuce, 2004 (Social Bluebook: An Analysis and Forecast of Social Situation in China, 2004)*, (Beijing: Shehui kexue wenxian chubanshe, 2004), p. 252.

the military under its control. In Beijing, many SARS cases developed in military hospitals, and the Beijing government was actually not supposed to know what was going on within them. Of course, military hospitals did not have an obligation to inform the civilian government about the SARS. So, when Beijing city officials claimed that the reported SARS cases included those in military hospitals, the world knew that this was not completely true.

All these factors led to the rapid spread of the SARS from Guangdong to other Chinese provinces and to different parts of the world. What broke China's information control was information technologies. When all newspaper reports on the SARS were suppressed in Guangdong, information on the SARS did not stop circulating among people, regions, and even countries via emails, short message service (SMS) transmissions, and other Internet-based communications. A few people who circulated such information were punished by Chinese authorities, but more people joined.

As shown in Table 6.1, the overwhelming majority of people were very much concerned about the spread of the SARS. This mysterious virus could kill them and their family members at any time. Despite tight information control by the regime, an essential portion of the population was aware of this deadly virus. Information technology played an important role in spreading the news about the SARS. Take Guangdong as an example. There were 40 million SMS transmissions recorded on April 8, 2003; 41 million on April 9 and 45 million on April 10.[35] Table 6.2 shows that, on average, about 41 percent of urban Chinese were aware of the SARS even before such information became available from official news media. Apparently, people in coastal areas such as Guangzhou were more conscious of the SARS than those in inland cities such as Chongqing. The rapid spread of the SARS in coastal cities made people pay attention to any information available.

The unavailability or lack of information on the SARS from official news

TABLE 6.2

"Were you aware of the SARS before such news became available in official news media?" (percentage)

	Beijing	Shanghai	Guangzhou	Chongqing	Nanjing	Total
Yes	39.5	37.9	58.2	29.4	39.6	40.9
No	59.0	60.6	39.4	70.1	58.0	57.5
Don't remember	1.0	1.5	2.3	5.0	2.4	1.5
Sample number	205	203	208	211	207	1,034

SOURCE: Adapted from Zhou, "SARS *liuxing qijian*," p. 254.

media forced residents to turn to other sources such as the Internet, SMS, and rumors. Needless to say, much of the news from such unofficial channels was frequently exaggerated. The widespread rumors actually led to several waves of panic among urban residents in cities like Guangzhou, Beijing, and Nanjing. People rushed to stores to buy and stock up on daily necessities. Public panic generated enormous pressure on local government officials and pushed them to tighten information control in order to avoid more panics. Thus, a vicious circle developed in the interaction between the government and urban citizens. What broke this vicious circle was a brave act by Jiang Yanyong, a retired military doctor in Beijing. On April 4, after he saw on TV that China's Minister of Health had lied to the world one day ago, he wrote an open letter to the CCP leadership about the seriousness of the SARS situation. Jiang first emailed a TV station in China and a pro-China TV station in Hong Kong but got no feedback from either station. Later, he mailed the letter to the *New York Times*, which published Jiang's letter immediately. Thus the whole world was informed of the actual situation of the SARS in China, and what happened in military hospitals came to be known.[36]

Once publicized, the Chinese leadership suddenly faced mounting pressure from both within and outside China. The new leadership began to take decisive measures to control the damage and to cope with the situation. Both Minister Zhang Wenkang and Beijing Mayor Meng Xuenong, who were regarded as responsible for not telling the truth about the SARS, were removed at the same time. At the top, the Political Bureau (party) and the State Council (government) held special meetings on the SARS, and all kinds of issues related to it were discussed. Consensus was reached among top leaders. A special task force was established, led by Premier Wen Jiabao. Madame Wu Yi, a member of the Political Bureau and deputy premier, was appointed as health minister.

With the removal of Zhang Wenkang and Meng Xuenong, a system of political accountability was implicitly coming into being. Relevant cadres and officials had to be responsible for containing the SARS, and those who failed to do so would be removed. In a short period of time, hundreds of government officials at different levels of government were punished for their misbehavior or irresponsibility.

To effectively contain the SARS, the government also revised the law on infectious diseases. Because the SARS was a new kind of infectious disease, it was not governed by the existing law. Early on, when the SARS was discovered in Guangdong, it was treated as a local medical issue. Indeed, government officials often justified the delayed response to the SARS by pointing out the fact that it was not listed in the law and national regulations, meaning therefore that it should be dealt with by local governments, not the central government. With the spread of the SARS, the central government immediately revised the law on infectious diseases to include the SARS. More importantly, the law legalizes punishment of those who fail to take effective measures to curb the spread of such infectious diseases. And those who intentionally spread the virus can even get the death penalty, a draconian measure.

It is also worth noting that the Chinese leadership changed its attitude toward the international community. The outbreak and spread of the SARS created enormous pressure for the Chinese government by both the domestic public and the international community. The regime was forced to show a degree of transparency. Initially, the regime was not happy with the World Health Organization (WHO), which accused the Chinese government of hiding information. All kinds of criticisms from the international community were regarded as politicizing the SARS outbreak, an ill-intentioned anti-China move. Nevertheless, with increasing international pressure and the rapid spread of the SARS, the Chinese government made a dramatic change. Under the leadership of Madame Wu Yi, the Chinese side began to work closely with WHO professionals to report the daily SARS situation in China to the world. The leadership was also willing to accept any useful advice to fight the SARS. When Madame Wu Yi attended the WHO conference in May 2003, she openly told the audience that in the initial stages, China mishandled the SARS due to certain complications.[37] When Premier Wen Jiabao was invited to attend an Association of Southeast Asian Nations conference on the SARS in Thailand, he was honest enough to recognize the shortcomings of the Chinese system in dealing with the SARS. Wen also called for multinational cooperation to combat this new virus.[38] Subsequently, State President Hu Jintao attended the G8 conference in France. Hu was questioned by many leaders on China's handling of the SARS and was asked to be forthcoming in this regard. Hu did not have any intention to hide the truth. Like Wu Yi and Wen Jiabao, he recognized the mishandling initially and promised to make greater efforts to contain the virus.[39]

162   The much greater transparency displayed by the Chinese government was a breath of fresh air after months of avoiding addressing the subject head-on. The international community reacted by making positive comments about China's efforts in combating the SARS.[40]

It is particularly worth noting a separate but related development. On May 2, 2003, the Chinese media suddenly reported that a Chinese Ming-class submarine had sunk in the East China Sea, causing the deaths of seventy men. This was extremely unusual in China. China had never before released such news promptly. Given the fact that the submarine's sinking was a military incident, the immediate release of the news was of some significance for the new leadership. Regardless of the real motivation behind the decision, such a move could become an example for Chinese leaders to follow in the future. Needless to say, without having been through the SARS situation, it would have been extremely difficult for the leadership to make such a move.[41]

How did the SARS affect China's politics? Despite its initial mishandling of the SARS, the Chinese leadership was actually able to win back people's confidence due to its concerted efforts in battling the virus. As shown in Table 6.3, most people believed that the central government had performed well in coping with the SARS. Different cities had a similar approval rate. Similarly, Table 6.4 shows that most urban residents had increased confidence in the central government or the Hu Jintao–Wen Jiabao leadership after the SARS event and that only a very small portion of urban residents stated that their confidence was negatively affected.

The SARS event has also generated other positive results. First, the new leadership began to focus on social and political transparency. As explained earlier, China's political system is generally regarded as one that lacks transparency. The SARS outbreak revealed the enormous negative impact of this system on the state's governing capability. It is understandable that the new leadership needs a greater degree of social and political transparency. Second, the leadership has also shown a willingness to establish a limited system of political accountability. Some efforts in this direction were already made in

TABLE 6.3

"What do you think of the performance of the central government in battling the SARS?" (percentage)

	Beijing	Shanghai	Guangzhou	Chongqing	Nanjing	Total
Excellent	53.1	59.7	48.5	64.7	53.6	55.8
Good	28.2	19.4	28.3	22.9	26.8	25.2
Not good	4.3	5.7	5.1	3.5	8.0	5.4
Do not know	14.4	15.2	18.2	9.0	11.6	13.6

SOURCE: Adapted from Zhou, "*SARS liuxing qijian de,*" p. 259.

TABLE 6.4 163

"Has your confidence toward the government increased or decreased after the SARS event?" (percentage)

	Beijing	Shanghai	Guangzhou	Chongqing	Nanjing	Total
Increased	45.5	57.3	32.3	55.7	50.0	48.4
No change	42.6	34.6	56.1	32.3	40.0	41.0
Decreased	1.4	0.9	2.0	2.0	2.8	1.9
Do not know	10.5	7.1	9.6	10.0	7.2	8.8

SOURCE: Adapted from Zhou, "SARS liuxing qijian de," p. 259.

dealing with the SARS. The removal of Zhang Wenkang, Meng Xuenong, and other lower-level government officials are signs that the leadership is keen to institute such a system. In June 2003, the Central Military Commission (CMC) also fired Navy Commander Shi Yunsheng and Political Commissar Yang Huaiqing, apparently for their responsibility in the Ming-class submarine tragedy.[42]

Third, since the SARS outbreak, the leadership has shown its willingness to allow social groups to play a more important role in providing input in the decision making process. The SARS outbreak demonstrated that without cooperation from social groups, the government will have greater difficulty in managing a crisis. Under central direction, grassroots communities played an important role in containing the SARS, especially in places like Shanghai. Even rural peasants banded together on their own to combat the SARS. While at times these grassroots groups might not necessarily see eye to eye with the government, the government does realize the role that such social organizations played in containing the SARS. On its own, the government would not have the means to cater to the specific needs of individuals or even small communities. Hence, there is value in adopting a decentralized approach to cope with emergencies at the people level.

Fourth, the the SARS event has created greater momentum for the leadership to improve the rural health care system. The most difficult aspect of dealing with the SARS was probably determining how to prevent it from spreading to rural areas. If the SARS had spread to rural areas, then very little could be done to curb its spread. Rural areas do not have a good health care system. This was a factor behind the leadership's decision to provide free medical treatment for rural peasants if they were infected. Furthermore, having a good rural health care system is also of political significance. Poor peasants have less capacity to resist a natural disaster like the SARS. When their survival is threatened, they are likely to take matters into their own hands and may even rebel. This is especially true in central China, like the Hebei, Hubei, and

164   Henan provinces, where a tradition of peasant rebellion is deep-rooted. It is no coincidence that during the SARS outbreak, the Falun Gong again became very active in Hebei and this made the leadership sit up and take notice. An immediate crackdown was initiated. The SARS outbreak has highlighted once again how rural problems can easily develop into a social stability issue. The SARS outbreak has undoubtedly provided an opportunity for the new leadership to push ahead with reform in the rural health care system.

CONCLUSION

How have all these collective actions led to some positive results? Information technology has presented opportunities for novel forms of collective action. All these cases involve unusual groupings of challengers organizing and using information technology in pursuit of political objectives. These cases demonstrate that information technology has empowered the organizers of collective action. Political entrepreneurs are able to overcome resource barriers by using comparatively inexpensive information technology. Without information technology, challengers would not have been able to organize nationwide collective actions quickly and efficiently. Events such as the FLG siege, the CDP movement, and the series of events that eventually led to the abolition of the C&R system were organized in a short period of time. Without the Internet, such quick collective actions would not have been possible.

Why did some collective actions fail and others succeed? The strategy that challengers choose in their interactions with the regime matters. An event usually involves two contending categories of agents — those who uphold a given order and those who challenge it. Nevertheless, in China's political context, whether a given collective action will succeed is largely dependent on what strategy will be taken because that strategy decides whether that collective action can attract those who observe — that is, a third set of participants. Given the fact that no formal opposition is allowed to exist, every participant to the collective action has to bear some cost. An "exit" option is unlikely to attract more observers due to its higher cost. Also, many people have learned from China's past experience that an exit approach in interacting with the regime is not necessarily productive. The existence of soft-liners (reformist leaders) and hard-liners (conservatives) inside the regime means that an exit option is likely to turn the soft-liners into hard-liners. With a few rare exceptions, political leaders do not like to see the regime they are part of be overthrown by challengers. When the regime is threatened by challengers, the soft-liners and hard-liners are likely to stand on the same side and fight the challengers.

The failure of direct challenges has led Chinese Internet users to turn to another important interaction strategy with the state, that is, "cooperation interaction" in Hardin's term, or the "voice" option in Hirschman's term. Such an interaction strategy was embedded in all the above-mentioned cases of successful challenges. The "voice" is acceptable to both the state and society. On the part of the state, the voice does not aim to undermine or overthrow the state. Instead, through a voice mechanism, the state can receive feedback from social groups to respond to state decline and improve its legitimacy.

On the part of social groups, the voice option is acceptable mainly for two reasons. First, it is a tactic with low risk and cost. As Hirschman pointed out, the voice option is the only way dissatisfied members can react whenever the exit option is unavailable.[43] As discussed earlier, a conflict interaction, or an exit option, is likely to invite a crackdown by the state and thus contains high political risks. Once challengers choose a conflict interaction or are identified as opposition to the state, the confrontation between them and the state becomes inevitable. Frequently, protesters are arrested, detained, and punished.

Second, the voice option can effectively introduce changes into political and policy practices on the part of the state and thus lead to incremental political changes. It seems that all the aforementioned cases posed serious challenges to the state. But a challenge does not necessarily amount to a threat. These cases exposed all kinds of malpractice and mismanagement in China's political system. They thus provided the reformist leadership with the opportunities to correct the system. For instance, measures taken in dealing with the SARS epidemic greatly promoted China's political transparency and political accountability on the part of the state. The death of Sun Zhigang pushed the government to abolish an old regulation that had led to serious human rights violations. The Sun Dawu case helped the government correct its old practice of discriminating against private entrepreneurs. It is in this sense that the Internet has enabled its users to participate in politics and have a say in what the government does, as discussed in the last chapter.

More importantly, the voice option is likely to lead to a tacit cooperation between the soft-liners (reformist leaders) and the challengers and thus is attractive to more observers. This is so partly because the voice option, a non-confrontational approach, reduces the risk that the participants have to bear in their interplay with the state and partly because it is more productive. As shown in the cases of Sun Zhigang and the SARS outbreak, when an event is not aimed at confronting the regime, reformist leaders can make use of such events to initiate reforms to existing policies and practices and thus result in incremental political changes.

7

INFORMATION TECHNOLOGY, TRANSFORMATION OF STATE-SOCIETY RELATIONS, AND POLITICAL CHANGES

INFORMATION TECHNOLOGY AND POLITICAL CHANGES

This book has so far examined the impact of the Internet on Chinese politics from three perspectives. The first was the impact of the Internet on the state. I have examined why the Internet has been an integral part of nation-state building on the part of the state and how the Internet has empowered the state in developing a national economy and improving its governance. The second was the impact of the Internet on society. The Internet has empowered society by providing new sources of information and channels for civic engagement. And the third was the impact of the Internet on state-society relations. The Internet opens up a new arena where both the state and society can empower themselves. It has enabled the state to deliver economic goods and services to the people more efficiently, and it has also enabled society to "voice" its interests and to facilitate policy changes on the part of the state. In this sense, the state and society can be mutually empowering over the Internet-mediated sphere. Furthermore, the Internet is also an arena in which the state and society compete for power and thus can confront each other. In competing for power, sometimes the state wins and sometimes social forces win. With the unlimited potential of information technology, the interaction between the state and society in the Internet-mediated sphere tends to become increasingly complicated. While the state and society are competing for power, they are also mutually transforming.

So, an ultimate question is this: Will information technology be able to promote political changes in China? In this concluding chapter, I shall sum-

marize the major findings and arguments of this study and provide an overall   167
analysis on the role of information technology in facilitating political changes
in China.

"Political change" is a broad term and means many things in the political realm. In previous chapters, I have made a distinction between political
liberalization and democratization and have argued that despite the still tight
political control, the Internet has promoted political liberalization in terms of
an increase in political transparency and accountability. Although these progresses have not yet enabled China to develop a democratic system, such developments can become part of the process of democratization in the long run.
All such developments might trigger a substantial political change, namely, a
transformation from authoritarianism to democracy. So, while previous chapters have focused on how the Internet facilitates political liberalization, this
final chapter shall narrow the question down: Will information technology be
able to promote the development of a democratic regime in China?

In this chapter, I will first answer the two relevant questions: What are regime changes — the core of political changes? What does political reform mean
for China's political leaders? These two questions are important. While regime
changes in general mean a transition from authoritarianism to democracy, the
Chinese leadership has struggled to manage the process of such a transition.
What role the Internet can play during this process to a great degree depends
on the perceptions of the Chinese leadership on political reform. Most states
are attempting to regulate the Internet to benefit from this new technology
and reduce its undesirable consequences. The Chinese communist state has
become one of the most sophisticated political organizations of today's world
in regulating the role of the Internet in China, even though it is almost impossible for the Chinese state to "eliminate" all undesirable political consequences resulting from the development of the Internet. The constraints that
the state places on the Internet have to be part of the exploration of dynamics
of political changes in China. I then identify three major scenarios of regime
changes and explore what role the Internet is playing and will play in each
of these scenarios. By doing so, I attempt to avoid technology-determinism
in explaining political changes associated with the Internet. I argue that the
Internet is a facilitating factor in leading political changes in China. To what
degree the Internet can promote political changes depends on the interaction
between the state and social forces in the opportunity structure that socioeconomic development provides. By analyzing the Internet in its relations with
other socioeconomic and political factors, one can reach a realistic assessment
of the role of the Internet in facilitating political changes in China.

REGIME CHANGE

Regime change is part of general political changes. There are Internet-facilitated political changes, as discussed throughout this book. But to many, the key question is, Will the Internet lead to regime change in China? To answer this question, one has to define what regime changes are. In the literature of political science, regime changes are often understood as transitions from authoritarian regimes toward an uncertain "something else." According to Guillermo O'Donnell and Philippe C. Schmitter, that "something else" can be the instauration of a political democracy or the restoration of a new, and possibly more severe, form of authoritarian rule.[1] In the case of China, most scholars would agree that a meaningful regime change will have to involve a transition from the existing communist authoritarian regime to one with some degree of political democracy. It is less meaningful to discuss regime changes in terms of restoring a new and more severe form of authoritarian rule. Over thousands of years, China experienced endless cycles of dynastic changes until the 1911 modern republic revolution. One dynastic regime was replaced by another with the same autocratic nature. Today, it is widely accepted that any meaningful regime change must involve some form of democratic transition. Will regime change mean that the current regime goes back to the Maoist era? It is quite unlikely, and it is also undesirable.

Then there is a question about democracy. While it is easy to define what democracy is by looking at the functioning of modern democratic systems,[2] one will find it rather difficult to identify what political changes can lead to democratization while other political changes cannot. Some forms of political changes might lead to meaningful regime transition, but others might not. This is the rationale behind the efforts of O'Donnell and Schmitter in distinguishing political liberalization and political democratization. Political liberalization might or might not lead to political democratization. As discussed in the previous chapters, information technology in China has enabled social groups to engage in collective actions that have promoted political liberalization in terms of an increase in political transparency and accountability on the part of the regime. While such collective actions have not been able to trigger political democratization, it is reasonable to argue that political liberalization is also an integral part of political changes toward democracy.

ELITE PERCEPTIONS ON POLITICAL CHANGE

In exploring the role of the Internet in facilitating political changes in general, and regime changes in particular, an equally significant question is, How do

Chinese political leaders perceive democracy? Elite perceptions of democra- 169 tization constrain the role of the Internet in mediating the relations between the state and society and thus democratization. I have demonstrated in my case studies that the leadership is the key factor behind the success or failure of Internet-mediated collective actions. If the leadership perceives a given collective action as favorable for the "right" policy changes, it is likely to be cooperative and even supportive of that collective action. On the other hand, if the leadership perceives a given collective action as undermining and threatening to the regime, it is likely to tighten control and even initiate a crackdown on that collective action. Whether the leadership perceives a given collective action as "right" or "wrong" depends on its perceptions of political changes and democracy. So, it is important to examine the perception of the leadership on political changes when one explores how information technology will affect political development in the future.

As a matter of fact, "political change" means different things to different persons. To the scholarly community, "political change" often refers to a political process toward Western-style democracies based on popular political participation, which usually refers to an open universal election. In this notion, political change in an authoritarian state like China implies the weakening of party control while empowering society. Nevertheless, this is not the case in the perceptions of Chinese ruling elites. Political changes, especially changes resulting from political reform, are not to decrease but to strengthen the power of the regime. During the processes of political changes, society might be empowered, but the power of the state over society should not be weakened.

Throughout reform years, Chinese political leaders from Deng Xiaoping and Jiang Zemin to Hu Jintao have strongly opposed developing any Western style of democracy in China. They do not believe that the Western style of democracy is suitable for China, either because they have learned from China's modern history and the recent history of the former Soviet Union that it will lead the country nowhere but instead bring chaos to, or even break up, the country or because they fear that the Communist party will lose its dominant position once radical democratization takes place.

However, top leaders have also argued that they have continuously taken the need for political reform into account.[3] Chinese political elites are reluctant to follow any models of democratization taking place either in the former Soviet Union and Eastern European communist states or in China's neighbors such as South Korea and Taiwan. The leadership wants to define political reforms on its own terms. To them, political changes must be managed and their undesirable consequences must be minimized. In this context, political reform has been characterized by incrementalism—progress by trial

170   and error — and does not mean that the political process will suddenly open to the general public. Rather, it refers to a managed process of institutional building.[4]

Because political reforms are aimed at strengthening the regime, the leadership has made every effort to lead and direct the country's development. Socioeconomic changes, however, often resulted in unintended consequences. The world has witnessed the constant rise of social demands for more radical political reform and the increased challenges to the authority of the ruling party. More often than not, the leadership has had to use coercive measures to cope with spontaneous social forces when the existing institutions were no longer able to accommodate them. But the frequent use of coercion does not necessarily mean that the leadership has declined to adjust its political institutions. Rather, it means that the leadership does not want social forces to lead the process of China's political development. Political incrementalism enables the Chinese leadership to continuously adjust its institutional framework to guarantee economic reforms on one hand and accommodate drastic changes resulting from socioeconomic development on the other.

It is in this context that the Chinese state has managed the development of the Internet and its consequences. The state has attempted to minimize any forms of undesirable impact that the Internet can bring on the regime. Like any other technology, information technology alone cannot decide the course of a country's political development. More important are political and social forces that apply the Internet in their daily struggle for political changes in China. Information technology functions in the context of the interaction between the state and social forces. So, while scholars like Benedict Anderson and Sidney Tarrow saw the important role of print media in the rise of social movements, they looked at how print helped the spread of nationalistic ideas or the formation of social movement networks and associations.[5] Social movements were more often than not the consequences of state building or national building. An ignorance of other important factors resulting from state building or national building, such as social grievances and national sentiments, will make one's arguments technologically deterministic. This argument can also be applied to the case of the Internet in China. The state is the most important political force in China, but it is not the only one. Rapid economic changes have given way to new social forces while weakening the power of the traditional social classes such as workers and peasants. Similarly, the state is not the only user of the Internet. While the state has attempted to manage the development of the Internet for its own purpose, other social forces have also used the Internet in their struggle for their own interests. The role of the Internet unfolds in the interaction between the state and social forces.

THREE SCENARIOS OF REGIME CHANGE

Because it is the interaction between the state and social forces or the interaction between different Internet users, not the Internet per se, that will bring about regime changes, one needs to identify how different social forces will interact with the state and in what opportunity structure. Empirically speaking, in today's world, three scenarios of regime change can be identified, scenarios in which the Internet and other information technology can play a part. First, the force of regime change could be external. In its crudest form, the regime could be removed by external forces and a new regime then imposed. Historically, colonialism and imperialism by Western powers created enormous "alien" regimes in the non-Western world before the onset of World War II. In the post–World War II era, the United States single-handedly built up a democratic regime in Japan. A similar development has been taking place in Iraq since the 9/11 terrorist attack on the United States. While such a scenario is unlikely to happen in China today, this does not mean that external forces are no longer important in influencing China's domestic political changes. Information technology can certainly facilitate this process because it can empower external forces to influence political changes in China, as it does domestic social forces.

Second, regime change can take place from below, that is, with a regime being overthrown by popular uprisings or revolutions. This was the case in the Philippines in the 1980s when people's power overthrew the Marcos dictatorship. More recently, in the late 1990s, it happened in Indonesia, where popular uprisings overthrew the Suharto presidency. Information technology can play an important role in this scenario. Indeed, as already mentioned, the Internet was believed to play an important role in overthrowing the Suharto regime.

Third, regime change can take place as a result of political reforms and liberalization initiated by the leadership as had happened in South Korea and Taiwan. In the following section, I shall discuss the possible role and limitations of information technology in each of these scenarios.

INFORMATION TECHNOLOGY AND EXTERNAL FORCES
OF REGIME CHANGE

Regime change by external forces is not an alien concept to the Chinese. In China's long history, the regimes in power were frequently removed by "barbarians" from the north, and China was frequently ruled by various "foreign" regimes. Wang Gungwu found that "in the last thousand years, the Chinese can only claim to have ruled their own country for 280 of those years."[6] National unity was a norm, but disunity often took place. While disunity often led to foreign aggression, foreign aggression could lead to China's disunity. In many periods of its history, China was unified only through "alien" forces. The Mongol and Manchu conquests are two examples.

Will foreign powers affect China's regime change as they did before? This is extremely unlikely in China today. China today is unified under one-party rule. It also has a relatively strong military force in the world. As long as the party and the army are united, foreign powers can hardly make a regime change in China. From Kuomintang (KMT) leaders such as Chiang Kai-shek to communist leaders such as Mao Zedong and Deng Xiaoping, Chinese ruling elites have undertaken every possible measure to prevent *neiluan* and *waihuan* (internal chaos and foreign aggression) from occurring. For them, the two are interconnected: a divided nation invites foreign aggression, and foreign aggression makes the nation divided. The deep fear of internal chaos and foreign aggression has been one of the fundamental reasons that Chinese political elites do not want to democratize the regime. More often than not, they regard democratization as a path down the slippery slope to a divided China. So, it is not uncommon for the leadership to crack down on pro-democracy movements in the name of national unity.

More importantly, an "alien" regime is impossible also because a modern form of nationalism has been firmly established among Chinese elites and ordinary people. The modern notions of nationalism did not exist in traditional China. The high culture and ideology in pre-modern China were principally forms of cultural consciousness. Confucianism was believed to represent a universal ethic distinguishing a "civilized" way of life accessible to any population through education, virtue, and good government. Accordingly, the traditional Chinese state was radically different from nation-states in the West. While modern nationalism entails an awareness of the nation-state as the ultimate goal of the community, Confucianism-based culturalism implies an identification with the moral goals and values of a universal civilization. In this sense, Lucian Pye argued that China is a civilization pretending to be a nation-state.[7] To a degree, Confucianism-educated Chinese elites were not so hostile to "alien rule" as long as the alien ruler could accept Confucianism as a way of governing China.

With the spread of modern nationalism, China has been transformed from a culturally defined entity to a politically defined one. A modern national identity came to Chinese intellectuals around the turn of the twentieth century. The May Fourth Movement helped cultivate a new Chinese consciousness while trying hard to destroy traditional Confucianism.[8] There were abor-

tive attempts by the KMT ruling class to revive Confucianism in the 1930s.[9]   173
The Japanese invasion of the 1930s helped Chinese communists mobilize
millions of peasants into the mainstream of modern nationalism.[10] Even Mao
Zedong recognized that without foreign aggression, modern Chinese nationalism could have hardly formed.

After thirty years of isolated national building under Mao Zedong, contemporary Chinese ruling elites have tirelessly pursued the goals of global-
izing China and integrating the country into the world community, and they
regard globalization and integration as the only way to build China into a
strong and modern nation-state. Nevertheless, Chinese ruling elites as well as
intellectuals have never forgotten to make greater efforts to nurture a new
nationalism—a new national identity—in accordance with the changing external and internal environment.[11] Hence, going too far ahead to bring the
country closer to international norms of behavior without being sensitive to
domestic sentiments could prove politically costly. For instance, when Zhu
Rongji tried to strike a deal with the Clinton administration in 1999 on China's
World Trade Organization entry, Zhu was blamed with betraying China's national interests. Consequently, any political leader that intends to use external
forces to drive domestic reform will have to strike a balance between globalism
and nationalism.

Such an environment decides how the Internet can empower external
forces to facilitate political changes in China. It is apparent that the Internet
or other information technology will not be able to empower external forces
to "overthrow" the regime. Indeed, the role of the Internet in facilitating political changes in this case is greatly constrained by not only the state but also
other nationalistic social forces. Michael Chase and James Mulvenon have
examined in detail overseas-based dissent Web sites such as those of the China
Democracy Party, the Falun Gong, Tibet in Exile, and the East Turkestan
Independence Movement.[12] These dissent groups are undoubtedly active outside China, but Chase and Mulvenon have shown that their influence inside
China is extremely limited. Quite effective counterstrategies on the part of the
Chinese state are an important factor in constraining the spread of dissident
influence inside China. But equally important is the rise of new Chinese nationalism.[13] It is a new national identity and a new national consciousness that
help the public resist foreign influence voluntarily. To a great degree, such
voluntary resistance is more effective than any measures imposed by the state.
More importantly, the Internet has been used by both the Chinese state and
the public to promote the new nationalism. The Internet has enabled the state
to extend its propaganda to an overseas audience. Now, people outside China
can easily access official Chinese Web sites and are thus subject to the state's

174   version of the world view. Moreover, the Internet has become an effective tool for Chinese nationalistic intellectuals and educated people to express their nationalistic voice.[14]

A simple conclusion can be drawn here: no foreign dissident groups or other external political forces can use information technology to make a regime change inside China. This, of course, does not mean that external factors will not have a major impact on China's political change in general. External factors work in a rather different way in driving China's political change. China is now an integral part of the world system. Globalization has created a new external structure and opportunities for political changes in China. The communist state has to continuously adjust itself to accommodate international norms. Despite all kinds of resistance, the Chinese state has been gradually socialized by international norms in its frequent interaction with the international community. Information technology, especially the Internet, plays an increasingly important role in this process. On the other hand, the state can now mobilize every possible means to bring Internet-facilitated foreign influences under control. This is certainly true in our cases of the China Democracy Party and the Falun Gong. Once dissident forces are exiled, the state can easily constrain the spread of their influence into China. The rising new nationalism makes the tight control on the part of the state acceptable to the public, but more important, it reinforces these control measures.

INFORMATION TECHNOLOGY AND A REVOLUTION FROM BELOW

Political or regime changes can result from a revolution from below. In China's long history, the replacement of one regime by another was often due to the rise of forces outside the regime. In other words, most regimes were not able to escape the fate of being overthrown by social forces. One classic case is the eventual success of the Chinese Communist Party in overthrowing the KMT regime after a long and arduous struggle. Information technology could play a part in a revolution from below.

While the communist regime is still coercive, there has been no lack of social movements since the reform and open door policy began in the late 1970s. The 1978 Democracy Wall movement in Beijing, the 1989 nationwide pro-democracy movement, the 1998 China Democracy Party (CDP) movement, and the 1999 Falun Gong (FLG) movement are well known to the world. As discussed in the previous chapters, the Internet played an important role in initiating and sustaining the CDP Movement and the FLG Movement. With the deepening of the reform and open door policy, China seems to have begun a stage of social resistance and popular rebellion, if not revolution. Recent

years have witnessed the rise of a new wave of collective actions by aggrieved   175
workers against the state. According to *The Outlook Weekly*, a Communist
party mouthpiece, China experienced more than 58,000 major incidents of
social unrest in 2003—up 15 percent from a year earlier—with more than
three million people taking part in the protests.[15] By 2004, the figure had
jumped to 74,000.[16]

Several main factors can be identified in explaining the rise of social
movements. First is capitalism-driven industrialization. Industrialization in a
European sense has just begun in China. The state-led industrialization and
a planned economy in the pre-reform era led to the dependency of workers
on the state. State-owned enterprises (SOEs) were not only economic entities;
more importantly, they were political entities, tools and mechanisms for the
party to control its people. The current wave of industrialization is radically
different from previous ones. It is driven by capitalism. While enterprises in
the non-state sector operate in accordance with market principles, the state is
also trying to shift the financial burden from SOEs to market forces. Industrialization has thus generated massive unemployment. China's entry into the
World Trade Organization has worsened the unemployment situation.

In Europe, industrialization created rich classes but also poor classes. Marx
saw the dynamics of historical changes from industrialization because it gave
rise to different social classes. As different classes compete with one another
for economic interests and political power, history progresses. The working
class movement was the dominant force for a long period of time in today's
advanced West. It seems that this process of capitalistic development is also
taking place in China. After the bitter and uncertain thirty years of experimentation of planned economy following the establishment of the People's
Republic in 1949, Chinese leaders have realized that learning from capitalism conforms to historical necessity, and capitalism is a stage that cannot be
skipped on the way to socialism. By the same logic, China is unlikely to escape working class movements. In advanced industrial states, it was the development of the welfare state that tamed working class movements. China's
capitalism resembles the one Marx and Engels described. Despite some good
efforts, the state is still not able to establish an effective social welfare system
and other relevant systems to protect the interests of workers. Workers' protests
have become widespread across the country.[17]

On top of its industrialization woes, the state also faces pressure from peasant movements. While the peasantry in the West was rapidly weakened by
industrialization, this is unlikely to happen in China. Given the fact that the
majority of the population is still made up of peasants, the regime has to
cope with an increasingly disgruntled peasantry. The impact of capitalism

176   on China's peasants is no less than that on workers. Capitalism has already generated a flowing rural population of millions, moving around the country in search of economic opportunities. On one hand, capitalism has forced peasants out of their homes in the countryside, while on the other, they are treated as second-class citizens in the cities where they work. Needless to say, there are enough reasons for them to resist and to rebel against perceived ill treatment and high-handedness of local authorities.[18]

A second main driving force behind social movements is globalization. Globalization can serve both as a source and a tool of social movements. It has linked China with the world economy, and this is beyond the control of the Chinese state. Any fluctuations in the world economy will inevitably have an impact on China. China's economy as a whole is still in the early stages of globalization, but in some parts of the country, especially coastal provinces, local economies are more closely integrated with the world market. In 1997, when most of China was relatively unscathed by the Asian Financial Crisis, the coastal provinces were hit badly. Thousands of township and village enterprises (TVEs) were wiped out by the financial crisis. With China becoming fully integrated into the world economy, external economic changes can easily trigger a domestic social movement.

Globalization is also a tool of social movements. Globalization helps provide a vital link between overseas opposition forces and domestic ones. The Internet serves as an important bridge linking the two forces together. Today, millions of emails flow between these two forces. The state is increasingly losing its grip on information flow. The FLG is an example. As discussed earlier, without modern communication technologies such as mobile phones and emails, FLG followers would not have been able to congregate so quickly and lay siege on Zhongnanhai in 1999. While the FLG has been suppressed within China, its followers all over the world continue to incite activities to show their displeasure with the state. Communication among its followers within and without China is still very much active. The SARS event serves as another good example. When SARS broke out in Guangdong, the government there suppressed all media reports, but this did not prevent people from emailing each other. Again, while the state was able to suppress the SARS news in the official media inside China, it was not able to stop Dr. Jiang Yanyong from telling the world the truth by emailing the foreign press.

Modern information technology has made it difficult for the Chinese communist state to ignore world opinions on domestic developments that generate a global impact. Even if the state is reluctant to respond to domestic forces, it cannot afford to ignore external opinions because China is now an integral part of global capitalism and its economy is increasingly reliant on world mar-

kets and foreign investors. The SARS event again serves as a good example.   177
Before the SARS spread from Guangdong to Hong Kong, Singapore, Canada,
and other foreign countries, it had spread to different parts of China such as
Beijing and Shanxi. But the state did not feel the urgency to respond to domestic pressure. Only after the SARS generated international pressure did the
state decide to react and take action against the SARS.

Despite an increase in incidents of rural and urban unrest, a nationwide revolution from below is quite unlikely in the foreseeable future. First, the state's
coercive forces have become more modernized. The military has become
more professional, and the state has also established a rapid-reaction force. Although these forces are mainly aimed at defending the nation, they also serve
a domestic function. To a great degree, these coercive forces have been used
to maintain domestic order. Due to the increasing urban and rural unrest, the
state has also made greater efforts in building an efficient armed police. In 1989,
the state mobilized the military to crack down on the pro-democracy movement. Today, the armed police are often used to maintain local social order.
In the future, if the state feels threatened by social movements, it may once
again decide to use force to suppress its people. Internal fragmentation does
not prevent the state from using coercive force when social threats emerge as in
the cases of the 1989 pro-democracy movement and the 1999 FLG movement.

Second, China's political structure has its advantages in containing a nationwide revolution. China is a unitary state, but in reality it has a de facto
federal structure.[19] Despite its highly centralized surface, the power structure
is actually decentralized. There is an implicit contract between Beijing and
the provinces (or between a provincial government and a city government
below it) that the latter has to be responsible for maintaining social order. If
chaos arises in a given area, it must be contained within that area. The state
tolerates no cross-border chaos. Although the number of incidents of rural and
urban unrest is increasing, most of them are small in scale and take place locally. Because they are easily isolated and contained by local governments, it
is quite unlikely that they will develop into a nationwide movement.

Third, China lacks effective agents to organize regional or nationwide social
movements. There are many agents for local instances of unrest such as de-
mobilized soldiers, local intellectuals, and other prestigious people, but their
appeal is limited to a locality. Traditionally, the state brooks no opposition to its
authority. As long as no opposition party can be established, these local agents
face insurmountable difficulties to rise regionally, let alone nationally.

Fourth, popular perceptions on regime changes have changed. Many indeed do not expect a rapid regime change as had occurred in Russia, Indonesia, and other places. Taiwan's experience with democratic transition has also

178   had a negative impact on many ordinary people. The state did not lose any chance to highlight the negative effects of democratization in Russia, Indonesia, and Taiwan. Historically, Chinese intellectuals have played an extremely important role in spreading revolutionary (liberal) ideas and in organizing social movements. This is hardly the case today. Since the early 1990s, most national intellectuals have become conservative in their orientation. Even the most radical intellectuals now advocate only gradual political reforms. Because there is no alternative to the CCP, most people are afraid that the country would be in chaos following a rapid regime change.

At the operational level, most rural and urban protesters are also realistic. In most cases, their goal is to satisfy their material interests more than anything else. Once that is done, they are ready to "cooperate" with the state. In recent years, rural unrest incidents have been aimed at reducing peasants' fiscal burdens, and the targets of these peasants are their immediate governments and government officials. For workers, their immediate concerns are unemployment, layoffs, medical care, and other social welfare benefits. As long as their goal is material interests, the state will be able to find a way to contain social movements and limit them within a certain boundary. Workers' protests in northeast provinces in recent years serve as an example. When a demonstration occurs, the state moves quickly to isolate its leaders and organizers but is willing to strike a compromise with the rest of the protesters.

The Internet has come to play an important part in both labor and rural protests. While there is still no study on how the Internet has helped protest organizers mobilize workers and farmers, the Internet has apparently helped frame public discourse on labor and rural problems and provided a virtual channel for political participation.[20] For many years, the "san-nong" issue, urban unemployment, and social security have been hot topics in Internet-mediated public discussions even on China's official Web sites such as *Qiangguo luntan* (Strong-Nation Forum), a Web site sponsored by *People's Daily*, the CCP's mouthpiece. The *san-nong* issue — that is, *nongye* (agriculture), *nongcun* (village), and *nongmin* (farmers) — has been a key concern of the Chinese leadership due to the rural decay resulting from rapid industrialization. Similarly, in urban areas, economic reforms and rapid industrialization have also created mounting problems of unemployment. The lack of a sound social security system has worsened the situation. The leadership has made greater efforts to cope with these rural and urban problems so that social stability can be maintained. The Internet has been an integral part of changing policy discourse on rural and urban issues. Internet-mediated political participation often creates intensive and extensive popular pressure for the state and pushes the latter to adjust its labor and rural policies.[21]

Nevertheless, the probability of the Internet's contributing to a revolution 179 from below is also limited. While the Internet enables protest organizers to engage in nationwide mobilization, it also empowers the state in initiating effective mobilization against its enemies. As discussed, Internet-mediated oppositions are possible, but once they formed, they are likely to be regarded as threats by the state. Once the state forms such a perception, it will use all possible coercive measures against them, as happened in the cases of the FLG and the CDP. Although political entrepreneurs in Chinese society can use the Internet to organize social protests, the state so far has been able to identify these organizers and thus crack down on these movements before they spread nationwide. To a great degree, the Internet has enabled the state to gain information more efficiently about social elements that are likely to lead to social protests and thus adjust its policies or implement measures to prevent such protests from taking place. Under these circumstances, it would be unrealistic to expect that the Internet will help political entrepreneurs to initiate a nationwide protest or revolution against the regime.

POLITICAL LIBERALIZATION AND MUTUAL TRANSFORMATION OF THE STATE AND SOCIETY

A more realistic scenario of regime change in China is a change from gradual political liberalization. In the process of political liberalization, the state and social forces interact with each other and their relations become mutually transformative.

In the multiple Internet-mediated meeting grounds between the state and social forces, some social forces have tied their own fortunes to those of the state or accepted it as the appropriate organization to represent the proper interests for all of society, as in the case of Internet-nationalism. In such cases, interactions between the state and social forces can create more power for both, and their relationship can be mutually empowering. But in many other instances, their interactions vitiate the power of each side, as in the case of the FLG and the CDP. Here, the struggle is one marked not by mutual empowerment but by mutually exclusive goals. So far, the state seems to have won the battle, but this does not mean that social forces are total losers. While the state wins, it also has to change its policy in order to prevent more social challenges from taking place. Such interactions often take place in the aforementioned two scenarios, namely, regime change from external forces and regime change from a revolution from below.

Within the arenas of political liberalization, the Internet-mediated interaction between the state and social forces is mutually transformative. Some of these interactions favor the state, while some favor social forces. Such interactions can produce a range of outcomes, depending on the opportunity structure that the political and socioeconomic environments provide. First, the state is able to impose its own version of political changes onto social forces. In this case, the state successfully changes how social forces identify themselves. Social forces are willing to accept the state as the agent for political changes. The second possible outcome is the absorption of social forces by the state. This implies that the state has to adjust its course of political changes in order to accommodate social forces. Third, the state may fail altogether in its attempt to impose its version onto or to accommodate social forces. In all these cases, while the interactions between the state and society are complicated, they are mutually transformative.

The dynamics of political liberalization range from high politics to low politics. At the top, the leadership can be disaggregated, as can the state. It is composed of different factions with different interests and policy preferences. Competition for power exists among them. Intensive power struggles could destabilize the Chinese regime. This was especially true during the 1989 pro-democracy movement. As discussed earlier, an open power struggle might result from different ideological orientations or policy ideas among key political leaders. It also might be a consequence of the interactions among individual leaders with different power ambitions. In reality, a power struggle is often a result of the interplay of these two factors. For example, during the 1989 movement, party secretary Zhao Ziyang's more liberal political orientation was in serious conflict with the more conservative line of Premier Li Peng and others. In the face of strong opposition, Zhao appealed to liberal forces among the various social groups for support. But in the end, the conservative forces were prevalent and the pro-democracy movement was crushed.

The appointment of Jiang Zemin as party secretary in 1989 initiated another round of power struggles. He was a compromise candidate among the party elders and was abruptly called up to Beijing from Shanghai immediately after the 1989 movement. He faced an uphill task in consolidating his power. In 1992, prior to the party's Fourteenth Party Congress, the Yang brothers (Yang Shangkun, the state president, and Yang Baibing, the general) initiated a political attack on Jiang Zemin. In 1996, Beijing Mayor Chen Xitong, who played a major role in cracking down on the 1989 movement, refused to be subordinated to the leadership of Jiang Zemin. In 1997, Qiao Shi, the chairman of the National People's Congress (NPC) and number three in the Standing Committee of the Political Bureau, challenged Jiang's conservative political stand. Nevertheless, through deft political maneuvering, Jiang was able to remove his political enemies one by one and consolidate power. The

party's Sixteenth Party Congress has been regarded as the first ever smooth and   181
peaceful transition of power in the CCP's history. But prior to the event, there
was still an intensive power struggle between Jiang Zemin and others, mainly
Li Ruihuan and Wei Jianxing.

Power struggles will continue, but a regime collapse resulting from a power
struggle is unlikely. The CCP leadership has learned a great deal from its
own experience and regime changes in other places. As a result of the 1989
pro-democracy movement, the leadership now knows that a divided leadership is detrimental to the survival of the party itself. It is acutely aware that if
factional politics goes out of control, social forces will be given opportunities
to challenge the power of the ruling party. Not only individual leaders but also
the ruling party per se will be threatened. From the experience of the former
Soviet Union, the leadership has learned that individual leaders' political ambitions have to be constrained in the interest of the party.

In order to allow power struggles to occur within permissible limits, the
leadership has established various explicit or implicit rules and norms. First,
top leaders have emphasized a collective leadership under which no leader
can dictate high politics, like Mao Zedong and Deng Xiaoping did before. In
the Jiang Zemin era, compromises among political figures became the norm.
To be sure, Jiang fought hard to fend off challenges mounted by the Yang
brothers, Chen Xitong, and Qiao Shi. But as long as he was not directly challenged, he was ready to strike compromises with other factions. Although he
had disagreements with Li Peng, Zhu Rongji, and other major political figures,
he was able to work with them and tap their expertise to manage the affairs of
the party and state. The current Hu Jintao–Wen Jiabao leadership continues
to practice this and comprises with different factions and their interests.

Second, the age factor has been most institutionalized in handling power
succession.[22] The retirement system for aged cadres was formally established
in the early 1980s. Candidates for ministers, provincial party secretaries, and
governors have to be younger than sixty-five years of age, and those for deputy
ministries, deputy provincial party secretaries, and deputy governors must be
younger than sixty years of age. The main problem lies in retiring top leaders,
namely those in the Political Bureau and especially in its Standing Committee. Nevertheless, since the 1990s, an unwritten practice has been established:
candidates for the premier and vice premier positions (or equivalent level
in the party sector) have to be younger than seventy years of age. At the Sixteenth Party Congress in 2002, all leaders in the Political Bureau and its Standing Committee who were older than seventy retired, and all the new leaders
are younger than seventy. Jiang Zemin was an exception, even though he no
longer held a position in the Political Bureau. Nevertheless, at the Fourth

182   Plenum in 2004, Jiang Zemin resigned from his last position as the chairman of the Central Military Commission and thus completed the whole process of power transition from the third generation to the fourth. The age system is unlikely to change because it has become a major mechanism in ensuring peaceful power succession.

Third, the system of graceful political exit for senior leaders has been institutionalized. Before Deng Xiaoping, China virtually did not have a system of political exit. Top leaders were able to hold onto their positions until their deaths. The "exit" problem had troubled both the top leadership and the country because it often had to be solved by a bitter power struggle. Since the 1990s, the leadership has made quite a commendable effort to build such an exit system. During the Fifteenth Party Congress, Qiao Shi retired gracefully from all power positions. Regardless of whether Qiao retired voluntarily or was pushed out, his retirement was widely regarded as a major step for the CCP to resolve its endemic problem of retiring senior leaders. At the same congress, General Liu Huaqing also gracefully exited from the Standing Committee. Since then, no military man has occupied a place in this most powerful decision-making body in China. This exit method was again practiced at the Sixteenth Party Congress. As mentioned above, all aged leaders exited from the Standing Committee. Li Ruihuan (at sixty-eight) was even under the age limit of seventy years.

All these measures have helped to constrain but not eliminate power struggles. As long as there is politics, there will be power struggles. The SARS outbreak in 2003 triggered a power struggle among top leaders, between Hu Jintao–Wen Jiabao and Jiang Zemin's faction. But again, the struggle occurred within permissible limits. Eventually, as a compromise, Minister of Health Zhang Wenkang (Jiang's man) and Beijing Mayor Meng Xuenong (Hu's man) were jointly fired.

Power struggles are unlikely to lead to a regime collapse but may lead to political liberalization. Due to drastic socioeconomic changes, even the most conservative political leader will not be able to turn the regime back to the days of Mao. Among top leaders, there is a gradual phenomenon of what may be termed "competitive liberalization." Certainly, no leader can propose any radical liberalization program. This is quite unlikely under the collective leadership system. Nevertheless, each leader has to propose and accomplish something that distinguishes his leadership from that of his predecessor and that conforms to existing socioeconomic reality. China's leaders after Deng Xiaoping are no longer revolutionaries but technocrats. Their legitimacy does not come from popular votes but from their performance, be it economic, social, or political.

The change from Jiang Zemin's "three represents" (*sange daibiao*) to Hu   183
Jintao–Wen Jianbao's "comfortable society" and "pro-people orientation"
serves as an example. After Jiang failed to promote his campaign of "three
talks" (talking about politics, virtue, and political learning) in 1998–1999, he
proposed a grand concept of "three represents," meaning that the CCP represents the most advanced production mode, the most advanced culture, and the
interests of the majority of the people. It is a great leap forward from the "three
talks" to the "three represents." If the "three represents" can be materialized
(e.g., the CCP begins to represent the interests of different social classes), that
could trigger political liberalization and even political democratization.

Even though Hu Jintao has claimed that the new leadership will emphasize
policy continuity, it has proposed something new — to build a comfortable society for all people (*xiaokang shehui*). The change from the "three represents" to
the "comfortable society" also involves a political process. Under Jiang Zemin,
the state had shifted its social base to include the capitalist class. This has significant political implications. After the 1989 pro-democracy movement, the party
leadership passed a regulation prohibiting private entrepreneurs from joining
the party, and Jiang Zemin was then one of the staunchest supporters of that
regulation. Nevertheless, Jiang was able to adjust his political orientation to suit
prevailing socioeconomic conditions. During his time, the state not only legalized the private sector and provided constitutional protection for private prop-
erties but also allowed private entrepreneurs or capitalists to join the party.

The accommodation of capitalists immediately resulted in strong reactions
from other social groups and party members such as old leftists like Deng
Liqun and new leftists like Lin Yanzhi. They initiated a campaign against the
party's tilting toward capitalists. They claim to represent the interests of the
working class and peasants. Many believe that if the trend continues, the CCP
will follow in the steps of the KMT under Chiang Kai-shek and become a
party for capitalists. In an effort to counter such criticisms, the Hu Jintao–Wen
Jiabao leadership has paid more attention to the needs of the lower social
classes while staying the course of expanding the class base of the CCP. Although it does not mean that the current regime will be able to represent
different class interests effectively, it does indicate that the younger leadership
has to be seen as relevant to different class interests.

One can reasonably argue that power struggles are inevitable in high politics. Power competition can generate a dynamic of competitive liberalization.
Due to socioeconomic changes, leaders generally have to compete with one
another to put forth a convincing case for political advancement.

At the societal level, China has become a typical class society, with different social classes struggling with one another for political participation.[23]

184   Private entrepreneurs are the most obvious. This is the rationale behind the party's decision to recruit capitalists. Capitalism-driven industrialization and globalization have resulted in greater class differentiation in China. The rise of social classes has created tremendous pressure for the regime. The leadership under Jiang Zemin raised the concept of the "three represents," but China still lacks formal institutions for interest aggregation and articulation. Without such institutions, the "three represents" can hardly materialize. In a democratic sense, no interest can be represented before it is articulated. Certainly, without establishing any representative mechanism, the regime will continue to face pressure for political participation by social classes.

At the grassroots level, the prospects for political participation appear brighter. In 1987, the village election system was established and villagers could elect their own leaders. The system has now been extended to all the provinces of the country, though the degree of democracy embedded in elections in different locations might vary. The village election system forms a meaningful basis for China's future democratization. Once an election system is established and benefits Chinese peasants, it is impossible for the state to withdraw such a system, even though elections could go against the interest of the regime. The village election system has indeed generated considerable pressure (both internal and external) for the regime to extend such a system to higher levels. Despite the regime's reluctance, elections of township heads were implemented in some places on an experimental basis. Such political pressure is likely to continue and increase over time as the democratic consciousness spreads among Chinese peasants.

It is in the areas of gradual political liberalization that the Internet becomes effective in facilitating political changes in China. The best results can occur if social interests and the regime's interests coincide. When such a condition is present, an implicit coalition between the reformist leadership and social groups is expected to form. The Internet can serve either as a forum in which the two actors can interplay or a tool for social groups to mobilize their support.

Our case studies in the previous chapters show that social groups have frequently undertaken political initiatives in promoting political changes in China. Without the Internet, it would not have been possible for social groups to set up their agendas. Internet-mediated public discussions more often than not can create enormous pressure for the regime. When the reformist leadership perceives such pressure from below in a "right" direction, social initiatives are likely to be accepted and become a force for policy changes and political changes. Our cases have also shown that while the regime has cracked down on Internet-mediated collective actions that were regarded as threatening, it has also accepted social initiatives and made great efforts in adjusting existing policy practices. This is especially apparent in the cases involving the death of Sun Zhigang, the release of Sun Dawu, and the SARS event. It is worth noting that while social groups succeeded in all these cases, the reformist leadership has also benefited from such social initiatives. These events not only helped the reformist leadership to consolidate its power vis-à-vis the conservative forces within the regime, but they also helped the leadership to change existing policy practices that would otherwise be difficult to change.

Internet-mediated political participation is important not only because it can create political pressure for the regime; more importantly, it can provide social support for a given reform policy. In China's authoritarian political system, major decisions are often made from above and without any social input. More often than not, the regime makes policies, but policy implementation is problematic. Policy initiatives often evaporate either during the process of power competition among key political figures or during the process of implementation. To change existing policy practice, the leadership must have a strong willingness to engage in reforms. Apart from such an inclination, the leadership must have the capability to devise and implement reform policies. Internet-mediated policy debates give the leadership not only a chance to take reform initiatives but also a sense of strong social support of these reform initiatives. In other words, Internet-mediated public discussions often grant the reformist leadership a mandate for policy initiation and implementation. This can partly explain why the reformist leadership was successful in making policy changes after the death of Sun Zhigang, the release of Sun Dawu, and the SARS event.

Needless to say, all these events have not resulted in political democratization, but they have benefited both the reformist leadership and Chinese society as well by facilitating gradual political liberalization. As discussed in earlier chapters, with the strong social support generated from these events, the leadership has focused its attention on limited social and political transparency.

More important, in all these cases, the interactions between the state and social forces are mutually transformative. The results of the engagement and disengagement of the state with social forces are tangible, even momentous, but outcomes rarely reflect the ultimate aims of either. The interaction between the state and social forces is mediated through struggles and accommodations in numerous arenas. These interactions cumulatively reshape the state and social forces, and they are the foundation of the recursive relationship between them. One can reasonably argue at this point that the state and social forces are transforming each other through their increasingly intensive

186   interactions over Internet-mediated platforms, and the mutual transformation of the state and social forces open opportunities for political changes and thus regime changes.

FROM THE IMPOSSIBLE TO THE INEVITABLE

Regime change in China is seemingly an enterprise of the impossible. But no Chinese regime has been able to survive forever. Regime changes do take place within and without China. Today, more and more authoritarian regimes have been democratized in other parts of the world. Will China buck the trend and become an exception? What role can modern information technology play in facilitating political changes in China? For the purpose of analysis, I have discussed three scenarios of regime change in China and possible roles of the Internet in these processes. Certainly, any regime change will not happen in a clear-cut way. There can be a mixture of different scenarios. Power struggles among leaders can trigger a social movement. Similarly, a social crisis or external shock can induce a power struggle among top leaders. Also, the regime's "competitive liberalization," despite its limitations, could encourage the rise of different political voices and create opportunities for social movements. These mixed scenarios are more likely in real politics.

It is important to note that Internet-based collective actions have their limitations in China. Such collective actions are able to promote political liberalization, but so far they have not been able to trigger political democratization. This is because democratization requires a structural change to the existing regime, but liberalization does not. With democratization taking off, the existing regime is likely to be replaced by a new one, and current power holders are likely to lose power. Furthermore, democratization requires that rulers are to increasingly become rule bound, and no one can control the free flow of information arbitrarily. Such a structural change is apparently not happening in China, as many studies of the Internet have proved.

But our cases show that Internet-based collective actions are promoting political openness, transparency, and accountability to a great degree. These developments are important aspects of political liberalization. Compared with the situation before the information age, the regime is now more accountable to citizens and is willing to change its old policies and political practices as long as the existence of the regime is not threatened. Such a change is partly due to the existence of new forms of collective actions that enable social forces to exert pressure over the regime.

Modern information technology alone cannot lead to meaningful regime changes in China. Other social forces for a regime change have to be present.

The reform and open door policy, market economy, globalization, capitalism, and class differentiation are all generating forces for regime change in China. All these forces, together with modern information technology, can generate significant dynamics for political changes and eventually regime changes in China. The political impact of modern information technology is still unfolding.

Selected Bibliography

Abramson, Jeffrey B., F. Christopher Arterton, and Gary R. Orren. 1988. *The Electronic Commonwealth: The Impact of New Media Technologies on Democratic Politics.* Cambridge, MA: Harvard University Press.

Alexander, Cynthia J. and Leslie A. Pal (eds.). 1998. *Digital Democracy: Policy and Politics in the Wired World.* Toronto: Oxford University Press.

Amnesty International. 2004. "People's Republic of China: Controls Tighten as Internet Activism Grows." *Amnesty International Journal.*

Anderson, Benedict. 1991. *Imagined Communities: Reflections on the Origin and Spread of Nationalism,* 2nd edition. London: Verso.

Arendt, Hannah. 1970. *On Violence.* New York: Harcourt Brace and Company.

Badie, Bertrand. 2000. *The Imported State: The Westernization of the Political Order,* translated by Claudia Royal. Stanford, CA: Stanford University Press.

Bakken, Borge. 2000. "State Capacity and Social Control in China," in Kjeld Erik Brødsgaard and Susan Young (eds.). *State Capacity in East Asia: Japan, Taiwan, China, and Vietnam.* Oxford: Oxford University Press, pp. 185–202.

Baldwin, Peter. 2003. "The Return of the Coercive State: Behavioral Control in Multicultural Society," in T. V. Paul, G. John Ikenberry, and John A. Hall (eds.). *The Nation-State in Question.* Princeton, NJ: Princeton University Press, pp. 106–35.

Bambauer, Derek, Ronald J. Deibert, John G. Palfrey Jr., Rafal Rohozinski, Nart Villeneuve, and Jonathan Zittrain. 2006. *Internet Filtering in China in 2004–2005: A Country Study.* Berkman Center for Internet and Society at Harvard Law School, Research Publication No. 2005-10. Available at SSRN: http://ssrn.com/abstract=706681. Accessed on May 15, 2006.

Barber, Benjamin. 1984. *Strong Democracy: Participatory Politics for a New Age.* Berkeley, CA: University of California Press.

Barber, Benjamin R. 1998. "The New Telecommunications Technology: Endless Frontier or End of Democracy," in Roger G. Noll and Monroe E. Price (eds.). *A Communications Cornucopia: Markle Foundation Essays on Information Policy.* Washington, D.C.: Brookings Institution, pp. 72–98.

190   Barber, Benjamin. 1998. *A Passion for Democracy: American Essays*. Princeton: Princeton University Press.

Barber, Benjamin. 1998. "Three Scenarios for the Future of Technology and Strong Democracy." *Political Science Quarterly*, 113:4, pp. 573–89.

Barber, Bernard. 1983. *The Logic and Limits of Trust*. New Brunswick, NJ: Rutgers University Press.

Bates, Robert H. 1988. "Contra Contractarianism: Some Reflections on the New Institutionalism." *Politics and Society*, 16: 2/3, pp. 387–99.

Beissinger, Mark R. 2002. *Nationalist Mobilization and the Collapse of the Soviet State*. New York: Cambridge University Press.

Bell, Daniel. 1973. *The Coming of Post-Industrial Society: A Venture in Social Forecasting*. New York: Basic Books.

Bernstein, Thomas P. and Xiaobo Lu. 2003. *Taxation without Representation in Contemporary Rural China*. New York: Cambridge University Press.

Bianco, William T. 1994. *Trust: Representatives and Constituents*. Ann Arbor: University of Michigan Press.

Bimber, Bruce. 2003. *Information and American Democracy: Technology in the Evolution of Political Power*. New York: Cambridge University Press.

Bright, Charles and Susan Harding. 1984. (eds.). *Statemaking and Social Movements: Essays in History and Theory*. Ann Arbor: The University of Michigan Press.

Brødsgaard, Kjeld Erik. 2002. "Institutional Reform and the Bianzhi System in China." *The China Quarterly*. 170, pp. 79–104.

Brødsgaard, Kjeld Erik. 2004. "Management of Party Cadres in China," in Kjeld Erik Brødsgaard and Zheng Yongnian (eds.). *Bringing the Party Back In: How China Is Governed*. Singapore, London, and New York: Eastern Universities Press, pp. 57–91.

Bunger, Karl. 1985. "The Chinese State between Yesterday and Tomorrow," in Stuart R. Schram (ed.). *The Scope of State Power in China*. Hong Kong: The Chinese University Press, pp. xiii–xxv.

Burchell, Graham, Colin Gordon, and Peter Miller (eds.). 1991. *The Foucault Effect: Studies in Governmentality*. Chicago: University of Chicago Press.

Cai, Yongshun. 2002. "The Resistance of Chinese Laid-Off Workers in the Reform Period." *The China Quarterly*, 170, pp. 327–44.

Calhoun, Craig (ed.). 1992. *Habermas and the Public Sphere*. Cambridge, MA: MIT Press.

Campbell, Angus, Philip Converse, Warren E. Miller, and Donald E. Stokes. 1960. *The American Voter*. New York: Wiley.

Cao, Cong. 2002. "Strengthening China Through Science and Education: China's Development Strategy toward the Twenty-First Century." *Issues and Studies*, 38:3, pp. 122–49.

Cao, Cong. 2003. "Zhongguancun Aspiring to Become China's Silicon Valley." *EAI Background Brief*, 152. East Asian Institute, National University of Singapore, April 24.

Cao, Cong. 2004. *China's Scientific Elite*. London and New York: Routledge-Curzon.

The Center for Social Development of the Chinese Academy of Social Sciences. 2003. 191 *2003nian hulianwang baogao (The 2003 Report on the Internet)*, Beijing.

Chan, Anita, Benedict J. Tria Kerkvliet, and Jonathan Unger. 1999. (eds.). *Transforming Asian Socialism: China and Vietnam Compared*. Lanham, MD: Rowman & Littlefield.

Chan, Joseph Man. 2003. "Administrative Boundaries and Media Marketization: A Comparative Analysis of the Newspaper, TV and Internet Market in China," in Chin-Chuan Lee (ed.). *Chinese Media, Global Contexts*. London and New York: RoutledgeCurzon, pp. 159–76.

Chang, Maria Hsia. 2004. *Falun Gong: The End of Days*. New Haven: Yale University Press.

Chao, Chien-min and Bruce Dickson (eds.). 2001. *Remaking the Chinese State: Strategies, Society, and Security*. New York: Routledge.

Chase, Michael S. and James C. Mulvenon. 2002. *You've Got Dissent! Chinese Dissident Use of the Internet and Beijing's Counter-Strategies*. Santa Monica, CA: Rand.

Cheek, Timothy and Tony Saich (eds.). 1997. *New Perspectives on State Socialism of China*. Armonk, NY: M. E. Sharpe.

Chen, An. 2002. "Capitalist Development, Entrepreneurial Class, and Democratization in China." *Political Science Quarterly* 117: 3 (Fall), pp. 401–22.

Chen Duxiu, 1919. "Xin qingnian zuian zhi dabianshu" ("*New Youth's* Reply to Charges against the Magazine"), *Xin Qingnian (New Youth)*, 6:1 (January 15), pp. 10–11.

Chen, Feng. 2000. "Subsistence Crisis, Managerial Corruption, and Labor Protest in China." *The China Journal*, 44, pp. 41–63.

Chen, Feng. 2003. "Between the State and Labor: The Conflict of Chinese Trade Unions' Dual Institutional Identity in Market Reform." *The China Quarterly*, 176, pp. 1006–28.

Chen, Feng. 2003. "Industrial Restructuring and Workers' Resistance in China." *Modern China*. 29:2, pp. 237–62.

The China Internet Network Information Center (CNNIC). 2002. *Zhongguo hulian wangluo nianjian 2002 (China Yearbook of Internet Network, 2002)*, Beijing.

The China Internet Network Information Center. 2004. *The Statistical Report of Internet Development in China*. Beijing: CNNIC, January.

Chow, Tse-tsung. 1960. *The May Fourth Movement: Intellectual Revolution in Modern China*. Cambridge, MA: Harvard University Press.

Chu, Samuel C. 1957. "The New Life Movement, 1934–1937," in John E. Lane (ed.). *Researches in the Social Sciences on China*. The East Asian Institute of Columbia University, pp. 1–19.

Cohen, Jean L. and Andrew Arato. 1992. *Civil Society and Political Theory*. Cambridge, MA: MIT Press.

Dahl, Robert A. 1989. *Democracy and Its Critics*. New Haven: Yale University Press.

Dahlgren, Peter. 1995. *Television and the Public Sphere: Citizenship, Democracy and the Media*. London: Sage Publications.

Dahlgren, Peter and Colin Sparks (eds.). 1991. *Communication and Citizenship: Journalism and the Public Sphere in the Media Age*. New York: Routledge.

192   Dai, Xiudian. 2003. "ICTs in China's Development Strategy," in Christopher R. Hughes and Gudrun Wacker (eds.). *China and the Internet: Politics of the Digital Leap Forward*. London and New York: RoutledgeCurzon, pp. 8–29.

Davis, Richard. 1999. *The Web of Politics: The Internet's Impact on the American Political System*. New York: Oxford University Press.

de Burgh, Hugo. 2003. *The Chinese Journalist: Mediating Information in the World's Most Populous Country*. London and New York: RoutledgeCurzon.

Deng Xiaoping. 1993. *Deng Xiaoping wenxuan (Selected Works of Deng Xiaoping)*, vol. 3. Beijing: Renmin chubanshe.

Deutsch, Karl W. 1966. *The Nerves of Government: Models of Political Communication and Control*, 2nd edition. New York: Free Press.

Di Palma, Giuseppe. 1991. "Legitimation from the Top to Civil Society: Politico-Cultural Change in Eastern Europe." *World Politics*, 44:1, pp. 49–80.

Diamond, Larry. 1993. "The Globalization of Democracy: Trends, Types, Causes, and Prospects," in Robert Slater, Barry M. Schutz, and Steven R. Dorr, *Global Transformation and the Third World*. Boulder, CO: Lynn Rienner, pp. 31–70.

Dirlik, Arif. 1975. "The Ideological Foundations of the New Life Movement: A Study in Counterrevolution." *Journal of Asian Study*, 34: 4, pp. 945–80.

Donald, Stephanie Hemelryk, Michael Keane, and Yin Hong (eds.). 2002. *Media in China: Consumption, Content and Crisis*. London: RoutledgeCurzon.

Donnithorne, Audrey. 1972. "China's Cellular Economy: Some Economic Trends since the Cultural Revolution." *The China Quarterly*, 52, pp. 605–19.

Downs, Anthony. 1957. *An Economic Theory of Democracy*. New York: Harper and Brothers.

Drori, Gili S., John W. Meyer, Francisco O. Ramirez, and Evan Schofer. 2003. *Science in the Modern World Polity: Institutionalization and Globalization*. Stanford, CA: Stanford University Press.

The Economist. 2006. "The Party, the People and the Power of Cyber-talk." *Special Report: China and the Internet*. April 29, pp. 27–30.

Eldridge, Michael. 1988. *Transforming Experience: John Dewey's Cultural Instrumentalism*. Nashville, TN: Vanderbilt University Press.

Etzioni, Amitai. 1993. *The Spirit of Community: Rights, Responsibilities, and the Communitarian Agenda*. New York: Crown Publishers.

Evans, Peter. 1995. *Embedded Autonomy: States and Industrial Transformation*. Princeton, NJ: Princeton University Press.

Evans, Peter B., Dietrich Rueschemeyer, and Theda Skocpol (eds.). 1985. *Bringing the State Back In*. New York: Cambridge University Press.

Fang Lizhi. 1990. *Bringing Down the Great Wall: Writings on Science, Culture and Democracy in China*. New York: A. A. Knopf.

Far Eastern Economic Review. 2003. *China's Elite 5: A Study of Affluent and Influential People in China*. Hong Kong.

Feigenbaum, Evan A. 2003. *China's Techno-Warriors: National Security and Strategic Competition from the Nuclear to the Information Age*. Stanford, CA: Stanford University Press.

Feinstein, Charles and Christopher Howe (eds.). 1997. *Chinese Technology Transfer in*   193
the 1990s: Current Experience, Historical Problems, and International Perspectives.
Lynn, NH: Edward Elgar.

Ferdinand, Peter (ed.). 2000. *The Internet, Democracy and Democratization.* London:
Frank Cass.

Fewsmith, Joseph. 2001. *China since Tiananmen: The Politics of Transition.* New York:
Cambridge University Press.

Foucault, Michel. 1991. *Discipline and Punish. The Birth of the Prison.* London:
Penguin.

Franda, Marcus. 2002. *Launching into Cyberspace: Internet Development and Politics*
in Five World Regions. Boulder, CO: Lynne Rienner.

Friedman, Thomas L. 2000. *The Lexus and the Olive Tree: Understanding Globaliza-*
tion. New York: Anchor Books.

Friedrich, Carl J., Michael Curtis, and Benjamin R. Barber. 1969. *Totalitarianism in*
Perspective: Three Views. New York: Praeger.

Fukuyama, Francis. 1995. *Trust: The Social Virtues and the Creation of Prosperity.* New
York: Free Press.

Gelman, Andrew and Gary King. 1993. "Why Are American Presidential Election
Campaign Polls So Variable When Votes Are So Predictable?" *British Journal of*
Political Science, 23, pp. 409–51.

Gernet, Jacques. 1985. "Introduction," in Stuart R. Schram (ed.), *The Scope of State*
Power in China. Hong Kong: The Chinese University Press, pp. xxvii–xxxiv.

Goldman, Merle. 1994. *Sowing the Seeds of Democracy in China: Political Reform in*
the Deng Xiaoping Era. Cambridge, MA: Harvard University Press.

Goldman, Merle and Leo Ou-fan Lee (eds.). 2002. *An Intellectual History of Modern*
China. Cambridge, MA: Harvard University Press.

Goodman, David and Beverly Hooper (eds.). 1994. *China's Quiet Revolution: New*
Interactions between State and Society. New York: St. Martin's Press.

Grieder, Jerome. 1970. *Hu Shih and the Chinese Renaissance: Liberalism in the Chi-*
nese Revolution, 1917–1937. Cambridge, MA: Harvard University Press.

Grieder, Jerome. 1972. "The Question of 'Politics' in the May Fourth Movement," in
Benjamin Schwartz (ed.). *Reflections on the May Fourth Movement.* Cambridge,
MA: Harvard University Press, pp. 95–101.

Gries, Peter Hays. 2004. *China's New Nationalism: Pride, Politics, and Diplomacy.*
Berkeley, CA: University of California Press.

Grossman, Lawrence K. 1995. *The Electronic Republic: Reshaping Democracy in the*
Information Age. New York: Viking.

Gu, Edward and Merle Goldman (eds.). 2004. *Chinese Intellectuals between State and*
Market. London: RoutledgeCurzon.

Gu, Edward X. 2001. "Who was Mr. Democracy? The May Fourth Discourse of
Populist Democracy and the Radicalization of Chinese Intellectuals (1915–1922)."
Modern Asian Studies, 35: 3, pp. 589–621.

Gu, Shulin. 1999. *China's Industrial Technology: Market Reform and Organizational*
Change. London: Routledge.

194   Guo, Liang. 2005. *Surveying Internet Usage and Impact in Five Chinese Cities.* Beijing: Research Center for Social Development, Chinese Academy of Social Sciences.

Gutmann, Ethan. 2004. *Losing the New China: A Story of American Commerce, Desire, and Betrayal.* New York: Encounter Books.

Habermas, Jurgen. 1989. *The Structural Transformation of the Public Sphere.* Cambridge, MA: Polity Press.

Hachigian, Nina. 2001. "China's Cyber-Strategy," *Foreign Affairs*, 80: 2, pp. 118–33.

Hague, Barry N. and Brian D. Loader (eds.). 1999. *Digital Democracy: Discourse and Decision Making in the Information Age.* London: Routledge.

Hall, David L. and Roger Ames. 1999. *The Democracy of the Dead: Dewey, Confucius, and the Hope for Democracy in China.* Chicago: Open Court Publishing Co.

Hamrin, Carol Lee. 1990. *China and the Challenge of the Future: Changing Political Patterns.* Boulder, CO: Westview Press.

Hardin, Russell. 1990. "The Social Evolution of Cooperation," in Karen Schweers Cook and Margaret Levi (eds.). *The Limits of Rationality.* Chicago: The University of Chicago Press, pp. 358–76.

Harford, Kathleen. 2000. "Cyberspace with Chinese Characteristics." *Current History*, pp. 255–62.

Harwit, Eric and Duncan Clark. 2001. "Shaping the Internet in China: Evolution of Political Control over Network Infrastructure and Content." *Asian Survey* xli: 3, pp. 377–408.

Hauben, Michael and Ronda Hauben. 1997. *Netizens: On the History and Impact of Usenet and the Internet.* Los Alamitos, CA: IEEE Computer Society Press.

He, Baogang. 1996. *The Democratization of China.* London: Routledge.

Held, David and Anthony McGrew, David Goldblatt and Jonathan Perraton. 1999. *Global Transformation: Politics, Economics and Culture.* Stanford, CA: Stanford University Press.

Hickman, Larry. 1995. "Pragmatism, Technology, and Scientism: Are the Methods of the Scientific-Technical Disciplines Relevant to Social Problems?" in Robert Hollinger and David Depew (eds.). *Pragmatism: From Progressivism to Postmodernism.* Westport, CT: Praeger, pp. 72–87.

Hill, David T. and Krishna Sen. 2000. "The Internet in Indonesia's New Democracy." *Democratization*, 7:1, pp. 119–36.

Hill, Kevin A. and John E. Hughes. 1998. *Cyberpolitics: Citizen Activism in the Age of the Internet.* Lanham, MD: Rowman & Littlefield Publishers.

Hirschman, Albert O. 1970. *Exit, Voice, and Loyalty: Responses to Decline in Firms, Organizations, and States.* Cambridge, MA: Harvard University Press.

Hirschman, Albert O. 1982. *Shifting Involvements: Private Interest and Public Action.* Princeton, NJ: Princeton University Press.

Hoff, Jens, Ivan Horrocks, and Pieter Tops (eds.). 2000. *Democratic Governance and New Technology: Technologically Mediated Innovations in Political Practice in Western Europe.* London: Routledge.

Holmes, David (ed.). 1997. *Virtual Politics: Identity and Community in Cyberspace.* London: Sage Publications.

Hook, Brian (ed.). 1996. *The Individual and the State in China.* New York: Oxford   195
University Press.

Hope, Nicholas C., Dennis Tao Yang, and Mu Yang Li. 2003 (eds.).. *How Far across the
River? Chinese Policy Reform at the Millennium.* Stanford, CA: Stanford University
Press.

Hung, Chin-Fu. 2003. "Public Discourse and 'Virtual' Political Participation in the
PRC: The Impact of the Internet." *Issues and Studies,* 39: 4, pp. 1–38.

Huntington, Samuel P. 1991. *The Third Wave: Democratization in the Late Twentieth
Century.* Norman, OK: University of Oklahoma Press.

Ji, You. 2004. "Learning and Catching Up: China's Revolution in Military Affairs Initiative," in Emily O. Goldman and Thomas G. Mahnken (eds.). *The Information
Revolution in Military Affairs in Asia.* New York: Palgrave, pp. 97–124.

Johnson, Chalmers A. 1962. *Peasant Nationalism and Communist Power: The Emergence of Revolutionary China, 1937–1945.* Stanford, CA: Stanford University Press.

Johnson, Thomas J., Carol E. Hays, and Scott P. Hays (eds.). 1998. *Engaging the
Public: How Government and the Media Can Reinvigorate American Democracy.*
Lanham: Rowman & Littlefield Publishers.

Jones, Colin and Roy Porter (eds.). 1994. *Reassessing Foucault: Power, Medicine and the
Body.* London: Routledge.

Kalathil, Shanthi and Taylor C. Boas. 2003. *Open Networks, Closed Regimes: The Impact of the Internet on Authoritarian Rule.* Washington D.C.: Carnegie Endowment
for International Peace.

Kasza, Gregory J. 1995. *The Conscription Society: Administered Mass Organizations.*
New Haven: Yale University Press.

Kedzie, Christopher R. 1997. *Communication and Democracy: Coincident Revolutions
and the Emergent Dictator's Dilemma.* Santa Monica, CA: Rand.

Kim, Taeho. 2003. "Leading Small Groups: Managing All under Heaven," in David M.
Finkelstein and Maryanne Kivlehan (eds.). *China's Leadership in the 21st Century:
The Rise of the Fourth Generation.* Armonk, NY: M. E. Sharpe, pp. 121–39.

Kohli, Atul. 1986. (ed.). *The State and Development in the Third World.* Princeton, NJ:
Princeton University Press.

Kornhauser, William. 1959. *The Politics of Mass Society.* Glencoe, IL: The Free Press.

Krasner, Stephen D. 1999. *Sovereignty: Organized Hypocrisy.* Princeton, NJ: Princeton
University Press.

Latham, K. 2000. "Nothing but the Truth: News Media, Power and Hegemony in
South China. *The China Quarterly,* 163, pp. 633–54.

Lee, Chin-Chuan (ed.). 1994. *China's Media, Media's China.* Boulder, CO:
Westview.

Lee, Chin-Chuan (ed.). 2000. *Power, Money and Media: Communication Patterns
and Bureaucratic Control in Cultural China.* Evanston, IL: Northwest University
Press.

Lee, Chin-Chuan (ed.). 2003. *Chinese Media, Global Contexts.* London: Routledge-
Curzon.

Lee, Hong Yung. 1991. *From Revolutionary Cadres to Party Technocrats in Socialist
China.* Berkeley, CA: University of California Press.

196   Lee, Paul S. N. (ed.). 1997. *Telecommunications and Development in China*. Cresskill, NJ: Hampton Press.

Lessig, Lawrence. 1999. *Code and Other Laws of Cyberspace*. New York: Basic Books.

Lessig, Lawrence. 2001. *The Future of Ideas: The Fate of the Commons in a Connected World*. New York: Vintage Books.

Li, Cheng. 2001. *China's Leaders: The New Generation*. Lanham, MD: Rowman & Littlefield Publishers.

Li, Lianjiang. 2001. "Elections and Popular Resistance in Rural China." *China Information*. xv:2, pp. 1–19.

Li, Lianjiang and Kevin J. O'Brien. 1996. "Villagers and Popular Resistance in Contemporary China." *Modern China*, 22:1, pp. 28–61.

Lieberthal, Kenneth. 1995. *Governing China: From Revolution through Reform*. New York: W. W. Norton & Company, Inc.

Lieberthal, Kenneth. 2004. *Governing China: From Revolution through Reform*, 2nd edition. New York: W. W. Norton.

Lieberthal, Kenneth and David M. Lampton (eds.). 1991. *Bureaucracy, Politics and Decision Making in Post-Mao China*. Berkeley, CA: University of California Press.

Lieberthal, Kenneth and Michel Oksenberg. 1988. *Policy Making in China: Leaders, Structures, and Processes*. Princeton, NJ: Princeton University Press.

Lin, Yu-Sheng. 1979. *The Crisis of Chinese Consciousness: Radical Antitraditionalism in the May Fourth Era*. Madison: The University of Wisconsin Press.

Linz, Juan J. and Alfred Stephan. 1996. *Problems of Democratic Transition and Consolidation: Southern Europe, South America, and Post-Communist Europe*. Baltimore, MD: Johns Hopkins University Press.

Lipset, Seymour Martin. 1959. "Some Social Requisites of Democracy: Economic Development and Political Legitimacy." *American Political Science Review*, 53, pp. 69–105.

Liu, Alan P. L. 1971. *Communications and National Integration in Communist China*. Berkeley, CA: University of California Press.

Liu, Shu-hsien. 1996. "Confucian Ideals and the Real World: A Critical Review of Contemporary Neo-Confucian Thought," in Tu Wei-ming (ed.). *Confucian Traditions in East Asian Modernity: Moral Education and Economic Culture in Japan and the Four Mini-Dragons*. Cambridge, MA: Harvard University Press, pp. 92–111.

Loader, Brian D. (ed.). 1997. *The Governance of Cyberspace: Politics, Technology and Global Restructuring*. London: Routledge.

Lu, Ding and Chee Kong Wong. 2003. *China's Telecommunications Market: Entering a New Competitive Age*. Cheltenham, UK: Edward Elgar.

Lu, Qiwen. 2000. *China's Leap into the Information Age: Innovation and Organization in the Computer Industry*. New York: Oxford University Press.

Lynch, Daniel C. 1999. *After the Propaganda State: Media, Politics, and "Thought Work" in Reformed China*. Stanford, CA: Stanford University Press.

McAdam, Doug. 1982. *Political Process and the Development of Black Insurgency, 1930–1970*. Chicago: University of Chicago Press.

McCord, Edward. 1993. *The Power of the Gun: The Emergence of Modern Chinese Warlordism*. Berkeley, CA: University of California Press.

McCormick, Barrett L. and Jonathan Unger (eds.). 1996. *China after Socialism: In the* 197
Footsteps of Eastern Europe or East Asia? Armonk, NY: M. E. Sharpe.

Meyer, John W., John Boli, George M. Thomas, and Francisco O. Ramirez. 2000.
"World Society and the Nation-State," in Frank J. Lechner and John Boli (eds.). *The Globalization Reader.* Blackwell Publishers, pp. 84–92.

Meynaud, Jean. 1969. *Technocracy.* New York: Free Press.

Migdal, Joel S. 1988. *Strong Societies and Weak States: State–Society Relations and State Capabilities in the Third World.* Princeton, NJ: Princeton University Press.

Migdal, Joel S. 2001. *State in Society: Studying How States and Societies Transform and Constitute One Another.* New York: Cambridge University Press.

Migdal, Joel S., Atul Kohli and Vivienne Shue. 1994. *State Power and Social Forces: Domination and Transformation in the Third World.* New York: Cambridge University Press.

Miles, James A.R. 1996. *The Legacy of Tiananmen: China in Disarray.* Ann Arbor: The University of Michigan Press.

Miller, H. Lyman. 1996. *Science and Dissent in Post-Mao China: The Politics of Knowledge.* Seattle, WA: University of Washington Press.

Ming, Yi. 2000. "Xinxi gaosu gonglu jiang ba Zhongguo daixiang hefang?" ("Where Will Information Highways Take China To?"). *Zhongguo zhichun (China Spring),* June.

Mueller, Milton and Tan Zixiang. 1997. *China in the Information Age: Telecommunications and the Dilemmas of Reform.* Westport, CT: Praeger Publishers.

Nathan, Andrew J. and Perry Link (eds.). 2001. *The Tiananmen Papers: The Chinese Leadership's Decision to Use Force Against Their Own People — In Their Own Words.* USA: Public Affairs.

Naughton, Barry. 1995. *Growing Out of the Plan: Chinese Economic Reform 1978–1993.* New York: Cambridge University Press.

Ning Zhaoxin. 2003. *Understanding Individual Resistance to Information Technology in E-Government.* Singapore: Department of Political Science, National University of Singapore, master's thesis.

Norris, Pippa. 2000. "The Impact of Television on Civic Malaise," in Susan J. Pharr and Robert D. Putnam (eds.). *Disaffected Democracies: What's Troubling the Trilateral Countries?* Princeton, NJ: Princeton University Press, pp. 231–51.

Norris, Pippa. 2001. *Digital Divide? Civic Engagement, Information Poverty, and the Internet Worldwide.* New York: Cambridge University Press.

O'Donnell, Guillermo and Philippe C. Schmitter. 1989. *Transitions from Authoritarian Rule: Tentative Conclusions about Uncertain Democracies.* Baltimore and London: The Johns Hopkins University Press.

Pan, Esther. 2005. "China's New Internet Restrictions," Council on Foreign Relations, September 27, 2005. Available at www.cfr.org/publication/8913/chinas_new_internet_restrictions.html. Accessed on May 24, 2006.

Perry, Elizabeth J. and Mark Selden (eds.). 2000. *Chinese Society: Change, Conflict and Resistance.* New York: Routledge.

Prins, J. E. J. 2001. *Designing E-Government: On the Crossroads of Technological Innovation and Institutional Change.* The Hague: Kluwer Law International.

198   Przeworski, Adam et al. 1995. *Sustainable Democracy*. New York: Cambridge University Press.

Putnam, Robert. 1993. *Making Democracy Work: Civic Traditions in Modern Italy*. Princeton, NJ: Princeton University Press.

Putnam, Robert. 1995. "Turning In, Turning Out: The Strange Disappearance of Social Capital in America." *PS: Politics and Political Science*, 28:4, pp. 664–83.

Putnam, Robert. 2000. *Bowling Alone: The Collapse and Revival of American Community*. New York: Simon and Schuster.

Pye, Lucian. 1990. "China: Erratic State, Frustrated Society." *Foreign Affairs*, 69:4, pp. 56–74.

Rau, Zbigniew (ed.). 1991. *The Reemergence of Civil Society in Eastern Europe and the Soviet Union*. Boulder, CO: Westview Press.

Rheingold, Howard. 2000. *The Virtual Community: Homesteading on the Electronic Frontier*. Cambridge, MA: MIT Press.

Rozman, Gilbert. 1987. *The Chinese Debate about Soviet Socialism, 1978–1985*. Princeton, NJ: Princeton University Press.

Ru Xing, Lu Xueyi, and Li Peilin (eds.). 2004. *Shehui lanpishu: Zhongguo shehui xingshi fenxi yu yuce, 2004 (Social Bluebook: An Analysis and Forecast of Social Situation in China)*. Beijing: Shehui kexue wenxian chubanshe.

Saich, Tony. 1989. *China's Science Policy in the 80s*. Manchester, England: Manchester University Press.

Saich, Tony (ed.). 1990. *The Chinese People's Movement: Perspectives on Spring 1989*. Armonk, NY: M. E. Sharpe.

Samuels, Richard. 1994. *Rich Nation, Strong Army: National Security and the Technological Transformation of Japan*. Ithaca, NY: Cornell University Press.

Schram, Stuart R. 1984. *Ideology and Policy in China since the Third Plenum, 1978–84*. London: University of London, School of Oriental and African Studies.

Schuler, Douglas. 1996. *New Community Networks: Wired for Change*. New York and Reading, MA: ACM Press and Addison-Wesley Publishing Company.

Schumpeter, Joseph A. 1975. *Capitalism, Socialism and Democracy*. New York: Harper & Row Publishers.

Schwarcz, Vera. 1986. *The Chinese Enlightenment: Intellectuals and the Legacy of the May Fourth Movement of 1919*. Berkeley, CA: The University of California Press.

Schwartz, Benjamin. 1983. "Themes in Intellectual History: May Fourth and After," in John K. Fairbank (ed.). *The Cambridge History of China: Republican China 1912–1949*, Vol. 12, Part I. Cambridge, MA: Cambridge University Press, pp. 406–50.

Science. 2000. "*Science* Interview: China's Leader Commits to Basic Research, Global Science," 288 (June 16), pp. 1950–53.

Segal, Adam. 2003. *Digital Dragon: High-Technology Enterprises in China*. Ithaca, NY: Cornell University Press.

Shi, Tianjian. 1997. *Political Participation in Beijing*. Cambridge, MA: Harvard University Press.

Smith, John E. 1985. "Pragmatism at Work: Dewey's Lectures in China." *Journal of Chinese Philosophy*, 12, pp. 231–59.

Strauss, Julia. 1998. *Strong Institutions in Weak Polities: State Building in Republic* 199
China, 1927–1940. Oxford: Clarendon Press.

Su Shaozhi. 1994. "Chinese Communist Ideology and Media Control," in Chin-Chuan Lee (ed.). *China's Media, Media's China.* Boulder, CO: Westview Press, pp. 75–88.

Sun, Yan. 1995. *The Chinese Reassessment of Socialism 1976–1992.* Princeton, NJ: Princeton University Press.

Sunstein, Cass. 2001. *Republic.com.* Princeton, NJ: Princeton University Press.

Suttmeier, Richard P. and Cong Cao. 2004. "China's Technical Community: Market Reforms and the Changing Policy Cultures of Science," in Edward Gu and Merle Goldman (eds.). *Chinese Intellectuals between State and Market.* London: RoutledgeCurzon, pp. 138–57.

Suttmeier, Richard P. and Yao Xiangkui. 2004. *China's Post-WTO Technology Policy: Standards, Software, and the Changing Nature of Techno-Nationalism*, NBR Special Report, no. 7. Seattle, Washington: The National Bureau of Asian Research, May.

Tarrow, Sidney, 1983. *Struggling to Reform: Social Movements and Policy Change during Cycles of Protest.* Western Societies Program Occasional Paper No. 15. Ithaca, NY: New York Center for International Studies, Cornell University.

Tarrow, Sidney. 1991. *Struggle, Politics, and Reform: Collective Action, Social Movements, and Cycles of Protest.* Cornell Studies in International Affairs, Western Societies Papers, No. 21. Ithaca, NY.

Tarrow, Sidney. 1994. *Power in Movement: Social Movements, Collective Action and Politics.* New York: Cambridge University Press.

Tarrow, Sidney. 1998. *Power in Movement: Social Movements and Contentious Politics*, second edition. New York: Cambridge University Press.

Taubman, Geoffry. 1998. "A Not-So World Wide Web: The Internet, China, and the Challenges to Nondemocratic Rule." *Political Communication*, 15, pp. 255–72.

Tian, Xiaowen. 2002. "The Private Economy: Will the Ugly Duckling Become a Swan?" in John Wong and Zheng Yongnian (eds.). *China's Post-Jiang Leadership Succession: Problems and Perspectives.* Singapore and London: Singapore University Press and World Scientific, pp. 261–84.

Tilly, Charles. 1978. *From Mobilization to Revolution.* Reading, MA: Addison-Wesley Publishing Co.

Tilly, Charles. 1990. *Coercion, Capital, and European States, A.D. 990–1990.* Cambridge, MA: Basil Blackwell.

Toulouse, Chris and Timothy W. Luke (eds.). 1998. *The Politics of Cyberspace: A New Political Science Reader.* New York: Routledge.

Truman, David. 1965. *The Governmental Process: Political Interest and Public Opinion.* New York: Alfred E. Knopf.

Tsagarousianou, Roza, Damian Tambini, and Cathy Bryan (eds.). 1998. *Cyberdemocracy: Technology, Cities, and Civic Networks.* London: Routledge.

Unger, Jonathan (ed.). 1991. *The Pro-Democracy Protests in China: Reports from the Provinces.* Armonk, NY: M. E. Sharpe.

200   Wacker, Gudrun. 2003. "The Internet and Censorship in China," in Christopher R. Hughes and Gudrun Wacker (eds.). *China and the Internet: Politics of the Digital Leap Forward*. London: RoutledgeCurzon, pp. 58–82.

Walder, Andrew G. 1986. *Communist Neo-Traditionalism: Work and Authority in Chinese Industry*. Berkeley, CA: University of California Press.

Walzer, Michael. 1980. *Radical Principles: Reflections of an Unreconstructed Democrat*. New York: Basic Books.

Wang Chunguang. 1998. "1997–1998 nian: Zhongguo shehui wending zhuangkuang de diaocha" ("A Survey on Social Stability in 1997–1998"), in Ru Xin et al. (eds.). *Shehui lanpishu 1998 (Social Bluebook)*. Beijing: Shehui kexue wenxian chubanshe, pp. 121–32.

Wang, Gungwu. 2000. *Joining the Modern World: Inside and Outside China*. Singapore and London: Singapore University Press and World Scientific.

Wang Gungwu and Zheng Yongnian. 2000. "Introduction: Reform, Legitimacy, and Dilemmas," in Wang Gungwu and Zheng Yongnian (eds.), *Reform, Legitimacy and Dilemmas: China's Politics and Society*. Singapore and London: Singapore University Press & World Scientific, pp. 1–20.

Wang Jun. 2006. "*Shixi dangdai Zhongguo de wangluo minzu zhuyi*" ("A Preliminary Analysis of Internet Nationalism in Contemporary China"), *Shijie jingji yu zhengzhi (World Economy and Politics)*, No. 2, pp. 1–13.

Wang, Shaoguang and Hu Angang. 1993. *Zhongguo guojia nengli baogao (A Report on State Capacity in China)*, Shenyang: Liaoning renmin chubanshe.

Wang, Shaoguang and Hu Angang. 2001. *The Chinese Economy in Crisis: State Capacity and Tax Reform*. Armonk, NY: M. E. Sharpe.

Wang, Xu. 1999. "Mutual Empowerment of State and Society: Its Nature, Conditions, Mechanisms, and Limits." *Comparative Politics*. 31:2, pp. 231–49.

Wang, Yue-Farn. 1993. *China's Science and Technology Policy, 1949–1989*. Aldershot, Hants: Avebury.

Wasserstrom, Jeffrey N. and Elizabeth Perry (eds.). 1994. *Popular Protest and Political Culture in Modern China*. Boulder: Westview Press.

Weber, Max. 1964. *The Theory of Social and Economic Organization*. Translated by A. M. Henderson & Talcott Parsons. New York: The Free Press.

Weigle, Narcia A. and Jim Butterfield. 1992. "Civil Society in Reforming Communist Regimes: The Logic of Emergence." *Comparative Politics* 25:1, pp. 1–23.

White, Gordon (ed.). 1991. *The Chinese State in the Era of Economic Reform: The Road to Crisis*. London: Macmillan.

White, Gordon. 1994. *Market Reforms and the Emergence of Civil Society in Post-Mao China*. Brighton, England: Institute of Development Studies, University of Sussex.

White, Gordon. 1995. *Chinese Trade Unions in the Transition from Socialism: The Emergence of Civil Society or the Road to Corporatism?* Brighton, England: Institute of Development Studies, University of Sussex.

White, Gordon, Jude Howell and Shang Xiaoyuan. 1996. *In Search of Civil Society: Market Reform and Social Change in Contemporary China*. New York: Oxford University Press.

Whitehead, Laurence (ed.). 1996. *The International Dimensions of Democratization:*
Europe and the Americas. New York: Oxford University Press.
Wilhelm, Anthony G. 2000. *Democracy in the Digital Age: Challenges to Political Life in Cyberspace.* New York: Routledge.
Wong, John and Nah Seok Ling. 2001. *China's Emerging New Economy: The Internet and E-Commerce.* London and Singapore: World Scientific and Singapore University Press.
Wong, John and William T. Liu. 1999. *The Mystery of China's Falun Gong: Its Rise and Its Sociological Implications.* London and Singapore: World Scientific & Singapore University Press.
Wong, John and Zheng Yongnian (eds.). 2004. *The SARS Epidemic: Challenges to China's Crisis Management.* Singapore and London: World Scientific.
Wright, Teresa. 2002. "The China Democracy Party and the Politics of Protest in the 1980s–1990s." *The China Quarterly,* 172, pp. 906–26.
Wu Guoguang. 1997. *Zhao Ziyang yu zhengzhi gaige (Political Reform under Zhao Ziyang).* Hong Kong: The Institute of Pacific Century.
Wu Guoguang. 2001. "The Return of Ideology? Struggling to Organize Politics During Socio-Economic Transitions," in John Wong and Zheng Yongnian (eds.). *The Nanxun Legacy and China's Post-Deng Development.* Singapore and London: Singapore University Press and World Scientific, pp. 221–46.
Xiao Gongqin. 2003. "The 'China Democratic Party' Event and Political Trends in Post-Deng China," in Wang Gungwu and Zheng Yongnian (eds.). *Damage Control: The Chinese Communist Party in the Jiang Zemin Era.* Singapore: Eastern Universities Press, pp. 320–49.
Xiao Gongqin. 2003. "The Falun Gong and Its Conflicts with the Chinese Government: A Perspective of Social Transformation," in Wang Gungwu and Zheng Yongnian (eds.). *Damage Control: The Chinese Communist Party in the Jiang Zemin Era.* Singapore: Eastern Universities Press, pp. 64–80.
Xu Liangying. 1999. "Chinese Officialdom's Miraculous and Unique Conception of Human Rights," in Orville Schell and David Shambaugh (eds.). *The China Reader: The Reform Era.* New York: Vintage Books, pp. 419–21.
Yang Taoyuan et al. 2004. "*Suzao daguo wangmin*" ("Creating Netizens in China"), *Liaowang xinwen zhoukan (Outlook News Weekly).* Beijing, February 23, pp. 24–31.
Yang, Andrew Nien-Dzu. 2004. "China's Revolution in Military Affairs: Rattling Mao's Army," in Emily O. Goldman and Thomas G. Mahnken (eds.). *The Information Revolution in Military Affairs in Asia.* New York: Palgrave, pp. 125–38.
Yang, Dali. 1996. *Calamity and Reform in China: State, Rural Society, and Institutional Change since the Great Leap Famine.* Stanford, CA: Stanford University Press.
Yang, Dali. 2004. *Remaking the Chinese Leviathan: Market Transition and the Politics of Governance in China.* Stanford, CA: Stanford University Press.
Yang, Guobin. 2003. "The Internet and Civil Society in China: A Preliminary Assessment." *Journal of Contemporary China,* 12: 36, pp. 453–75.
Yu, Mok Chiu and J. Frank Harrison. 1990. *Voices from Tiananmen Square: Beijing Spring and the Democracy Movement.* New York: Black Rose Books.

202 Yu, Q. Y. 1999. *The Implementation of China's Science and Technology Policy*. Westport, CT: Quorum.

Zang, Xiaowei. 2004. *Elite Dualism and Leadership Selection in China*. New York: RoutledgeCurzon.

Zhang, Junhua. 2003. "Network Convergence and Bureaucratic Turf Wars," in Christopher R. Hughes and Gudrun Wacker (eds.). *China and the Internet: Politics of the Digital Leap Forward*. London and New York: RoutledgeCurzon, pp. 83–101.

Zhao, Dingxin. 2001. *The Power of Tiananmen: State-Society Relations and the 1989 Beijing Student Movement*. Chicago: University of Chicago Press.

Zhao, Yuezhi. 1998. *Media, Market and Democracy in China: Between the Party Line and the Bottom Line*. Urbana and Chicago: University of Illinois Press.

Zheng, Shiping. 2003. "The Age Factor in Chinese Politics," in Wang Gungwu and Zheng Yongnian (eds.). *Damage Control: The Chinese Communist Party in the Jiang Zemin Era*. Singapore and London: Eastern Universities Press, pp. 173–189.

Zheng, Yongnian. 1999. "Political Incrementalism: Political Lessons from China's 20 Years of Reform." *Third World Quarterly*, 20:6, pp. 1157–77.

Zheng, Yongnian. 1999. *Discovering Chinese Nationalism in China: Modernization, Identity, and International Relations*. Cambridge, England: Cambridge University Press.

Zheng, Yongnian. 2000. "Institutionalizing de facto Federalism in Post-Deng China," in Hung-mao Tien and Yun-han Chu (eds.). *China under Jiang Zemin*. Boulder, CO: Lynne Rienner Publishers, pp. 215–32.

Zheng, Yongnian. 2000. "The Politics of Power Succession," in Wang Gungwu and Zheng Yongnian (eds.). *Reform, Legitimacy and Dilemmas: China's Politics and Society*. London and Singapore: World Scientific and Singapore University Press, pp. 23–50.

Zheng, Yongnian. 2002. "State Rebuilding, Popular Protest and Collective Action in China." *Japanese Journal of Political Science*, 3: 1, pp. 45–70.

Zheng, Yongnian. 2002. "Technocratic Leadership, Private Entrepreneurship, and Party Transformation in the Post-Deng Era" in John Wong and Zheng Yongnian (eds.). *China's Post-Jiang Leadership Succession: Problems and Perspectives*. London and Singapore: World Scientific and Singapore University Press, pp. 87–118.

Zheng, Yongnian. 2004. *Globalization and State Transformation in China*. Cambridge, England: Cambridge University Press.

Zheng, Yongnian. 2004. *Will China Become Democratic? Elite, Class and Regime Transition*. London and New York: Eastern Universities Press.

Zheng, Yongnian. 2005. "The New Policy Initiatives in China's 11th 5-Year Plan." *Briefing Series*, Issue 1. China Policy Institute, University of Nottingham, November.

Zheng, Yongnian. 2006. "Explaining the Sources of de facto Federalism in Reform China: Intergovernmental Decentralization, Globalization, and Central-Local Relations." *Japanese Journal of Political Science*, vol. 7, no. 2, pp. 101–26.

Zheng, Yongnian and Lye Liang Fook. 2004. "SARS and China's Political System," in Wong and Zheng (2004), pp. 45–75.

Zheng, Yongnian, Zhengxu Wang and Sow Keat Tok. 2006. "China's National People's Congress 2006: Policy Shifts Amidst Growing Dissatisfaction with Existing Devel-

opment Patterns," *Briefing Series*, Issue 7. China Policy Institute, University of Not-   203
tingham, March.
Zhou Jiang. 2003. "*2002 nian zhongguo chengshi redian wenti diaocha*" (Investigation
of the hot issues in Chinese cities in 2002), in Ru Xin, Lu Xueyi and Li Peilin (eds.).
Shehui lanpishu 2003 nian: Zhongguo shehui xingshi fenxi yu yuce (*Blue Book of
the Chinese Society in 2003: An Analysis and Forecast of Chinese Social Situation*),
Beijing: Shehui kexue wenxian chubanshe, pp. 151–61.
Zhou Runjian, Song Changqing and Cai Yugao. 2006. "*Shangwang shimingzhi 'min-
gcunshiwang' shuizhiguo?*" ("The System of Accessing the Internet by Real Name
Has Ceased to Exist but in Name, Whose Fault Is This?"). The Xinhua News Agency,
May 24, 2006. Available at www.xinhuanet.com. Accessed on May 24, 2006.
Zhu Lilan et al. 1996. *Kejiao xingguo: Zhongguo maixiang ershiyi shiji de zhongda
zhanlue juece* (*To Revitalize the Nation through Science and Education: China's
Important Strategic Decision toward the Twenty-First Century*). Beijing: Zhonggong
zhongyang dangxiao chubanshe.
Zittrain, Jonathan and Benjamin Edelman. 2002. *Empirical Analysis of Internet
Filtering in China*. Harvard Law School. December.

NOTES

PREFACE

1. "Congressman Christopher Smith Statement for Hearing on 'The Internet in China: A Tool for Freedom or Suppression?'" February 15, 2006. Available at www .house.gov/international_ relations/109/smith021506.pdf. Accessed on May 15, 2006.

CHAPTER 1

1. For example, Gili S. Drori, John W. Meyer, Francisco O. Ramirez, and Evan Schofer, eds., *Science in the Modern World Polity: Institutionalization and Globalization* (Stanford, CA: Stanford University Press, 2003).
   2. In his essay published in January 1919, Chen Duxiu, one of the intellectual leaders of the New Culture Movement, gave democracy and science the nicknames "Mr. Democracy" (*de xiansheng*) and "Mr. Science" (*sai xiansheng*) and argued that "only these two gentlemen can save China from the political, moral, academic, and intellectual darkness in which it finds itself." See Chen Duxiu, "Xin qingnian zuian zhi dabianshu" ("*New Youth's* Reply to Charges against the Magazine"), *Xin Qingnian* (*New Youth*), vol. 6, no. 1 (January 15, 1919), pp. 10–11. Cited in Edward X. Gu, "Who Was Mr. Democracy? The May Fourth Discourse of Populist Democracy and the Radicalization of Chinese Intellectuals (1915–1922)," *Modern Asian Studies*, 35: 3 (2001), p. 580. Also, see Merle Goldman and Leo Ou-fan Lee, eds., *An Intellectual History of Modern China* (Cambridge, MA: Harvard University Press, 2002).
   3. For some liberal interpretations of the May Fourth Movement, see Tse-tsung Chow, *The May Fourth Movement: Intellectual Revolution in Modern China* (Cambridge, MA: Harvard University Press, 1960); and Vera Schwarcz, *The Chinese Enlightenment: Intellectuals and the Legacy of the May Fourth Movement of 1919* (Berkeley, CA: The University of California Press, 1986).
   4. For a discussion of Dewey's lectures in China, see John E. Smith, "Pragmatism

206   at Work: Dewey's Lectures in China," *Journal of Chinese Philosophy*, 12 (1985), pp. 231–59.

    5. Jerome B. Grieder, *Hu Shih and the Chinese Renaissance: Liberalism in the Chinese Revolution, 1917–1937* (Cambridge, MA: Harvard University Press, 1970); Grieder, "The Question of 'Politics' in the May Fourth Movement," in Benjamin I. Schwartz, ed., *Reflections on the May Fourth Movement: A Symposium* (Cambridge, MA: Harvard University Press, 1972), pp. 95–101.

    6. Benjamin Schwartz, "Themes in Intellectual History: May Fourth and After," in John K. Fairbank, ed., *The Cambridge History of China: Republican China 1912–1949*, Vol. 12, Part I (Cambridge, MA: Cambridge University Press, 1983), pp. 406–50. On pragmatism and scientism, see Larry Hickman, "Pragmatism, Technology, and Scientism: Are the Methods of the Scientific-Technical Disciplines Relevant to Social Problems?" in Robert Hollinger and David Depew, eds., *Pragmatism: From Progressivism to Postmodernism* (Westport, CT: Praeger, 1995), pp. 72–87; and Michael Eldridge, *Transforming Experience: John Dewey's Cultural Instrumentalism* (Nashville, TN: Vanderbilt University Press, 1988). On Dewey and Confucianism, see David Hall and Roger Ames, *The Democracy of the Dead: Dewey, Confucius, and the Hope for Democracy in China* (Chicago, IL: Open Court Publishing Co., 1999).

    7. For a discussion of this perceptional transformation, see Gu, "Who Was Mr. Democracy?"

    8. For various perceptions on democracy among different scholarly communities in contemporary China, see Baogang He, *The Democratization of China* (London: Routledge, 1996).

    9. On the 1989 pro-democracy movement, see Joseph Fewsmith, *China since Tiananmen: The Politics of Transition* (New York: Cambridge University Press, 2001); Zhang Liang, Andrew J. Nathan, and Perry Link, eds., *The Tiananmen Papers: The Chinese Leadership's Decision to Use Force Against Their Own People — In Their Own Words* (USA: Public Affairs, 2001); Dingxin Zhao, *The Power of Tiananmen: State-Society Relations and the 1989 Beijing Student Movement* (Chicago: University of Chicago Press, 2001); James A. R. Miles, *The Legacy of Tiananmen: China in Disarray* (Ann Arbor: The University of Michigan Press, 1996); Jonathan Unger, ed., *The Pro-Democracy Protests in China: Reports from the Provinces* (Armonk, NY: M. E. Sharpe, 1991); Mok Chiu Yu and J. Frank Harrison, *Voices from Tiananmen Square: Beijing Spring and the Democracy Movement* (New York: Black Rose Books, 1990); and Tony Saich, ed., *The Chinese People's Movement: Perspectives on Spring 1989* (Armonk, NY: M. E. Sharpe, 1990).

    10. For a discussion of the involvement of Chinese scientists in the 1989 pro-democracy movement, see Merle Goldman, *Sowing the Seeds of Democracy in China: Political Reforms in the Deng Xiaoping Era* (Cambridge, MA: Harvard University Press, 1994); and H. Lyman Miller, *Science and Dissent in Post-Mao China: The Politics of Knowledge* (Seattle, WA: University of Washington Press, 1996). For the thoughts of this scientific community, see, for example, Fang Lizhi, *Bringing Down the Great Wall: Writings on Science, Culture, and Democracy in China* (New York: A. A. Knopf, 1990); and Xu Liangying, "Chinese Officialdom's Miraculous and Unique Conception of Human Rights," in Orville Schell and David Shambaugh, eds., *The China Reader: The Reform Era* (New York: Vintage Books, 1999), pp. 419–21.

11. Yongnian Zheng, *Globalization and State Transformation in China* (Cambridge,   207
England: Cambridge University Press, 2004); and Dali Yang, *Remaking the Chinese
Leviathan: Market Transition and the Politics of Governance in China* (Stanford, CA:
Stanford University Press, 2004).

12. Yongnian Zheng, "The New Policy Initiatives in China's 11th 5-Year Plan," Briefing Series, Issue 1, China Policy Institute, University of Nottingham, November 2005;
and Yongnian Zheng, Zhengxu Wang, and Sow Keat Tok, "China's National People's
Congress 2006: Policy Shifts Amidst Growing Dissatisfaction with Existing Development Patterns," *Briefing Series*, Issue 7, China Policy Institute, University of Nottingham, March 2006.

13. Drori, Meyer, Ramirez, and Schofer, *Science in the Modern World Polity*.

14. See discussions in ibid.

15. David Hill and Krishna Sen, "The Internet in Indonesia's New Democracy,"
in Peter Ferdinand, ed., *Internet, Democracy, and Democratization*, 3rd ed. (London:
Frank Cass, 2000), pp. 119–36.

16. Drori, Meyer, Ramirez, and Schofer, *Science in the Modern World Polity*.

17. Q. Y. Yu, *The Implementation of China's Science and Technology Policy* (Westport, CT: Quorum, 1999); Charles Feinstein and Christopher Howe, eds., *Chinese
Technology Transfer in the 1990: Current Experience, Historical Problems, and International Perspectives* (Lynn, NH: Edward Elgar, 1997); Yue-Farn Wang, *China's Science
and Technology Policy, 1949–1989* (Aldershot, Hants: Avebury, 1993); and Tony Saich,
China's Science Policy in the 80s (Manchester, England: Manchester University Press,
1989).

18. Anita Chan, Benedict J. Tria Kerkvliet, and Jonathan Unger, eds., *Transforming
Asian Socialism: China and Vietnam Compared* (Lanham, MD: Rowman & Little-
field, 1999); Timothy Cheek and Tony Saich, eds., *New Perspectives on State Socialism
of China* (Armonk, NY: M. E. Sharpe, 1997); Barrett L. McCormick and Jonathan
Unger, eds., *China after Socialism: In the Footsteps of Eastern Europe or East Asia?*
(Armonk, NY: M. E. Sharpe, 1996); Yan Sun, *The Chinese Reassessment of Socialism
1976–1992* (Princeton, NJ: Princeton University Press, 1995); and Gilbert Rozman, *The
Chinese Debate about Soviet Socialism, 1978–1985* (Princeton, NJ: Princeton University Press, 1987).

19. An incomplete list includes the following: Edward Gu and Merle Goldman,
eds., *Chinese Intellectuals between State and Market* (London: RoutledgeCurzon,
2004); Chien-min Chao and Bruce Dickson, eds., *Remaking the Chinese State: Strategies, Society, and Security* (New York: Routledge, 2001); Gordon White, Jude Howell,
and Shang Xiaoyuan, *In Search of Civil Society: Market Reform and Social Change
in Contemporary China* (New York: Oxford University Press, 1996); Brian Hook, ed.,
The Individual and the State in China (New York: Oxford University Press, 1996); Gordon White, *Chinese Trade Unions in the Transition from Socialism: The Emergence
of Civil Society or the Road to Corporatism?* (Brighton, England: Institute of Development Studies, University of Sussex, 1995); David Goodman and Beverly Hooper,
eds., *China's Quiet Revolution: New Interactions between State and Society* (New York:
St. Martin's Press, 1994); Gordon White, *Market Reforms and the Emergence of Civil
Society in Post-Mao China* (Brighton, England: Institute of Development Studies,
University of Sussex, 1994); Jeffrey N. Wasserstrom and Elizabeth Perry, eds., *Popular*

208   *Protest and Political Culture in Modern China* (Boulder, CO: Westview Press, 1994); and Gordon White, ed., *The Chinese State in the Era of Economic Reform: The Road to Crisis* (London: Macmillan, 1991).

20. For example, Richard P. Suttmeier and Cong Cao, "China's Technical Community: Market Reforms and the Changing Policy Cultures of Science," in Gu and Goldman, eds., *Chinese Intellectuals between State and Market*, pp. 138–57. For a discussion on how key leaders in the scientific community influenced decision making in the 1980s, see Carol Lee Hamrin, *China and the Challenge of the Future: Changing Political Patterns* (Boulder, CO: Westview Press, 1990).

21. Jean Meynaud, *Technocracy* (New York: Free Press, 1969).

22. Daniel Bell, *The Coming of Post-Industrial Society: A Venture in Social Forecasting* (New York: Basic Books, 1973).

23. Meynaud, *Technocracy*.

24. Cheng Li, *China's Leaders: The New Generation* (Lanham, MD: Rowman & Littlefield Publishers, 2001); and Hong Yung Lee, *From Revolutionary Cadres to Party Technocrats in Socialist China* (Berkeley, CA: University of California Press, 1991).

25. Lee, *From Revolutionary Cadres to Party Technocrats*, p. 404.

26. On scientific decision making, see Hamrin, *China and the Challenge of the Future*. On elite recruitment, see Li, *China's Leaders*; Lee, *From Revolutionary Cadres to Party Technocrats*; and Xiaowei Zang, *Elite Dualism and Leadership Selection in China* (New York: RoutledgeCurzon, 2004). On cadre management, see Kjeld Erik Brødsgaard, "Institutional Reform and the Bianzhi System in China," *The China Quarterly*, 170 (June 2002), pp. 79–104; and Brødsgaard, "Management of Party Cadres in China," in Kjeld Erik Brødsgaard and Zheng Yongnian, eds., *Bringing the Party Back In: How China Is Governed* (Singapore, London, and New York: Eastern Universities Press, 2004), pp. 57–91.

27. Zheng Yongnian, "Technocratic Leadership, Private Entrepreneurship, and Party Transformation in the Post-Deng Era," John Wong and Zheng Yongnian, eds., *China's Post-Jiang Leadership Succession: Problems and Perspectives* (London and Singapore: World Scientific and Singapore University Press, 2002), pp. 87–118.

28. This body of the literature is growing, and an incomplete list includes the following: Hugo de Burgh, *The Chinese Journalist: Mediating Information in the World's Most Populous Country* (London and New York: RoutledgeCurzon, 2003); Chin-Chuan Lee, ed., *Chinese Media, Global Contexts* (London: RoutledgeCurzon, 2003); Stephanie Hemelryk Donald, Michael Keane, and Yin Hong, eds., *Media in China: Consumption, Content and Crisis* (London: RoutledgeCurzon, 2002); Chin-Chuan Lee, ed., *Power, Money, and Media: Communication Patterns and Bureaucratic Control in Cultural China* (Evanston, IL: Northwestern University Press, 2000); Daniel C. Lynch, *After the Propaganda State: Media, Politics, and "Thought Work" in Reformed China* (Stanford, CA: Stanford University Press, 1999); Yuezhi Zhao, *Media, Market and Democracy in China: Between the Party Line and the Bottom Line* (Urbana and Chicago: University of Illinois Press, 1998); and Chin-Chuan Lee, ed., *China's Media, Media's China* (Boulder, CO: Westview, 1994).

29. Lawrence Lessig, *Code and Other Laws of Cyberspace* (New York: Basic Books, 1999).

30. Ibid., p. 57.

31. Ibid., p. 60.

32. Ibid., p. 97.

33. Cited in Gudrun Wacker, "The Internet and Censorship in China," in Christopher R. Hughes and Gudrun Wacker, eds., *China and the Internet: Politics of the Digital Leap Forward* (London: RoutledgeCurzon, 2003), pp. 58–82.

34. Michel Foucault, *Discipline and Punish: The Birth of the Prison* (London: Penguin, 1991). On Foucault, see Colin Jones and Roy Porter, eds., *Reassessing Foucault: Power, Medicine and the Body* (London: Routledge, 1994); and Graham Burchell, Colin Gordon, and Peter Miller, eds., *The Foucault Effect: Studies in Governmentality* (Chicago: University of Chicago Press, 1991).

35. Shanthi Kalathil and Taylor C. Boas, *Open Networks, Closed Regimes: The Impact of the Internet on Authoritarian Rule* (Washington, D.C.: Carnegie Endowment for International Peace, 2003), p. 136.

36. Ibid., p. 136.

37. Wacker, "The Internet and Censorship in China."

38. Derek Bambauer, Ronald J. Deibert, John G. Palfrey Jr., Rafal Rohozinski, Nart Villeneuve, and Jonathan Zittrain, *Internet Filtering in China in 2004–2005: A Country Study*, Berkman Center for Internet and Society at Harvard Law School, Research Publication No. 2005-10. Available at SSRN: *http://ssrn.com/abstract=706681*. Accessed on May 15, 2006.

39. George W. Bush, "Remarks by the President at the 20th Anniversary of the National Endowment for Democracy," October 16, 2003, Washington, D.C.: The National Endowment of Democracy.

40. Geoffry Taubman, "A Not-So World Wide Web: The Internet, China, and the Challenges to Nondemocratic Rule," *Political Communication*, 15 (1998), pp. 255–72; Kathleen Harford, "Cyberspace with Chinese Characteristics," *Current History* (September 2000), pp. 255–62; and Nina Hachigian, "China's Cyber-Strategy," *Foreign Affairs*, 80: 2 (March/April 2001), pp. 118–33.

41. Michael S. Chase and James C. Mulvenon, *You've Got Dissent! Chinese Dissident Use of the Internet and Beijing's Counter-Strategies* (Santa Monica, CA: Rand, 2002).

42. Eric Harwit and Duncan Clark, "Shaping the Internet in China: Evolution of Political Control over Network Infrastructure and Content," *Asian Survey* xli: 3 (May/June 2001), pp. 377–408.

43. Guobin Yang, "The Internet and Civil Society in China: A Preliminary Assessment," *Journal of Contemporary China*, 12: 36 (August 2003), pp. 453–75.

44. For example, Peter B. Evans, Dietrich Rueschemeyer, and Theda Skocpol, eds., *Bringing the State Back In* (New York: Cambridge University Press, 1985).

45. For example, Joel S. Migdal, *Strong Societies and Weak States: State-Society Relations and State Capabilities in the Third World* (Princeton, NJ: Princeton University Press, 1988); and Atul Kohli, ed., *The State and Development in the Third World* (Princeton, NJ: Princeton University Press, 1986).

46. For example, Wang Shaoguang and Hu Angang, *The Chinese Economy in Crisis: State Capacity and Tax Reform* (Armonk, NY: M. E. Sharpe, 2001). The original

210 Chinese version was published in 1993 when the Chinese government began to recentralize its fiscal power; see Wang Shaoguang and Hu Angang, *Zhongguo guojia nengli baogao* (*A Report on State Capacity in China*) (Shenyang: Liaoning renmin chubanshe, 1993). For a discussion of statism in China, see Yongnian Zheng, *Discovering Chinese Nationalism in China: Modernization, Identity, and International Relations* (Cambridge, England: Cambridge University Press, 1999), pp. 38–44.

47. For example, Joel S. Migdal, Atul Kohli, and Vivienne Shue, eds., *State Power and Social Forces: Domination and Transformation in the Third World* (New York: Cambridge University Press, 1994); Peter Evans, *Embedded Autonomy: States and Industrial Transformation* (Princeton, NJ: Princeton University Press, 1995); Joel S. Migdal, *State in Society: Studying How States and Societies Transform and Constitute One Another* (New York: Cambridge University Press, 2001).

48. Xu Wang, "Mutual Empowerment of State and Society: Its Nature, Conditions, Mechanisms, and Limits," *Comparative Politics*, vol. 31, no. 2 (1999), p. 232.

49. Adam Przeworski et al., *Sustainable Democracy* (New York: Cambridge University Press, 1995).

50. Migdal, Kohli, and Shue, "Introduction," in Migdal, Kohli, and Shue, eds., *State Power and Social Forces*, p. 2.

51. In this study, the "state" refers to the "party-state" given the fact that China is a one-party state. For a description of China's political system, see Kenneth Lieberthal, *Governing China: From Revolution through Reform* (New York: W.W. Norton & Company, INC, 1995).

CHAPTER 2

1. Gili S. Drori, John W. Meyer, Francisco O. Ramirez, and Evan Schofer, *Science in the Modern World Polity: Institutionalization and Globalization* (Stanford, CA: Stanford University Press, 2003).

2. Ibid., p. 268.

3. Ibid., p. 278.

4. Bertrand Badie, *The Imported State: The Westernization of the Political Order*, translated by Claudia Royal (Stanford, CA: Stanford University Press, 2000), pp. 1–2.

5. Stephen D. Krasner, *Sovereignty: Organized Hypocrisy* (Princeton, NJ: Princeton University Press, 1999); and David Held and Anthony McGrew, David Goldblatt and Jonathan Perraton, *Global Transformation: Politics, Economics and Culture* (Stanford, CA: Stanford University Press, 1999).

6. John W. Meyer, John Boli, George M. Thomas, and Francisco O. Ramirez, "World Society and the Nation-State," in Frank J. Lechner and John Boli, eds., *The Globalization Reader* (Blackwell Publishers, 2000), pp. 84–92.

7. Ibid.

8. Liu Shu-hsien, "Confucian Ideals and the Real World: A Critical Review of Contemporary Neo-Confucian Thought," in Tu Wei-ming, ed., *Confucian Traditions in East Asian Modernity: Moral Education and Economic Culture in Japan and the Four Mini-Dragons* (Cambridge, MA: Harvard University Press, 1996), p. 100.

9. Karl Bunger, "The Chinese State between Yesterday and Tomorrow," in Stuart R.　211
Schram, ed., *The Scope of State Power in China* (Hong Kong: The Chinese University
Press, 1985), p. xvii.

10. For a study of such a mind-set in Japan, see Richard Samuels, *Rich Nation,
Strong Army: National Security and the Technological Transformation of Japan* (Ithaca,
NY: Cornell University Press, 1994).

11. Jacques Gernet, "Introduction," in Schram, ed., *The Scope of State Power in
China*, p. xxxii.

12. Bunger, "The Chinese State," p. xxii.

13. Edward McCord, *The Power of the Gun: The Emergence of Modern Chinese
Warlordism* (Berkeley, CA: University of California Press, 1993).

14. Julia Strauss, *Strong Institutions in Weak Polities: State Building in Republican
China, 1927–1940* (Oxford: Clarendon Press, 1998).

15. Cong Cao, *China's Scientific Elite* (London and New York: RoutledgeCurzon,
2004), p.26.

16. Arif Dirlik, "The Ideological Foundations of the New Life Movement: A Study
in Counterrevolution," *Journal of Asian Study*, 34: 4 (August 1975), pp. 945–80; and
Samuel C. Chu, "The New Life Movement, 1934–1937," in John E. Lane, ed., *Researches in the Social Sciences on China* (The East Asian Institute of Columbia University, 1957), pp. 1–19.

17. Evan A. Feigenbaum, *China's Techno-Warriors: National Security and Strategic
Competition from the Nuclear to the Information Age* (Stanford, CA: Stanford University Press, 2003), p. 14.

18. Ibid.

19. Dali Yang, *Calamity and Reform in China: State, Rural Society, and Institutional
Change since the Great Leap Famine* (Stanford, CA: Stanford University Press, 1996).

20. Richard P. Suttmeier and Yao Xiangkui, *China's Post-WTO Technology Policy:
Standards, Software, and the Changing Nature of Techno-Nationalism*, NBR Special
Report, no. 7 (Seattle, Washington: The National Bureau of Asian Research, May 2004),
p. 13. Also see Gu Shulin, *China's Industrial Technology: Market Reform and Organizational Change* (London: Routledge, 1999).

21. Alan P. L. Liu, *Communications and National Integration in Communist China*
(Berkeley, CA: University of California Press, 1971).

22. Adam Segal, *Digital Dragon: High-Technology Enterprises in China* (Ithaca, NY:
Cornell University Press, 2003); and Qiwen Lu, *China's Leap into the Information Age:
Innovation and Organization in the Computer Industry* (New York: Oxford University
Press, 2000).

23. Max Weber, *The Theory of Social and Economic Organization*. Translated by
A. M. Henderson & Talcott Parsons (New York: The Free Press, 1964).

24. Deng Xiaoping, "*Women ba gaige dangzuo yizhong geming*" ("We Regard the
Reform as a Revolution," October 10, 1984), and "*Gaige shi Zhongguo de dierci geming*"
("The Reform Is China's Second Revolution," March 28, 1985), in Deng, *Deng Xiaoping wenxuan* (Selected Works of Deng Xiaoping), vol. 3 (Beijing: Renmin chubanshe,
1993), pp. 81–82, and 113–14.

25. For a discussion on China's reform process, see Barry Naughton, *Growing Out*

212   *of the Plan: Chinese Economic Reform 1978–1993* (New York: Cambridge University Press, 1995).

26. Carol Lee Hamrin, *China and the Challenge of the Future: Changing Political Patterns* (Boulder, CO: Westview Press, 1990).

27. Naughton, *Growing Out of the Plan.*

28. Many of Deng's speeches touched on the issue of political reform and democratization. For examples, see Deng Xiaoping, "*Zhengzhi shang fazhan minzhu, jingji shang shixing gaige*" ("To Develop Democracy in Politics, and to Implement Reform in Economics," April 15, 1985); "*Guanyu zhengzhi tizhi gaige wenti*" ("On the Problems of Reforming the Political System," September–November 1986); and "*Zenyang pingjie yige guojia de zhengzhi tizhi*" ("How a Country's Political System Should Be Evaluated," March 27, 1987). All in Deng, *Deng Xiaoping wenxuan* (Selected Works of Deng Xiaoping), vol. 3 (Beijing: Renmin chubanshe, 1993), pp. 115–18, 176–80, and 213–14, respectively.

29. This period of history is detailed by Wu Guoguang, who served Zhao Ziyang during that period. See Wu Guoguang, *Zhao Ziyang yu zhengzhi gaige* (Political Reform under Zhao Ziyang) (Hong Kong: The Institute of Pacific Century, 1997).

30. Merle Goldman, *Sowing the Seeds of Democracy in China: Political Reform in the Deng Xiaoping Era* (Cambridge, MA: Harvard University Press, 1994).

31. For a discussion on changing bases of the political legitimacy of the Chinese state, see Wang Gungwu and Zheng Yongnian, "Introduction: Reform, Legitimacy, and Dilemmas," in Wang Gungwu and Zheng Yongnian, eds., *Reform, Legitimacy and Dilemmas: China's Politics and Society* (Singapore and London: Singapore University Press & World Scientific, 2000), pp. 1–20.

32. Xiudian Dai, "ICTs in China's Development Strategy," in Christopher R. Hughes and Gudrun Wacker, eds., *China and the Internet: Politics of the Digital Leap Forward* (London and New York: RoutledgeCurzon, 2003), pp.8–29.

33. Zhu Lilan et al., *Kejiao xingguo: Zhongguo maixiang ershiyi shiji de zhongda zhanlue juece* (To Revitalize the Nation through Science and Education: China's Important Strategic Decision toward the Twenty-first Century) (Beijing: Zhonggong zhongyang dangxiao chubanshe, 1996). For a discussion of this strategy, see Cong Cao, "Strengthening China through Science and Education: China's Development Strategy toward the Twenty-First Century," *Issues and Studies*, 38: 3 (September 2002), pp. 122–49.

34. "*Science* Interview: China's Leader Commits to Basic Research, Global Science," *Science* 288 (June 16, 2000): 1950–53.

35. Jiang's emphasis on the development of information technology was also due to his personal experience and his extensive knowledge on information technology. He was educated at Jiaotong University in Shanghai, majoring in electrical engineering. In the 1980s, he served as the Minister of Electronics Industry.

36. The impact of information technology on China's military goes beyond the scope of this study. For discussions in this regard, see Ji You, "Learning and Catching Up: China's Revolution in Military Affairs Initiative," and Andrew Nien-Dzu Yang, "China's Revolution in Military Affairs: Rattling Mao's Army," both in Emily O. Goldman and Thomas G. Mahnken, eds., *The Information Revolution in Military Affairs in Asia* (New York: Palgrave, 2004), pp. 97–124, 125–38, respectively.

37. Suttmeier and Yao, *China's Post-WTO Technology Policy*, p. 3. 213

38. For a discussion on the connections between globalism and nationalism, see Yongnian Zheng, *Globalization and State Transformation in China* (Cambridge, England: Cambridge University Press, 2004).

39. Ding Lu and Chee Kong Wong, *China's Telecommunications Market: Entering a New Competitive Age* (Cheltenham, UK: Edward Elgar, 2003), p. 2.

40. Cong Cao, "Zhongguancun Aspiring to Become China's Silicon Valley," *EAI Background Brief*, no. 152, East Asian Institute, National University of Singapore, April 24, 2003.

41. John Wong and Nah Seok Ling, *China's Emerging New Economy: The Internet and E-Commerce* (London and Singapore: World Scientific and Singapore University Press, 2001).

42. Segal, *Digital Dragon*.

43. *People's Daily*, "Zhongguo hulianwang: meili shuzi di beihou" ("China's Internet: Behind the Wonderful Figures"), January 16, 2004.

44. Lu and Wong, *China's Telecommunications Market*.

45. Shanthi Kalathil and Taylor C. Boas, *Open Networks, Closed Regimes: The Impact of the Internet on Authoritarian Rule* (Washington, D.C.: Carnegie Endowment for International Peace, 2003).

46. *People's Daily*, "Zhongguo hulianwang: meili shuzi de beihou."

47. China Internet Network Information Center (CNNIC), *The Statistical Report of Internet Development in China* (Beijing: CNNIC, January 2004), p. 57.

48. The survey was conducted by face-to-face interviews with 1,019 top management executives and entrepreneurs between September and October 2002 in three major Chinese cities — Beijing, Guangzhou, and Shanghai. See *Far Eastern Economic Review, China's Elite 5: A Study of Affluent and Influential People in China* (Hong Kong, 2003).

49. Zheng Yongnian, *Will China Become Democratic? Elite, Class and Regime Transition* (London and New York: Eastern Universities Press, 2004), Part III.

50. Karl W. Deutsch, *The Nerves of Government: Models of Political Communication and Control*, 2nd ed. (New York: Free Press, 1966), p. 82.

51. Kalathil and Boas, *Open Networks, Closed Regimes*.

52. Daniel C. Lynch, *After the Propaganda State: Media, Politics, and "Thought Work" in Reformed China* (Stanford, CA: Stanford University Press, 1999).

53. The Xinhua News Agency, "Zhongyang lingdao gaodu zhongshi wangluo yulun, minyi huiru Zhongnanhai" ("Central leaders Appreciate Internet Discussions, and Public Opinions Are Channeled into Zhongnanhai"), April 10, 2006.

54. The survey was sponsored by a foreign foundation and conducted by the Chinese Academy of Social Sciences. *Renmin ribao*, September 28, 2003, p. 1.

55. Guo Liang, *Surveying Internet Usage and Impact in Five Chinese Cities* (Beijing: Research Center for Social Development, Chinese Academy of Social Sciences, 2005).

56. Ning Zhaoxin, *Understanding Individual Resistance to Information Technology in E-Government* (Singapore: Department of Political Science, National University of Singapore, master's thesis, 2003).

57. Lu and Wong, *China's Telecommunications Market*.

58. China Internet Network Information Center, *Zhongguo hulian wangluo nianjian 2002* (China Yearbook of Internet Network, 2002), 2002, Beijing, p. 112.

59. China Internet Network Information Center, *Zhongguo hulian wangluo nianjian 2002* (China Yearbook of Internet Network, 2002), 2002, Beijing, p. 92.

60. Kalathil and Boas, *Open Networks, Closed Regimes*.

61. Lu and Wong, *China's Telecommunications Market*, p. 109.

62. Sidney Tarrow, *Power in Movement: Social Movements, Collective Action and Politics* (New York: Cambridge University Press, 1994), pp. 3–4.

63. For example, Charles Bright and Susan Harding, eds., *Statemaking and Social Movements: Essays in History and Theory* (Ann Arbor: The University of Michigan Press, 1984).

64. Tarrow, *Power in Movement*, p. 62.

65. Charles Tilly, *From Mobilization to Revolution* (Reading, MA: Addison-Wesley Publishing Co., 1978); Tarrow, *Struggling to Reform: Social Movements and Policy Change during Cycles of Protest*. Western Societies Program Occasional Paper No. 15 (Ithaca, NY: New York Center for International Studies, Cornell University, 1983); Tarrow, *Struggle, Politics, and Reform: Collective Action, Social Movements, and Cycles of Protest*, Cornell Studies in International Affairs, Western Societies Papers, No. 21 (Ithaca, NY: 1991); and Doug McAdam, *Political Process and the Development of Black Insurgency, 1930–1970* (Chicago: University of Chicago Press, 1982).

66. Bright and Harding, "Processes of Statemaking and Popular Protest," in Bright and Harding, eds., *Statemaking and Social Movements*, p. 3.

67. Ibid., pp. 3–4. Also see a more recent study: Joel S. Migdal, Atul Kohli, and Vivienne Shue, *State Power and Social Forces: Domination and Transformation in the Third World* (New York: Cambridge University Press, 1994).

68. Bright and Harding, "Processes of Statemaking and Popular Protest," in Bright and Harding, eds., *Statemaking and Social Movements*, p. 4.

69. Ibid., p. 10.

70. Ibid., p. 4.

71. Ibid., p. 10.

72. Tarrow, "States and Opportunities: The Political Structuring of Social Movement," in Doug McAdam, John D. McCarthy, and Mayer N. Zald, eds., *Comparative Perspectives on Social Movements: Political Opportunities, Mobilizing Structures, and Cultural Framings* (Cambridge, England: Cambridge University Press, 1996), pp. 48–49.

73. Ibid., p. 49.

74. Tarrow, *Power in Movement*, p. 66.

75. Charles Tilly, "Social Movements and National Politics," in Bright and Harding, eds., *Statemaking and Social Movements*, pp. 297–317; Tilly, *From Mobilization to Revolution*; and Tilly, *Coercion, Capital, and European States, A.D. 990–1992* (Cambridge, MA: Basil Blackwell, 1990).

76. For example, Yongnian Zheng, "State Rebuilding, Popular Protest and Collective Action in China," *Japanese Journal of Political Science*, 3: 1 (May 2002), pp. 45–70. Also see Elizabeth J. Perry and Mark Selden, eds., *Chinese Society: Change, Conflict and Resistance* (New York: Routledge, 2000).

77. It has to be pointed out that the figure of 29 million living below the poverty

line was slightly higher than the figure of 28.2 million in 2002. This is the first time the number of needy people increased since China embarked on its reform and open door policy in the late 1970s. See "Number of Indigent Chinese Rises by 800,000 in 2003," The Xinhua News Agency, 20 July 2004, and "Rise in Country's Poor Calls for Attention," *China Daily*, 20 July 2004.

78. Some Chinese scholars such as An Chen have argued that China's entrepreneurial class and other middle classes that have benefited most from the reform and open door policy see it in their continued interest to work closely with existing political leaders to ensure that they are able to continue to reap economic benefits. The entrepreneurial class and other middle classes are generally distrustful of the lower classes because there is a fear that if the lower classes are allowed a greater say in the political process, the economic interests of the higher classes would be jeopardized. Therefore, the entrepreneurial class and other middle classes, unlike their counterparts in the West, are not really supportive of greater democratization in the country. See An Chen, "Capitalist Development, Entrepreneurial Class, and Democratization in China," *Political Science Quarterly*, vol. 117, no. 3, Fall 2002, pp. 401–22.

79. Zhou Jiang, "2002 nian zhongguo chengshi redian wenti diaocha" (Investigation of the Hot Issues in Chinese Cities in 2002), in Ru Xin, Lu Xueyi, and Li Peilin, eds., *Shehui lanpishu 2003 nian: Zhongguo shehui xingshi fenxi yu yuce* (Blue Book of the Chinese Society in 2003: An Analysis and Forecast of the Chinese Social Situation), Beijing: Shehui kexue wenxian chubanshe, 2003, p. 160.

80. Zheng, "State Rebuilding, Popular Protest and Collective Action in China."

81. "Social Development Draws Attention from Chinese Government," The Xinhua News Agency, 1 March 2004. See also "Urgent—China Working to Narrow Growing Income Gaps—Premier," The Xinhua News Agency, 15 March 2004.

82. Johann Graf Lambsdorff, "Corruption Perceptions Index 2003," pp. 282–87, in *Global Corruption Report 2004*, available at http://www.globalcorruptionreport.org/index.shtml.

83. The annual survey reports are organized by the Institute of Sociology of the Chinese Academy of Social Sciences. See its annual report: Ru Xin et al., eds., *Shehui lanpishu: Zhongguo shehui xingshi fenxi yu yuce* (Social Bluebook: Analysis and Forecast of the Social Situation in China), various issues. Beijing: Shehui kexue wenxian chubanshe.

84. Wang Chunguang, "1997–1998 nian: Zhongguo shehui wending zhuangkuang de diaocha" ("A Survey on Social Stability in 1997–1998"), in Ru Xin et al., eds., *Shehui lanpishu 1998* (Social Bluebook). Beijing: Shehui kexue wenxian chubanshe, 1998, p. 127.

85. Borge Bakken, "State Capacity and Social Control in China," in Brødsgaard and Young, eds., *State Capacity*, pp. 185–202.

86. Sidney Tarrow, *Power in Movement: Social Movements and Contentious Politics*, Second Edition (New York: Cambridge University Press, 1998), p. 43.

CHAPTER 3

1. On the reform of China's telecommunications sector, see Ding Lu and Chee Kong Wong, *China's Telecommunications Market: Entering a New Competitive Age*

(Cheltenham, UK: Edward Elgar, 2003); Milton Mueller and Tan Zixiang, *China in the Information Age: Telecommunications and the Dilemmas of Reform* (Westport, CT: Praeger Publishers, 1997); and Paul S. N. Lee, ed., *Telecommunications and Development in China* (Cresskill, NJ: Hampton Press, 1997).

2. On fragmented authoritarianism in the Chinese political and economic system, see Kenneth Lieberthal and David M. Lampton, eds., *Bureaucracy, Politics, and Policy Making in Post-Mao China* (Berkeley, CA: University of California Press, 1991); Kenneth Lieberthal and Michel Oksenberg, *Policy Making in China: Leaders, Structures, and Processes* (Princeton, NJ: Princeton University Press, 1988); and Audrey Donnithorne, "China's Cellular Economy: Some Economic Trends since the Cultural Revolution," *China Quarterly*, 52 (October–December 1972), pp. 605–19.

3. Yongnian Zheng, *Globalization and State Transformation in China* (Cambridge, England: Cambridge University Press, 2004), Chapter 5.

4. *China Online News*, "Wu Said China ISPs, ICPs Regulated Separately," December 17, 1999, http://www.chinaonline.com. Cited in Lu and Wong, *China's Telecommunications Market*, pp. 55–6.

5. Lu and Wong, *China's Telecommunications Market*.

6. Ibid. Also see Junhua Zhang, "Network Convergence and Bureaucratic Turf Wars," in Hughes and Wacker, eds., *China and the Internet*, pp. 83–101. The origins of the SARFT go back to 1954, when the Administration of Broadcasting Affairs was created as an institution responsible for governance of the voice medium. In 1987, the organization became the Ministry of Radio, Film, and TV. After restructuring in 1998, it was reincarnated as the SARFT.

7. Worth elaborating on here is the NCNA, which is also known as the Xinhua News Agency. Xinhua is the state news agency of China and an authoritative source of information on various issues. Very often, Xinhua is the channel through which the CCP or government announces important policies and key decisions. Other media channels often have to reproduce in full what is already carried by Xinhua.

8. Hugo de Burgh, *The Chinese Journalist: Mediating Information in the World's Most Populous Country* (London and New York: RoutledgeCurzon, 2003), pp. 19–21.

9. *Ming pao*, "Shiliuda qian yue shuaixian qingwang" ("Prior to 16th Party Congress, Guangdong Takes the Lead to Clean the Web"), Hong Kong, May 3, 2002.

10. For a discussion of the concept *xitong* in China's political system, see Kenneth Lieberthal, *Governing China: From Revolution through Reform* (New York: W. W. Norton & Company, Inc., 1995), Chapter 7.

11. *Ming pao*, "Chuanmei biancai jinqu neirong" ("Media Editing and Usage of Taboo Subjects"), June 21, 2002.

12. For a discussion of *lingdao xiaozu*, see Taeho Kim, "Leading Small Groups: Managing All under Heaven," in David M. Finkelstein and Maryanne Kivlehan, eds., *China's Leadership in the 21st Century: The Rise of the Fourth Generation* (Armonk, New York: M. E. Sharpe, 2003), pp. 121–39.

13. Article 6, The Administrative Provisions on Secrecy of Computer Information Systems.

14. Article 2, The State Secrecy Law.

15. Article 6, The Administrative Provisions on Secrecy of Computer Information Systems.

16. The State Council Information Office and the Ministry of Information Industry, *Rules on the Administration of Internet News Information Services*, Beijing: The Xinhua News Agency, September 25, 2005.

17. Article 6(1), The Interim Provisions on the Administration of International Wiring of Computer Information Networks.

18. Article 2, The Rules for the Administration of International Wiring Gateway for Inbound and Outbound Computer Information.

19. *Lianhe Zaobao* (Singapore), December 6, 1998.

20. Jonathan Zittrain and Benjamin Edelman, *Empirical Analysis of Internet Filtering in China*, Harvard Law School, December 2002.

21. Derek Bambauer, Ronald J. Deibert, John G. Palfrey Jr., Rafal Rohozinski, Nart Villeneuve, and Jonathan Zittrain, *Internet Filtering in China in 2004–2005: A Country Study*, Berkman Center for Internet and Society at Harvard Law School, Research Publication No. 2005-10. Available at SSRN: http://ssrn.com/abstract=706681. Accessed on May 15, 2006.

22. "Chinese Internet Service Providers Pledge 'Self-Discipline,'" Xinhua/BBC, December 12, 2003.

23. Ethan Gutmann, *Losing the New China: A Story of American Commerce, Desire, and Betrayal* (New York: Encounter Books, 2004).

24. Kevin Poulsen, "Critics Squeeze Cisco over China," *Wired* News, July 29, 2005, at http://www.wired.com. Accessed on May 17, 2006.

25. Peter S. Goodman, "Yahoo Says It Gave China Internet Data," *Washington Post*, September 11, 2005.

26. Associated Press, "Microsoft Censors Chinese Blogs," *Wired* News, June 13, 2005, at http://www.wired.com. Accessed on May 17, 2006.

27. Allison Linn, "Microsoft Amends Policies Regarding Blog Shutdowns," The Associated Press, February 5, 2006.

28. Esther Pan, "China's New Internet Restrictions," Council on Foreign Relations, September 27, 2005. Available at http://www.cfr.org/publication/8913/chinas_new_internet_restrictions.html. Accessed on May 24, 2006.

29. Zhou Runjian, Song Changqing, and Cai Yugao, "Shangwang shimingzhi 'mingcunshiwang' shuizhiguo?" ("The System of Accessing the Internet by Real Name Has Ceased to Exist but in Name. Whose Fault Is This?"), The Xinhua News Agency, May 24, 2006. Available at www.xinhuanet.com. Accessed on May 24, 2006.

30. *The Economist*, "The Party, the People and the Power of Cyber-talk," *Special Report: China and the Internet*, April 29, 2006, p. 30.

CHAPTER 4

1. For example, Cynthia J. Alexander and Leslie A. Pal, eds., *Digital Democracy: Policy and Politics in the Wired World* (Toronto: Oxford University Press, 1998); Barry N. Hague and Brian D. Loader, eds., *Digital Democracy: Discourse and Decision Making in the Information Age* (London: Routledge, 1999); Jens Hoff, Ivan Horrocks, and Pieter Tops, eds., *Democratic Governance and New Technology: Technologically Mediated Innovations in Political Practice in Western Europe* (London: Routledge, 2000), esp. Christine Bellamy, "Modelling Electronic Democracy: Towards Democratic Discourses for

218   an Information Age," pp. 33–54; Peter Ferdinand, ed., *The Internet, Democracy and Democratization* (London: Frank Cass, 2000), esp. Beth Simone Noveck, "Paradoxical Partners: Electronic Communication and Electronic Democracy," pp. 18–35; Brian D. Loader, ed., *The Governance of Cyberspace: Politics, Technology and Global Restructuring* (London: Routledge, 1997), esp. Ralph Schroeder, "Virtual Worlds and the Social Realities of Cyberspace," pp. 97–110; Roza Tsagarousianou, Damian Tambini, and Cathy Bryan eds., *Cyberdemocracy: Technology, Cities, and Civic Networks* (London: Routledge, 1998).

2. Larry Diamond, "The Globalization of Democracy: Trends, Types, Causes, and Prospects," in Robert Slater, Barry M. Schutz, and Steven R. Dorr, *Global Transformation and the Third World* (Boulder, CO: Lynn Rienner, 1992); Philippe C. Schmitter, "The Influence to the International Context upon the Choice of National Institutions and Policies in Neo-Democracies," in Laurence Whitehead, ed., *The International Dimensions of Democratization: Europe and the Americas* (New York: Oxford University Press, 1996); Juan J. Linz and Alfred Stephan, *Problems of Democratic Transition and Consolidation: Southern Europe, South America, and Post-Communist Europe* (Baltimore, MD: Johns Hopkins University Press, 1996).

3. Samuel P. Huntington, *The Third Wave: Democratization in the Late Twentieth Century* (Norman, OK: University of Oklahoma Press, 1991).

4. David T. Hill and Krishna Sen, "The Internet in Indonesia's New Democracy," *Democratization*, vol. 7, no. 1 (Spring 2000), pp. 119–36.

5. For example, Michael S. Chase and James Mulvenon, *You've Got Dissent! Chinese Dissident Use of the Internet and Beijing's Counter-Strategies* (Santa Monica, CA: Rand, 2002).

6. Christopher R. Kedzie, *Communication and Democracy: Coincident Revolutions and the Emergent Dictator's Dilemma* (Santa Monica, CA: Rand, 1997).

7. Pippa Norris, *Digital Divide: Civic Engagement, Information Poverty, and the Internet Worldwide* (New York: Cambridge University Press, 2001).

8. For example, Shanthi Kalathil and Taylor C. Boas, *Open Networks, Closed Regimes: The Impact of the Internet on Authoritarian Rule* (Washington, D.C.: Carnegie Endowment for International Peace, 2003); Eric Harwit and Duncan Clark, "Shaping the Internet in China: Evolution of Political Control over Network Infrastructure and Content," *Asian Survey*, 41:3 (May/June, 2001); Nina Hachigian, "China's Cyber-Strategy," *Foreign Affairs*, 80: 2 (March/April 2001), pp. 118–33.

9. Chase and Mulvenon, *You've Got Dissent!*

10. Seymour Martin Lipset, "Some Social Requisites of Democracy: Economic Development and Political Legitimacy," *American Political Science Review*, 53 (1959), pp. 69–105.

11. Robert A. Dahl, *Democracy and Its Critics* (New Haven, CT: Yale University Press, 1989).

12. Benjamin Barber, *Strong Democracy: Participatory Politics for a New Age* (Berkeley, CA: University of California Press, 1984); and Barber, "Three Scenarios for the Future of Technology and Strong Democracy," *Political Science Quarterly*, 113 (4), 1998, pp. 573–89.

13. For example, Amitai Etzioni, *The Spirit of Community: Rights, Responsibilities, and the Communitarian Agenda* (New York: Crown Publishers, 1993).

14. For example, Angus Campbell, Philip Converse, Warren E. Miller, and Donald E. Stokes, *The American Voter* (New York: Wiley, 1960).

15. Andrew Gelman and Gary King, "Why Are American Presidential Election Campaign Polls So Variable When Votes Are So Predictable?" *British Journal of Political Science*, 23 (1993), pp. 409–51.

16. Pippa Norris, "The Impact of Television on Civic Malaise," in Susan J. Pharr and Robert D. Putnam, eds., *Disaffected Democracies: What's Troubling the Trilateral Countries?* (Princeton, NJ: Princeton University Press, 2000), pp. 233–34.

17. Richard Davis, *The Web of Politics: The Internet's Impact on the American Political System* (New York: Oxford University Press, 1999); J. E. J. Prins, *Designing E-Government: On the Crossroads of Technological Innovation and Institutional Change* (The Hague: Kluwer Law International, 2001); Lawrence K. Grossman, *The Electronic Republic: Reshaping Democracy in the Information Age* (New York: Viking, 1995); Michael Hauben and Ronda Hauben, *Netizens: On the History and Impact of Usenet and the Internet* (Los Alamitos, CA: IEEE Computer Society Press, 1997); Thomas J. Johnson, Carol E. Hays, and Scott P. Hays, eds., *Engaging the Public: How Government and the Media Can Reinvigorate American Democracy* (Lanham, MD: Rowman & Littlefield Publishers, 1998).

18. Schumpeter defines democracy as follows: "The democratic method is that institutional arrangement for arriving at political decisions in which individuals acquire the power to decide by means of a competitive struggle for the people's vote." Joseph A. Schumpeter, *Capitalism, Socialism and Democracy* (New York: Harper & Row Publishers, 1975), p. 269.

19. David Truman, *The Governmental Process: Political Interests and Public Opinion* (New York: Alfred E. Knopf, 1965), p. 55.

20. Ibid.

21. Richard Davis, *The Web of Politics* (New York: Oxford University Press, 1999).

22. Anthony G. Wilhelm, *Democracy in the Digital Age: Challenges to Political Life in Cyberspace* (New York: Routledge, 2000), p. 34.

23. Lawrence Lessig, *Code and Other Laws of Cyberspace* (New York: Basic Books, 1999); Lessig, *The Future of Ideas: The Fate of the Commons in a Connected World* (New York: Vintage Books, 2001).

24. Wilhelm, *Democracy in the Digital Age*, p. 6.

25. Ibid., p. 37.

26. Ibid., p. 7.

27. Jeffrey B. Abramson, F. Christopher Arterton, and Gary R. Orren, *The Electronic Commonwealth: The Impact of New Media Technologies on Democratic Politics* (Cambridge, MA: Harvard University Press, 1988).

28. Robert Putnam, "Turning In, Turning Out: The Strange Disappearance of Social Capital in America," in *PS: Politics and Political Science*, 28: 4 (1995), pp. 664–83. Also see Putnam, *Bowling Alone: The Collapse and Revival of American Community* (New York: Simon and Schuster, 2000).

220   29. Benjamin R. Barber, "The New Telecommunications Technology: Endless Frontier or End of Democracy?" in Roger G. Noll and Monroe E. Price, eds., *A Communications Cornucopia: Markle Foundation Essays on Information Policy* (Washington, D.C.: Brookings Institution, 1998), pp. 72–98.

30. Cass Sunstein, *Republic.com* (Princeton, NJ: Princeton University Press, 2001).

31. Jean L. Cohen and Andrew Arato, *Civil Society and Political Theory* (Cambridge, MA: MIT Press, 1992).

32. Benjamin Barber, *A Passion for Democracy: American Essays* (Princeton: Princeton University Press, 1998), p. 268.

33. Guillermo O'Donnell and Philippe C. Schmitter, *Transitions from Authoritarian Rule: Tentative Conclusions about Uncertain Democracies* (Baltimore and London: The Johns Hopkins University Press, 1989), p. 7.

34. Ibid., p. 8.

35. Ibid., p. 9.

36. For example, Merle Goldman, *Sowing the Seeds of Democracy in China: Political Reform in the Deng Xiaoping Era* (Cambridge, MA: Harvard University Press, 1994); Joseph Fewsmith, *China since Tiananmen: The Politics of Transition* (New York: Cambridge University Press, 2001); and Xiao Gongqin, "The 'China Democratic Party' Event and Political Trends in Post-Deng China," in Wang Gungwu and Zheng Yongnian, eds., *Damage Control: The Chinese Communist Party in the Jiang Zemin Era* (Singapore: Eastern Universities Press, 2003), pp. 320–49.

37. Mark R. Beissinger, *Nationalist Mobilization and the Collapse of the Soviet State* (New York: Cambridge University Press, 2002).

38. Ibid., p. 13.

39. Ibid., p. 14.

40. Hannah Arendt, *On Violence* (New York: Harcourt Brace and Company, 1970), p. 7.

41. Beissinger, *Nationalist Mobilization and the Collapse of the Soviet State*, pp. 14–15.

42. Dahl, *Democracy and Its Critics*, p. 338.

43. Bruce Bimber, *Information and American Democracy: Technology in the Evolution of Political Power* (New York: Cambridge University Press, 2003), p. 17.

44. Joseph A. Schumpeter, *Capitalism, Socialism, and Democracy*, 4th ed. (London: Allen and Unwin, 1952).

45. Carl J. Friedrich, "The Evolving Theory and Practice of Totalitarian Regimes," in Carl J. Friedrich, Michael Curtis, and Benjamin R. Barber, *Totalitarianism in Perspective: Three Views* (New York: Praeger, 1969).

46. Su Shaozhi, "Chinese Communist Ideology and Media Control," in Chin-Chuan Lee, ed., *China's Media, Media's China* (Boulder, CO: Westview Press, 1994), pp. 75–88.

47. Stuart R. Schram, *Ideology and Policy in China since the Third Plenum, 1978–84* (London: University of London, School of Oriental and African Studies, 1984), p. 112.

48. Alan P. L. Liu, *Communications and National Integration in Communist China* (Berkeley, CA: University of California Press, 1971).

49. Su, "Chinese Communist Ideology and Medial Control."

50. Peter Baldwin, "The Return of the Coercive State: Behavioral Control in Multicultural Society," in T. V. Paul, G. John Ikenberry, and John A. Hall, eds., *The Nation-State in Question* (Princeton, NJ: Princeton University Press, 2003), pp. 106–35.

51. Gregory J. Kasza, *The Conscription Society: Administered Mass Organizations* (New Haven, CT: Yale University Press, 1995).

52. William Kornhauser, *The Politics of Mass Society* (Glencoe, IL: The Free Press, 1959), p. 32.

53. Ibid., p. 62.

54. Andrew G. Walder, *Communist Neo-Traditionalism: Work and Authority in Chinese Industry* (Berkeley, CA: University of California Press, 1986), pp. 2–3.

55. Chin-Chuan Lee, ed., *Power, Money and Media: Communication Patterns and Bureaucratic Control in Cultural China* (Evanston, IL: Northwest University Press, 2000); and K. Latham, "Nothing but the Truth: News Media, Power and Hegemony in South China," *The China Quarterly*, 163 (2000), pp. 633–54.

56. Marcus Franda, *Launching into Cyberspace: Internet Development and Politics in Five World Regions* (Boulder, CO: Lynne Rienner, 2002), p. 94.

57. Russell Hardin, "The Social Evolution of Cooperation," in Karen Schweers Cook and Margaret Levi, eds., *The Limits of Rationality* (Chicago: The University of Chicago Press, 1990), pp. 358–76. Hardin divided what he called "strategic interaction" into three categories, namely, conflict, coordination, and cooperation. "In a pure conflict one party can gain only if another loses. Coordination interactions are the virtual opposite of this. In such interactions each party can gain only if others also gain. . . . Cooperation interactions involve elements of both conflict and coordination. I have something you want and you have something I want. . . . There is conflict because each of us has to give up something in order for the other to gain. And there is coordination because we can both be made better off at once by exchanging," pp. 359–60.

58. Ibid., p. 359.

59. In the case of China, see Daniel C. Lynch, *After the Propaganda State: Media, Politics, and "Thought Work" in Reformed China* (Stanford, CA: Stanford University Press, 1999).

60. Kenneth Lieberthal, *Governing China: From Revolution through Reform*, 2nd ed. (New York: W. W. Norton, 2004); Kenneth Lieberthal and David M. Lampton, eds., *Bureaucracy, Politics, and Decision Making in Post-Mao China* (Berkeley, CA: University of California Press, 1992); and Kenneth Lieberthal and Michel Oksenberg, *Policy Making in China: Leaders, Structures, and Processes* (Princeton, NJ: Princeton University Press, 1988). On leadership fragmentation in the event of a political crisis in the post-Mao era, see Fewsmith, *China since Tiananmen*; and Goldman, *Sowing the Seeds of Democracy in China*.

61. O'Donnell and Schmitter, *Transitions from Authoritarian Rule*, pp. 15–16.

62. Amnesty International, "People's Republic of China: Controls Tighten as Internet Activism Grows," *Amnesty International Journal 2004*, p. 3.

63. Larry J. Griffin, "Temporality, Events, and Explanation in Historical Sociology: An Introduction," *Sociological Methods and Research*, 20: 4 (1992), p. 413.

1. See, for example, Giuseppe Di Palma, "Legitimation from the Top to Civil Society: Politico-Cultural Change in Eastern Europe," *World Politics* 44, 1 (October 1991), pp. 49–80; Narcia A. Weigle and Jim Butterfield, "Civil Society in Reforming Communist Regimes: The Logic of Emergence," *Comparative Politics* 25, 1 (October 1992), pp. 1–23; Zbigniew Rau, ed., *The Reemergence of Civil Society in Eastern Europe and the Soviet Union* (Boulder, CO: Westview Press, 1991).

2. Douglas Schuler, *New Community Networks: Wired for Change* (New York and Reading, MA: ACM Press and Addison-Wesley Publishing Company, 1996); David T. Hill and Krishna Sen, "The Internet in Indonesia's New Democracy," in Peter Ferdinand, *The Internet, Democracy and Democratization* (London: Cass Publishers, 2000), pp. 119–36; David Holmes, ed., *Virtual Politics: Identity and Community in Cyberspace* (London: Sage Publications, 1997); Ronald J. Deibert, "Altered Worlds: Social Forces in the Hypermedia Environment," and Dineh M. Davis, "Women on the Net: Implications of Informal International Networking Surrounding the Fourth World Conference on Women," in Cynthia J. Alexander and Leslie A. Pal, *Digital Democracy: Policy and Politics in the Wired World* (Toronto: Oxford University Press, 1998); Howard Rheingold, *The Virtual Community: Homesteading on the Electronic Frontier* (Cambridge, MA: MIT Press, 2000); Roza Tsagarousianou, Damian Tambini, and Cathy Bryan, *Cyberdemocracy: Technology, Cities, and Civic Networks* (London: Routledge, 1998); Kevin A. Hill and John E. Hughes, *Cyberpolitics: Citizen Activism in the Age of the Internet* (Lanham, MD: Rowman & Littlefield Publishers, 1998).

3. Jurgen Habermas, *The Structural Transformation of the Public Sphere* (Cambridge, MA: Polity Press, 1989); Craig Calhoun, ed., *Habermas and the Public Sphere* (Cambridge, MA: MIT Press, 1992).

4. Peter Dahlgren, *Television and the Public Sphere: Citizenship, Democracy and the Media* (London: Sage Publications, 1995); Peter Dahlgren and Colin Sparks, eds., *Communication and Citizenship: Journalism and the Public Sphere in the Media Age* (New York: Routledge, 1991); Roza Tsagarousianou, "Electronic Democracy and the Public Sphere: Opportunities and Challenges," in Tsagarousianou, Tambini, and Bryan, *Cyberdemocracy*; Kees Schalken, "Virtual Communities: New Public Spheres on the Internet?" in Jens Hoff, Ivan Horrocks, and Pieter Tops, *Democratic Governance and New Technology: Technologically Mediated Innovations in Political Practice in Western Europe* (London: Routledge, 2000); Douglas Kellner, "Intellectuals, the New Public Spheres, and Techno-Politics," in Chris Toulouse and Timothy W. Luke, eds., *The Politics of Cyberspace: A New Political Science Reader* (New York: Routledge, 1998); Schuler, *New Community Networks*.

5. Robert Putnam, *Making Democracy Work: Civic Traditions in Modern Italy* (Princeton, NJ: Princeton University Press, 1993).

6. Michael Walzer, *Radical Principles: Reflections of an Unreconstructed Democrat* (New York: Basic Books, 1980), p. 64.

7. For example, Tianjian Shi, *Political Participation in Beijing* (Cambridge, MA: Harvard University Press, 1997).

8. Yang Taoyuan, et al., "Suzao daguo wangmin" ("Creating Netizens in China"),

Liaowang xinwen zhoukan (Outlook News Weekly), Beijing, February 23, 2004, pp.
24–31.

9. Anthony Downs, *An Economic Theory of Democracy* (New York: Harper and Brothers, 1957), pp. 13–77.

10. Bruce Bimber, *Information and American Democracy: Technology in the Evolution of Political Power* (New York: Cambridge University Press, 2003).

11. For a discussion on how the private concerns differ from those in the public arena and how the transformation possibly takes place, see Albert O. Hirschman, *Shifting Involvements: Private Interest and Public Action* (Princeton, NJ: Princeton University Press, 1982).

12. Putnam, *Making Democracy Work*. For applications of the concept of "social capital" or "trust," see, for example, Bernard Barber, *The Logic and Limits of Trust* (New Brunswick, NJ: Rutgers University Press, 1983); William T. Bianco, *Trust: Representatives and Constituents* (Ann Arbor: University of Michigan Press, 1994); Francis Fukuyama, *Trust: The Social Virtues and the Creation of Prosperity* (New York: Free Press, 1995).

13. Putnam, *Making Democracy Work*, p. 167.

14. Robert H. Bates, "Contra Contractarianism: Some Reflections on the New Institutionalism," in *Politics and Society*, 16 (1988), p. 398.

15. Sidney Tarrow, *Power in Movement: Social Movements and Contentious Politics*, 2nd ed. (Cambridge, England: Cambridge University Press, 1998), p. 21.

16. Putnam, *Making Democracy Work*, p. 173.

17. Ibid.

18. Thomas L. Friedman, *The Lexus and the Olive Tree: Understanding Globalization* (New York: Anchor Books, 2000), pp. 62–3.

19. Ibid., pp. 67–8.

20. Joseph Man Chan, "Administrative Boundaries and Media Marketization: A Comparative Analysis of the Newspaper, TV and Internet Markets in China," in Chin-Chuan Lee, ed., *Chinese Media, Global Contexts* (London and New York: Routledge-Curzon, 2003), p. 169.

21. Ibid., p. 170.

22. *People's Daily*, "Zhongguo hulianwang:meili shuzi de beihou" ("China's Internet: Behind the Wonderful Figures"), January 16, 2004.

23. These figures are calculated from the respondents' multiple choices. The Center for Social Development of the Chinese Academy of Social Sciences, *2003nian hulianwang baogao (The 2003 Report on the Internet)*, Beijing, 2003. The survey was conducted among citizens in China's twelve major cities.

24. Ibid.

25. Ibid.

26. Ibid.

27. Yi Ming, "Xinxi gaosu gonglu jiang ba Zhongguo daixiang hefang?" ("Where Will Information Highways Take China To?"), *Zhongguo zhichun (China Spring)*, June 2000.

28. Merle Goldman, *Sowing the Seeds of Democracy in China: Political Reform in the Deng Xiaoping Era* (Cambridge, MA: Harvard University Press, 1994).

29. *Ming pao* (Hong Kong), February 21, 2004.

30. *Ming pao* (Hong Kong), February 2, 2004.

31. The Xinhua News Agency, February 15, 2004.

32. The Xinhua News Agency, December 29, 2003.

33. The Xinhua News Agency, December 15, 2003.

34. Agence France-Presse, "Chinese Mafia Figure Executed after Landmark Ruling," December 23, 2003.

35. *People's Daily*, "External Influence Complicates Court Ruling on Chinese Mafia Kingpin," October 25, 2003.

36. *China Daily*, Hong Kong edition, "External Influence Complicates Court Ruling," October 24, 2003.

37. John Pomfret, "Execution Reveals Party's Grip in China: Case Highlights Flaws in Legal System," *Washington Post*, December 23, 2003.

38. Sophie Beach, "A Brave Student Becomes a Symbol of Modern China," *The Asian Wall Street Journal*, November 7, 2003.

39. Agence France-Presse, "For Chinese Internet Dissident, Protest Runs in the Family," December 16, 2002. Many of Liu's Internet writings can be found at http://boxun.com/hero/liudi. Accessed on December 26, 2003.

40. Beach, "A Brave Student Becomes a Symbol of Modern China."

41. BBC News, "China Internet Dissidents Freed," November 30, 2003.

42. Beach, "A Brave Student Becomes a Symbol of Modern China."

43. Agence France-Presse, "Chinese Press Ridicules Jailed Shanghai Lawyer Zheng Enchong," October 28, 2003.

44. For more information about the case of Zheng Enchong, see Stacy Mosher, "Prisoner Profile: Zheng Enchong," *China Rights Forum*, No. 4, 2003, pp. 124–29.

45. *China Daily*, "BMW Drives Wedge between Rich, Poor," January 18, 2004.

46. *China Daily*, "Roaring BMW: Was It 'Road Rage' or an Accident?" January 6, 2004.

47. Ibid.

48. Ibid.

49. Jim Yardley, "Chinese Go Online in Search of Justice against Elite Class," *New York Times*, January 16, 2004.

50. *Shenzhen Daily*, "BMW Case's Verdict Upheld," March 29, 2004.

CHAPTER 6

1. Albert O. Hirschman, *Exit, Voice, and Loyalty: Responses to Decline in Firms, Organizations, and States* (Cambridge, MA: Harvard University Press, 1970).

2. Ibid., p. 77.

3. For a comprehensive discussion of Internet nationalism in China, see Wang Jun, "Shixi dangdai Zhongguo de wangluo minzu zhuyi" ("A Preliminary Analysis of Internet Nationalism in Contemporary China"), *Shijie jingji yu zhengzhi* (*World Economy and Politics*), No. 2 (2006), pp. 1–13.

4. Ibid., pp. 77–8.

5. Ibid., p. 82.

6. Ibid., p. 4.

7. Ibid., p. 37.

8. Ibid., p. 36.

9. Michael Chase and James Mulvenon, *You've Got Dissent! Chinese Dissident Use of the Internet and Beijing's Counter-Strategies* (Santa Monica, CA: Rand, 2002).

10. Hirschman, *Exit, Voice, and Loyalty*, p. 4.

11. Ibid., p. 30.

12. Ibid., p. 33.

13. Russell Hardin, "The Social Evolution of Cooperation," in Karen Schweers Cook and Margaret Levi, eds., *The Limits of Rationality* (Chicago: The University of Chicago Press, 1990), p. 359.

14. Ibid., p. 360.

15. Ibid., p. 358.

16. Ibid., p. 363.

17. Ibid.

18. Willy Wo-Lap Lam, "Fear of Non-Party Faithful," *South China Morning Post*, April 29, 1999.

19. John Wong and William T. Liu, *The Mystery of China's Falun Gong: Its Rise and Its Sociological Implications* (London and Singapore: World Scientific & Singapore University Press, 1999), pp. 14–15. For an introduction of the FLG and its interaction with the state, see Maria Hsia Chang, *Falun Gong: The End of Days* (New Haven, CT: Yale University Press, 2004).

20. Wu Guoguang, "The Return of Ideology? Struggling to Organize Politics during Socio-Economic Transitions," in John Wong and Zheng Yongnian, eds., *The Nanxun Legacy and China's Post-Deng Development* (Singapore and London: Singapore University Press and World Scientific, 2001), pp. 221–46.

21. Xiao Gongqin, "The Falun Gong and Its Conflicts with the Chinese Government: A Perspective of Social Transformation," in Wang Gungwu and Zheng Yongnian, eds., *Damage Control: The Chinese Communist Party in the Jiang Zemin Era* (Singapore: Eastern Universities Press, 2003), pp. 64–80.

22. *Ming pao*, Hong Kong, June 6, 2003.

23. The author is grateful to Xiao Gongqin (professor at the Shanghai Normal University) for sharing the information he contributed to this case. For more information about this event of the China Democracy Party movement in 1998, see Xiao Gongqin, "The 'China Democratic Party' Event and Political Trends in Post-Deng China," in Wang and Zheng, eds., *Damage Control*, pp. 320–49.

24. This discussion focuses on the China Democracy Party movement in 1998. For a discussion of the historical development of the China Democracy Party, see Teresa Wright, "The China Democracy Party and the Politics of Protest in the 1980s–1990s," *The China Quarterly*, 172 (December 2002), pp. 906–26.

25. The Xinhua News Agency, Beijing, June 28, 2003.

26. Proposal to Examine the "Measures for Custody and Repatriation of Urban Vagrants and Beggars," Submitted to the National People's Congress Standing Committee on May 16, 2003 (*Guanyu shencha "chengshi liulang qitao renyuan shourong yisong banfa de jueyishu"*), available at http://www.southcn.com/weekend/commend/200305220015.htm (20 June 2003). These scholars argued that the regulations were il-

226   legal because (1) under Articles 8 and 9 of the Legislation Law and Article 8 of the
Administrative Punishments Law, the freedom of citizens can be restricted only by law
(not by administrative regulations such as the Measures for Custody and Repatriation
of Urban Vagrants and Beggars) and (2) under Article 37 of China's constitution, no
citizen may be arrested except with the approval of a people's procuratorate or people's
court, and unlawful deprivation of freedom by detention or other means is prohibited.
As such, the measures were illegal under Article 87 of the Legislation Law, which states
that administrative regulations may not contravene the Constitution or the law.

27. Proposal Submitted to the Standing Committee of the National People's Congress on Initiating a Special Investigation into the Sun Zhigang Case and the Implementation of the Custody and Repatriation System (*Tiqing quanguo changweihui jiu
Sun Zhigang an ji shourong yisong zhidu shishi zhuangkuang qidong tebie diaocha
chengxu de jianyishu*), submitted to the National People's Congress, 22 May 2003, available at http://www.china-review.com/everyday/jianyishu.htm (20 June 2003).

28. For a report of the Sun Dawu event, see Wang Jianmin, "*Zhongguo minqi yu
zhengzhi bodou*" ("Chinese Private Entrepreneurs and Their Political Struggles"), *Ya-
zhou zhoukan* (*Asian Weekly*), November 16, 2003, pp. 26–33.

29. *China Daily*, "Entrepreneur Sun Dawu Gets 3-Year Sentence," November 1,
2003.

30. *Ming pao*, Hong Kong, November 21, 2003.

31. The Xinhua News Agency, "*Jiang Zemin tongzhi zai quanguo dangxiao gongzuo
huiyi shan de jianghua*" (June 9, 2000) ("Comrade Jiang Zemin's Talk in National
Party Schools Working Conference"), *Renmin ribao*, July 17, 2000.

32. On policy changes over the private sector and private entrepreneurs, see Zheng
Yongnian, "Ideological Decline, the Rise of an Interest-Based Social Order, and the
Demise of Communism in China," "Technocratic Leadership, Private Entrepreneur-
ship, and Party Transformation," and "The Party, Class, and Democracy in China."
All three are in Zheng Yongnian, *Will China Become Democratic? Elite, Class and Re-
gime Transition* (Singapore, New York, and London: Eastern Universities Press, 2004),
Chapters 9–10.

33. For example, see Tian Xiaowen, "The Private Economy: Will the Ugly Duck-
ling Become a Swan?" in John Wong and Zheng Yongnian, eds., *China's Post-Jiang
Leadership Succession: Problems and Perspectives* (Singapore and London: Singapore
University Press and World Scientific, 2002), pp. 261–84.

34. This description is based on Zheng Yongnian and Lye Liang Fook, "SARS and
China's Political System," in John Wong and Zheng Yongnian, eds., *The SARS Epidemic: Challenges to China's Crisis Management* (Singapore and London: World Scientific, 2004), pp. 45–75.

35. Zhou Xiaohong, "*SARS liuxing qijian de shehui chuanyan yu gongzhong yulun
diaocha*" ("An Investigation of Social Rumors and Public Opinions during the SARS"),
in Ru Xing, Lu Xueyi, and Li Peilin, eds., *Shehui lanpishu: Zhongguo shehui xingshi
fenxi yu yuce, 2004* (*Social Bluebook: An Analysis and Forecast of Social Situation in
China, 2004*), (Beijing: *Shehui kexue wenxian chubanshe*, 2004), p. 254.

36. Jiang Yanyong had first emailed his letter to CCTV and Phoenix TV (a pro-
China TV station in Hong Kong) on April 4, 2003. After his email was ignored, Jiang
was interviewed by Susan Jakes, a correspondent with *Time* Magazine, on April 8,

2003, and she published the interview on the same day. See "Feature: A Chinese Doctor's Extraordinary April in 2003" at http://english.peopledaily.com.cn/200306/13/
print20030613_118182.html.

37. See Statement by Madame Wu Yi Head of the Chinese Delegation, Vice Premier and Minister of Health of the People's Republic of China at the General Debate
of the 56th World Health Assembly, May 20, 2003, at http://www.casy.org/Chindoc/
wuyi_0503.htm. Accessed on April 14, 2007. See also "*Wu Yi: zhongguo yuan chengdan
zeren, luxing yiwu yingdui yiqing*" ("Wu Yi: China Is Willing to Take Responsibility,
Carry Out Its Duty to Deal with the SARS"), *Xinhuanet*, May 21, 2003.

38. See Speech by Premier Wen Jiabao of China at the Special-ASEAN Leaders'
Meeting on the SARS, April 29, 2003, at http://www.fmprc.gov.cn/eng/topics/zgcydyhz/
t26292.htm. Accessed on April 14, 2007.

39. "Chinese President's Euro-Asian Tour Fruitful - FM," The Xinhua News Agency,
June 5, 2003.

40. At their bilateral meeting in Evian in France in June 2003, President Bush
praised Hu for his handling of the SARS crisis, especially his efforts to improve transparency. See "Bush Invites Hu to Pay a Visit to Washington," *South China Morning
Post*, June 3, 2003, and "Hu, Bush Pledge to Further Develop Constructive Relations
of Cooperation," The Xinhua News Agency, June 2, 2003.

41. "*Jiang Zemin fa yandian aidao 361hao qianting yunan guanbin weiwen qinshu*"
("Jiang Issues Condolence Message to the Relatives of Officers and Soldiers of the 361
Submarine Mishap"), The Xinhua News Agency, May 2, 2003 (http://www.chinanews
.com.cn/n/2003-05-02/26/299688.html). See also "Seventy Crew Killed in Submarine
Accident," *China Daily*, May 3, 2003, and "Suffocation Killed 70 on Sub, Says Report,"
South China Morning Post, May 5, 2003.

42. "*Jing zhonggong zhongyang pizhun, zhongyangjunwei fabu mingling tiaozheng
haijun junzheng zhuguan*" ("Upon Approval by Central Committee, the Central Military Commission Issues Order to Reshuffle Key Military and Political Leaders in the
Navy"), *Xinhuanet*, June 13, 2003.

43. Hirschman, *Exit, Voice, and Loyalty*, p. 33.

CHAPTER 7

1. Guillermo O'Donnell and Philippe C. Schmitter, *Transitions from Authoritarian
Rule: Tentative Conclusions about Uncertain Democracies* (Baltimore, MD: The Johns
Hopkins University Press, 1989), p. 3.

2. For example, according to Held et al., modern states have the following unique
features. First, while all states have made claims on territories, it is only with the modern nation-state system that exact borders have been gradually fixed. Second, the claim
to hold a monopoly on force and the means of coercion became possible only with
the "pacification" of people, the breaking down of rival centers of power and authority within the nation-state. Third, the modern state is an impersonal and sovereign
political order—that is, a legally circumscribed structure of power—with supreme
jurisdiction over a territory. It became prevalent when political rights, obligations, and
duties were no longer conceived as closely tied to religion and claims of the traditionally privileged, such as the monarchy and nobility. Fourth, the modern state enjoys

228   the loyalty of its citizens and claims to be legitimate because it reflects and represents the needs, wishes, and interests of its citizens. See David Held and Anthony McGrew, David Goldblatt, and Jonathan Perraton, *Global Transformations: Politics, Economics and Culture* (Stanford, CA.: Stanford University Press, 1999). Modern nation-states especially in Europe and North America have acquired a particular political form — liberal democracy. Liberal democracy means that decisions affecting a community are made by a subgroup of representatives who have been chosen through the electoral process to govern within the framework of the rule of law. In the arena of national politics, liberal democracy is distinguished by the presence of a cluster of rules and institutions, all of which are necessary to its successful functioning. See Robert Dahl, *Democracy and Its Critics* (New Haven, CT: Yale University Press, 1989), pp. 221, 223.

3. Deng Xiaoping, "*Guanyu zhengzhi tizhi gaige wenti*" ("Issues Related to Political System Reform, September–November, 1986"), in Deng, *Deng Xiaoping wenxuan* (*Selected Works of Deng Xiaoping*), vol. 3 (Beijing: Renmin chubanshe, 1993), p. 176.

4. On political incrementalism, see Yongnian Zheng, "Political Incrementalism: Political Lessons from China's 20 Years of Reform," *Third World Quarterly*, vol. 20, no. 6 (1999), pp. 1157–77.

5. Benedict Anderson, *Imagined Communities: Reflections on the Origin and Spread of Nationalism*, 2nd ed. (London: Verso, 1991); Sidney Tarrow, *Power in Movement: Social Movements and Contentious Politics*, 2nd ed. (New York: Cambridge University Press, 1998).

6. Wang Gungwu, *Joining the Modern World: Inside and Outside China* (Singapore and London: Singapore University Press and World Scientific, 2000), p. 11.

7. Lucian Pye, "China: Erratic State, Frustrated Society," *Foreign Affairs*, 69:4 (Fall 1990), pp. 56–74.

8. Yu-Sheng Lin, *The Crisis of Chinese Consciousness: Radical Antitraditionalism in the May Fourth Era* (Madison: The University of Wisconsin Press, 1979).

9. Arif Dirlik, "The Ideological Foundations of the New Life Movement: A Study in Counterrevolution," *Journal of Asian Study*, 34:4 (August 1975), pp. 945–80.

10. Chalmers A. Johnson, *Peasant Nationalism and Communist Power: The Emergence of Revolutionary China, 1937–1945* (Stanford, CA: Stanford University Press, 1962).

11. Yongnian Zheng, *Discovering Chinese Nationalism in China: Modernization, Identity, and International Relations* (Cambridge, England: Cambridge University Press, 1999).

12. Michael Chase and James Mulvenon, *You've Got Dissent! Chinese Dissident Use of the Internet and Beijing's Counter-Strategies* (Santa Monica, CA: Rand, 2002).

13. For example, Peter Hays Gries, *China's New Nationalism: Pride, Politics, and Diplomacy* (Berkeley, CA: University of California Press, 2004); Zheng, *Discovering Chinese Nationalism*.

14. Gries, ibid.

15. *Reuters*, "China to Curb Demolitions to Defuse Unrest," June 15, 2004.

16. *The Economist*, "The Cauldron Boils; Protests in China," October 1, 2005.

17. Feng Chen, "Between the State and Labor: The Conflict of Chinese Trade Unions' Dual Institutional Identity in Market Reform," *The China Quarterly*, no. 176

(December 2003), pp. 1006–28; Feng Chen, "Industrial Restructuring and Workers' 229 Resistance in China," *Modern China*, vol. 29, no. 2 (April 2003), pp. 237–62; and Feng Chen, "Subsistence Crisis, Managerial Corruption, and Labor Protest in China," *The China Journal*, 44 (July 2000), pp. 41–63. Also see *The China Quarterly*, special feature, "China's Workers: Reform, Resistance and Reticence," 170 (June 2002), especially the paper by Yongshun Cai, "The Resistance of Chinese Laid-Off Workers in the Reform Period," pp. 327–44.

18. Joseph Kahn, "China Crushes Peasant Protest, Turning 3 Friends into Enemies," *New York Times*, October 13, 2004. For scholarly analyses on rural social movements, see Thomas P. Bernstein and Xiaobo Lu, *Taxation without Representation in Contemporary Rural China* (New York: Cambridge University Press, 2003); Lianjiang Li, "Elections and Popular Resistance in Rural China," *China Information*, vol. xv, no. 2 (2001), pp. 1–19; and Lianjiang Li and Kevin J. O'Brien, "Villagers and Popular Resistance in Contemporary China," *Modern China*, vol. 22, no. 1 (1996), pp. 28–61.

19. Yongnian Zheng, "Explaining the Sources of de facto Federalism in Reform China: Intergovernmental Decentralization, Globalization, and Central-Local Relations," *Japanese Journal of Political Science*, vol. 7, no. 2 (2006), pp. 101–26.

20. For a discussion, see Chin-Fu Hung, "Public Discourse and 'Virtual' Political Participation in the PRC: The Impact of the Internet," *Issues and Studies*, vol. 39, no. 4 (December 2003), pp. 1–38.

21. For social policy reforms, see articles in Nicholas C. Hope, Dennis Tao Yang, and Mu Yang Li, eds., *How Far across the River? Chinese Policy Reform at the Millennium* (Stanford, CA: Stanford University Press, 2003).

22. Zheng Shiping, "The Age Factor in Chinese Politics," in Wang Gungwu and Zheng Yongnian, eds., *Damage Control: The Chinese Communist Party in the Jiang Zemin Era* (Singapore and London: Eastern Universities Press, 2003), pp. 173–89; Zheng Yongnian, "The Politics of Power Succession," in Wang Gungwu and Zheng Yongnian, eds., *Reform, Legitimacy and Dilemmas: China's Politics and Society* (London and Singapore: World Scientific and Singapore University Press, 2000), pp. 23–50.

23. Zheng Yongnian, "The Party, Class, and Democracy in China," in Zheng, *Will China Become Democratic? Elite, Class and Regime Transition* (Singapore, London, and New York: Eastern Universities Press, 2004), pp. 282–316.

INDEX

Italic page numbers indicate material in figures and tables; n indicates material in endnotes.

Academic Sinica, 22
"accessing card," 68–69
"accessing the Internet by real identity" system, 68–69
addresses, electronic, 65, 67. *See also* domains
"administered mass organizations," 91
Administration of Broadcasting Affairs, 216n6
Administrative Procedural Law, 121
Administrative Punishment Act, 150, 226n26
Adopt-a-Blogger program, 68
advertisements, 93, 112
age: business use and, 34; home use and, 34; interpersonal relationships and, 115; news use by, 111; proficiency and, 35; for retirement, 181–82
agricultural reforms: beneficiaries of, 44, 44, 215n78; industrialization and, 178; political legitimacy and, 25
Altavista, 64
Amnesty International, 67, 100–101
Anderson, Benedict, 170
anti-bourgeois campaigns, 25
Arato, Andrew, 86

Arendt, Hannah, 89
arrests, 41, 67, 67–68, 70–78, 100
Association of Southeast Asian Nations, 161
"atomized society," 91–92, 119, 133
August coup, 17
authoritarian states: design and development by, 9; information in, 96–97, 116–17; political change in, 169; political liberalization in, 88–89, 98–101; proactive and reactive measures by, 80; regime change in, 168

Badie, Bertrand, 18–19
banks, 93, 95, 109, 152
Barber, Benjamin, 82, 86
Bates, Robert, 106
Beach, Sophie, 127
Beijing: arrests in, 70–77; business use in, 34; CDP in, 146; democratic movement in, 146; "Digital Beijing" plan, 37; FLG event in, 155; home use in, 34; interpersonal relationships in, 115; news use in, 111; polls on SARS in, 159, 160, 162, 163; proficiency in, 35; SARS in, 156, 158–60, 177
Beissinger, Mark, 89
Bimber, Bruce, 105
blogs, 66–68
BMW case, the, 130–32
Boas, Taylor, 9

232

bourgeois liberalization, 117
Boyle, James, 8, 9
Bright, Charles, 41–42
Bunger, Karl, 20–21, 22
Bush, George W., 10, 227n40
bu xiu gang laoshu (Stainless Steel Mouse), 125

cable services, 69
Cai Lujun, 70
Canada, SARS in, 156
C&R system, 81, 147–51, 225–26nn26–27
capitalism, 6, 153–54, 175–77, 183–84
CASS surveys. *See* Chinese Academy of Social Sciences (CASS) surveys
CCDI survey on corruption, 120, 121, 122
CCP. *See* Chinese Communist Party (CCP)
CDP. *See* China Democracy Party (CDP)
censorship, 9, 58–63, 66–68
Central Commission for Discipline Inspection (CCDI), 120, 121, 122
Central Committee, 55
Central Military Commission, 163, 182
Chan, Joseph, 109
Changjiang (Yangtze River) Delta software park, 29
Chase, Michael S., 10, 138, 173
chat rooms: corruption stories in, 122; "A Life Likes Fire," 125; MII and, 61; SSB and, 60; trust of data from, 112
Chen, An, 215n78
Chen Duxiu, 205n2
Chen Shaowen, 70
Chen Weigao, 121
Chen Xitong, 180, 181
Chiang Kai-shek, 22, 172, 183
China Academy of Sciences, 52
China Auditing Administration, 121
China Construction Bank, 121
China Corporation of Aerospace Industry, 53
China Corporation of Aviation Industry, 53
China Daily news Web site, 64
China Democracy Party (CDP): arrests for, 71, 73–74; in Beijing, 146; Clinton and, 145; founding of, 67, 144; in Hubei

province, 146; interaction strategies of, 138, 142, 147; Jiang Zemin and, 145, 147; Li Peng and, 146–47; National Congress of, 146; objective of, 145; organization of, 138; radicalization of, 146; regime's response to, 81, 145–47, 174; rise of, 96, 174; in Shandong province, 145–46; in Tianjin, 146; in United States, 147; Web sites, 173; in Zhejiang province, 145
China International Broadcast Web site, 64
China Internet Network Information Center (CNNIC), 59. *See also* CNNIC *Survey Report on the Development of China's Internet*
China Network 2 (CN2), 66
China Telecom, 51, 53
China United Telecommunication Corporation (Unicom), 52, 53
Chinese Academy of Social Sciences (CASS) surveys: on civic engagement, 116, *116*; on digital divide, 107–8, *108*; on interpersonal relationships, 111, 113–15, *114*; on politics, *118*, 118–19, *119*; on reasons for use, 109; on trust of Internet, 111–12, *114*
Chinese Communist Party (CCP): age factor in, 181–82; class and membership in, 183; crackdown costs, 97–98; entrepreneurs in, 154, 183, 184; FLG members in, 143; hard-liners in (*see* hard-liners); on "ideology," 90; intermediary organizations and, 91; on International Covenant on Civil and Political Rights, 145; Japanese invasion and, 173; KMT and, 174; leadership style in, 180–82; media policies of, 7, 91; modern state model of, 23; in *san ge dai biao* concept, 154, 183; on social organizations, 91; soft-liners in (*see* soft-liners); Sun Dawu on, 151–52
Chinese News Agency Web site, 64
Chinese People's Political Consultative Conference, 37
Chi Shouzhu, 70
Chong, Dennis, 106
Chongqing: arrests in, 74; polls on SARS in, 159, *159*, *160*, *162*, *163*
Cisco Systems, 65–66

civic engagement: barriers to, 84; CASS surveys on, 116, *116*; class and, 183–84; collective actions and, 133–34; definition of, 104; digital divide and, 85, 107, 133; events by social movements as, 123; IT and, 81–87, 103–5, 116–18, 178; networks of, 106; political democratization and, 103; political liberalization and, 103, 134; social capital and, 106; societal empowerment and, 10, 166; trust and, 133–34

Clark, Duncan, 10

class: CCP membership and, 183; civic engagement and, 183–84; collective actions and, 106; Constitution on, 153; digital divide and, 85; globalization and, 184; industrialization and, 175, 184; regime's response to, 183–84

Clinton, Bill, 10, 145

CNNIC *Survey Report on the Development of China's Internet*: on access locations, 39; on computer hosts, 31; on data searched for, 93; on domains, 33; on factors affecting use, 107; on income of users, 40; on Internet users, 92–93; on number of users, 32; on occupations of users, 33; on privacy concerns, 112; on reasons for use, 92; on regionalism of use, 39; on services used, 95; on social acceptance of Internet, 109, 110; on trust of virtual community, 110–11, 112, 113; on work, 110

coercion: forces for, 177; forms of, 8; interaction strategies and, 94–96, 141–42; in modern state, 9, 91, 227n2; political reform and, 170; state empowerment from, 8, 91

Cohen, Jean, 86

collective actions: civic engagement and, 133–34; class and, 106; conflict strategy (*see* conflict strategy); control over, 116; cooperation strategy (*see* cooperation strategy); coordination strategy, 94–95, 140–42, 221n57; on corruption, 120, 122; elites on, 169; exit activities (*see* exit activities); IT and, 105; loyalty activities, 137, 141, 147; motivation for, 106; organization of, 106; participants in, 164–65;

political liberalization and, 168, 184; statistics on, 175; voice activities (*see* voice activities). *See also* social movements

"comfortable society" concept, 183

Commission on Radio Frequencies, 53

Committee of Politics and Law, 125

communism, technocrats and, 6

communitarian theory, 82

Computer Aided Office, 37

computer hosts, 31, *31*, 38, 39

Computer Information Network and Internet Security, Protection, and Management Regulations, 60

computers: number of, 31–32; searches for, 93

conflict strategy: against CDP, 147; definition of, 96, 140, 221n57; exit activities and, 142, 165; against FLG, 144

Confucian politics: elites in, 5, 172–73; Japanese invasion and, 173; KMT and, 172–73; Maoist politics and, 23; May Fourth Movement and, 172; nationalism and, 172; technocrats and, 5; Western modern state and, 19–22, 172

"conscription society," 91

Constitution, 150, 153–54, 183, 226n26

Contemporary Business News, 66

cooperation strategy: definition of, 221n57; of FLG, 142–43; hard- vs. soft-liners and, 140, 165; social capital and, 106; societal and state empowerment and, 165; voice activities and, 140–42, 165

coordination strategy, 94–95, 140–42, 221n57

Corporation Law, 51

corruption: Administrative Procedural Law, 121; in C&R system, 149–50; CCDI survey on, 120, 121, 122; collective actions on, 120, 122; CPI score, 46; crime and, 47; in education sector, 120, *120*; exposure of, 38, 122; in Guangzhou, 149; in Guizhou province, 121; in Hebei province, 121; investigation of, 46, 120–22; in judicial system, 120, 120–21, 132, 149–50; in Liaoning province, 123–25; in medical and health care sector, 120, *120*; in Ministry of Land and Resources, 121; People's

234

Movement and, 120, 121; punishment of, 46; rule of law and, 46–47; in Shanghai, 128; social movements and, 46–47, 120; in Yunnan province, 121
Corruption Perception Index (CPI), 46
credit unions, 152
crime, 47, 59, 60, 86
Criminal Law articles, 59
Criminal Procedure Law, 127
Cuba, IT in, 80
Cultural Revolution, 6, 24
"cultural scripts," 18
custody and repatriation (C&R) system, 81, 147–51, 225–26nn26–27
Customs, 37
cyber cafés: access from, 39, 40; identity registration at, 69; license for, 65; Ministry of Culture on, 61, 65; rules and regulations on, 61, 69; surveillance software installation by, 65

Dahl, Robert, 82, 90
Dai Mengyao, 131
Dai Qingjiang, 131
Dai Yiquan, 130, 131
Dawu Farming and Husbandry Group, 151, 152
death penalty, 61
Decision of the NPC Standing Committee on Safeguarding Internet Safety, The, 61
democracy: deliberations in, 86–87; Deng Xiaoping on, 25, 169; direct mass, 83; election systems, 184; elites and, 90, 169; entrepreneurs and, 215n78; Hu Jintao on, 169; information flow in, 90; IT and, 79, 82–83; Jiang Zemin on, 169; liberal, 228n2; Mr. Democracy, 1–2, 18, 205n2; neiluan, waihuan, and, 172; populism and, 2; regime change and, 168; "rich nation and strong army" and, 2; Schumpeterian, 83, 219n18; state capacity and, 12; Sun Dawu on, 152; weaknesses of, 83. See also China Democracy Party (CDP); 1989 pro-democracy movement
Democracy Wall movement, 96, 174
Deng Liqun, 56, 183

Deng Xiaoping: Constitution revision by, 153; death of, 27, 182; on democracy, 25, 169; elite recruitment policies of, 6; leadership of, 181, 182; on neiluan and waihuan, 172; reforms of, 25–27, 140, 169–70, 212n28; on state structure, 24·
Department of Propaganda (DOP), 54–57, 55, 158
Deutsch, Karl, 36
Dewey, John, 1–2
de xiansheng (Mr. Democracy), 1–2, 18, 205n2
digital divide: CASS surveys on, 107–8, 108; civic engagement and, 85, 107, 133; class and, 85; creation of, 38; decentralized development and, 11, 38–39, 108–9, 133; reasons for, 85, 107, 107–8, 108; regionalism of, 38, 107–8; social movements and, 97
digital empowerment, 82–83
Ding Guan'gen, 56, 57
direct mass democracy, 83
Directorate General of Posts, 51
Directorate General of Telecommunications, 51
domains: business' share of, 32; government, 33, 38; ISP records on visited, 60; MII on, 61, 65; registration of, 61; rules and regulations on, 61; statistics on, 33
Dong Yanhong, 70
DOP, 54–57, 55, 158
Downs, Anthony, 105
Drori, Gili S., 18
Du Daobin, 70

Eastern Europe: civil society in, 103; democratization in, 169; Soviet Union (see Soviet Union); television in, 79
East Turkestan Independence Movement, 173
economic development: beneficiaries of, 44, 44–45, 47, 215n78; Constitution on, 153–54; growth rate of, 43; information flow and, 94, 97–98, 157; in Maoist politics, 175; 1997 Asian financial crisis and, 43, 176; NPC on, 153–54; political legitimacy from, 43; political reform

and, 170; in *san ge dai biao* concept, 154; social movements and, 175–77; social stability and, 157; state empowerment and, 32, 166

Economist, The, 69

education, online access to, 92, 93, 95

education sector: corruption in, 120, 120; Internet use by, 32, 33

e-government project, 36–38, 93, 95

1898 reforms, 21

"electoral legitimation," 98

electronic bulletin boards, 60, 61, 95, 100

Elias, Norbert, 91

elites: business use by, 34; centralization and, 11; on collective actions, 169; in Confucian politics, 5, 172–73; Constitution and, 150; "cultural scripts" and, 18; democracy and, 90, 169; in domestic business, 31; *Far Eastern Economic Review* on, 32, 109–10, 115; home use by, 34; information advantage of, 82; interpersonal relationships of, 115; in Maoist politics, 5–6; nationalism among, 172–73; on *neiluan* and *waihuan*, 172; news for, 111; political legitimacy of, 24; proficiency of, 35; recruitment of by Deng Xiaoping, 6; in technocracy, 5–6; work use by, 34

email: August coup and, 17; corruption stories in, 122; to dissents, 67; events by social movements and, 17; Google-hosted, 67; on SARS, 159, 176; from social movements, 100; Suharto overthrow and, 17; survey on use of, 95; trust of data in, 112; Yahoo! account records, 66

Engels, Friedrich, 175

entertainment, online access to, 92, 93, 95, 109

entrepreneurs: bank loans for, 152; capital for, 152, 153; in CCP, 154, 183, 184; censorship and, 9; democracy and, 215n78; in Hebei province, 152; People's Movement and, 183; political control of, 35–36; property rights of, 36

ethnic discrimination/hatred, 60

events by social movements: as civic engagement, 123; conflict strategy (*see*

conflict strategy); cooperation strategy (*see* cooperation strategy); coordination strategy, 94–95, 140–42, 221n57; creation of, 100, 123; definition of, 89; email and, 17; as exit activities (*see* exit activities); as loyalty activities, 137, 141, 147; participants in, 164–65; political democratization and, 101–2, 185; political liberalization and, 101–2, 155, 185; public opinion and, 133; as voice activities (*see* voice activities). *See also specific events*

exit activities: CDP events as, 142, 147; conflict strategy and, 142, 165; definition of, 138; FLG events as, 142, 144; hard-liners and, 164; loyalty activities and, 141; participants in, 164; political liberalization and, 138–39, 141–42; regime's response to, 164, 165; soft-liners and, 164; voice activities and, 138, 139, 141, 165

Explanations on Requirements to Provide Domain Registration Services, 61

Falun Gong (FLG): arrests for, 67, 70–78, 142–43; email use by, 17; events by, 97, 100, 142–44, 155, 176; interaction strategies of, 138, 142, 144; organization of, 138, 143, 176; regime's response to, 81, 143–44, 155, 174, 177; rise of, 174; SARS and, 144, 164; science/technology and, 17; Web sites, 173

Fang Lizhi, 3

Far Eastern Economic Review: on business elites, 32, 109–10, 115; on business use, 34; on home use, 34; on interpersonal relationships, 115; on news, 111; on proficiency, 35; on work use, 34

farmers' issues, 178

"Field of Ideas," 64, 116

Fifteenth Party Congress (1997), 145, 153, 182

firewalls, "proxy" technologies and, 94

"flash mobs," 97

"Forbidding Free Movement of the Population," 149

foreign aggression, prevention of, 172

Foucault, Michel, 8, 9, 91

Fourteenth Party Congress (1992), 180

236   Fourth Plenum (2004), 181–82
Franda, Marcus, 94
Friedman, Thomas, 108–9
Friedrich, Carl, 90
friends, online access to, 92, 93, 109
fuguo qiangbing. *See* "rich nation and strong army"
Fujian, digital plan for, 37

gambling, rules and regulations on, 60
games, online access to, 93, 95
game theory, 140
Gansu province, arrests in, 73
Geological Research Institute, 22
Gernet, Jacques, 21
Gini coefficient, 45
globalization: class and, 184; crackdown costs and, 97; definition of, 18–19; modern statehood and, 18–19, 43, 173; neo-technonationalism and, 27; political change and, 174; social movements and, 176–77
Google, 64–67
Government Online Project (GOP), 37
Great Leap Forward, 23, 24
Griffin, Larry, 101
gross domestic product (GDP), 28
Guangdong province: arrests in, 71–74, 76, 78; government of, 157; MOH and, 157, 158; newspapers in, 148; SARS in, 154, 156–59, 161, 176; SMS messages on SARS in, 159; trade in, 157
Guangming Daily, 117
Guangxi province, arrests in, 75
Guangzhou: business use in, 34; C&R system in, 147–48; corruption in, 149; home use in, 34; interpersonal relationships in, 115; news use in, 111; polls on SARS in, 159, 159, 160, 162, 163; proficiency in, 35; SARS, reaction to, 160
Guizhou province, corruption in, 121
Guo Qinghai, 71

Habermas, Jurgen, 103
Hainan province, arrests in, 75
Han Guizhi, 131
Harbin City, 130, 132
Hardin, Russell, 94, 96, 140–41, 221n57

Harding, Susan, 41–42
hard-liners: on capitalists, 183; cooperation strategy and, 140, 165; definition of, 98; exit activities and, 164; political liberalization and, 98–99; voice activities and, 140, 165
Harvard Law School Web site study, 65
Harwit, Eric, 10
health insurance, 120, 131
"Heaven, The" Web site, 64, 126
Hebei province: arrests in, 70–71; on bank loans, 152; corruption in, 121; FLG in, 144, 164; rebellions in, 144, 163–64; Sun Dawu and, 151–54
He Depu, 71
Heilongjiang province, arrests in, 77
Held, David, 227–28n2
Henan province: arrests in, 78; e-government project and, 38; rebellions in, 164
Hirschman, Albert, 137–42
homicide, rules and regulations on, 60
Hong Kong: Guangdong province and, 157; Phoenix TV in, 226n36; SARS in, 156
Household Registration System, 149
Huang Kui, 71
Huang Qi, 67, 71, 126
Huang Qunwei, 71
Hubei province: arrests in, 74; CDP in, 146; rebellions in, 163–64
Hu Jintao: Bush on, 227n40; class issues and, 183; on democracy, 169; at G8 conference, 161; Jiang Zemin and, 127; leadership of, 181, 183; Liu Di and, 127; policy agenda of, 3; reforms of, 169–70; SARS and, 161, 182, 227n40; SILG and, 57; *xiaokang shehui* concept of, 183; on Zheng Enchong, 129
hukou zhidu (Household Registration System), 149
Hunan province: arrests in, 70, 73; newspapers in, 66
Hungary, political survey of, 118, 119
Huntington, Samuel, 79
Hu Shih, 2, 20
Hu Yaobang, 56

income level: business use and, 34; Gini coefficient for, 45; home use and, 34;

interpersonal relationships and, 115; news use by, 111; proficiency and, 35; urban vs. rural, 45, 45
incrementalism, 169–70
Indonesia: democratization in, 178; regime change in, 4, 17, 79, 171
industrialization: beneficiaries of, 44, 44, 215n78; class and, 175, 184; political legitimacy and, 25; social movements and, 175, 178
INE program, 27
information, online access to, 92, 93, 95, 109
information technology (IT): in communitarian theory, 82; crackdown costs and, 97–98; in Cuba, 80; development of, 18, 80, 97; governance and, 36; interest group theory on, 4–5, 84; in modernization theory, 82; research on impact of, 7–8; in Vietnam, 80
Informatization of the National Economy (INE) program, 27
Informatization Plan for National Economy and Society, The, 37
Instructions on Building E-Government, 37
interest group theory, 4–5, 84
Interim Regulations on Management of Computer Information Networks–International Connections, 59
Interim Regulations on Management of URL Registration, 59
internal chaos, prevention of, 172
International Commission of Jurists, 129
Internet: attacks on, 66; cyber café access to, 39; data sought on, 92–94, 93; designing of, 84; growth rate, 32; home use of, 34, 39; length of time on, 111; library use of, 39; mobile subscribers to, 39; MPS and, 57; vs. newspapers, 109; occupations of users, 33; OpenNet Initiative on, 9; reasons for use of, 92, 92, 109; regionalism of, 39; regulation of, 8–9, 53–54, 57, 58, 94–96; school use of, 39; services from, 94, 95; state-society relations and, 8–13, 108, 166; surveillance of, 9; trust of data from, 36, 110–13, 112, 113, 114; vs. TV, 109; work use of, 34, 39. *See also* World Wide Web

Internet channel providers, regulation of, 57
Internet content providers, regulation of, 9, 54
"Internet nationalism," 137, 173–74, 179
Internet News Information Service Self-Pledge, 65
Internet service providers (ISPs): "accessing the Internet by real identity" system, 68–69; license for, 53, 60, 63; MII and, 53, 61; MPS and, 61; prosecution of, 64; Public Security Bureau and, 60; regulation of, 9, 53–54; SILG and, 57; SSB and, 61; subscribers' records, 60, 61, 64
Internet Society of China, 65
interpersonal relationships: business elites on, 115; CASS surveys on, 111, 113–15, 114; facilitation of, 118; social atomization in, 91–92, 119
Iraq, regime change in, 171
Italy, political survey of, 119

Jakes, Susan, 226–27n36
Japan: invasion by, 173; political survey of, 118, 118, 119; regime change in, 171; "rich nation and strong army" mind-set in, 21
Jiang Fuzhen, 145
Jiang Lijun, 72
Jiang Meili, 129
Jiangsu province, arrests in, 78
Jiang Yanyong, 160, 176, 226n36
Jiang Yuxia, 72
Jiang Zemin: appointment of, 180; capitalism and, 183; CDP and, 145, 147; Chen Xitong and, 180; on democracy, 169; education of, 212n35; FLG and, 144; on GOP, 37; Hu Jintao and, 127; leadership of, 181; Li Peng and, 181; MEI and, 212n35; military and, 27; People's Movement and, 27, 183; political legitimacy of, 26, 180–81; reforms of, 169–70; resignation of, 181–82; *san ge dai biao* concept of, 154, 183, 184; SARS and, 182; on science/technology, 27, 212n35; "three talks" campaign of, 183; Yang brothers and, 180; Zhou Zhengyi and, 129
Jiayang Group, 123
Jilin province, arrests in, 70, 74, 77

238

jingji mingmai (economic lifeline), 53
Jinguan (Customs Intranet System), 37
Jin Haike, 72
Jinshui (Taxation Intranet System), 37
"Jin Yong Martial Arts Novels" Web site,
    117
Joint Conference on State Economic Infor-
    mation, 52, 53
judicial system: C&R system, 81, 147–51,
    225–26nn26–27; confidence in, 133;
    corruption in, 120, 120–21, 132, 149–50;
    criminal investigation in, 148; indepen-
    dence in, 124–25; political prisoners and,
    127; regionalism of, 125
June Fourth Incident, 145
Juniper Networks, 66

Kalathil, Shanthi, 9
Kedzie, Christopher, 80
kejiao xingguo ("revitalizing the nation")
    strategy, 27
kexue shehui zhuyi ("scientific socialism"),
    1, 2, 4, 23
key word filters, 65, 68
Kong Youping, 72
Kornhauser, William, 91
Kuomintang (KMT), 172, 173, 174, 183

large enterprises, 34, 35
Legislation Law, 150, 226n26
Lessig, Lawrence, 8–9, 85
liangdao xiaozu ("leading small group"), 57
Liaoning province: arrests in, 72; corrup-
    tion in, 123–25
liberal democracy, 228n2
Li Changchun, 157
Li Chunyan, 72
Li Dawei, 73
"Life Likes Fire, A" chat room, 125
Li Hongmin, 73
Li Hongzhi, 143
Li Jiating, 121
Li Lanqing, 57
Lin Hai, 67
Lin Hui, 145
Lin Yang, 73
Lin Yanzhi, 183

Li Peng: CDP and, 146–47; Jiang Zemin
    and, 181; MPT and, 51; problem-solving
    by, 7; reforms of, 51; Zhao Ziyang and,
    7, 180
Li Ruihuan, 181, 182
Li Shenzhi, 151
Liu, Alan, 23–24, 90–91
Liu Di, 70, 125–27
Liu Fangren, 121
Liu Haofeng, 73
Liu Heng, 125
Liu Huaqing, 182
Liu Lianjun, 145, 146
Liu Weifang, 73
Liu Wenyu, 74
Liu Xiaobo, 127
Liu Yong, 123–25, 133
Liu Yunshan, 55
Liu Zhongxia, 130–31
Li Yanfang, 73
Li Zhi, 73
loyalty activities, 137, 141, 147
Luo Changfu, 74
Luo Yongzhong, 74
Lu Xinhua, 74

Macao, Guangdong province and, 157
Malaysia, Web sites in, 127
Manchu conquest, 172
manufacturing sector, Internet use by,
    32, 33
Maoist politics: Confucian politics and, 23;
    Cultural Revolution, 6, 24; economic
    development in, 175; elites in, 5–6;
    Great Leap Forward, 23, 24; nationalism
    and, 173; neo-technonationalism and, 27;
    socioeconomic impact of, 24; state struc-
    ture and, 23, 24; technocrats and, 5–6
Mao Qingxiang, 74
Mao Zedong: agenda of, 91; belief in sci-
    ence/technology, 23; leadership of, 181;
    on *neiluan* and *waihuan*, 172, 173; on
    party history, 99; reforms of, 140; on
    "scientific socialism," 23; Sun Dawu
    on, 152
Marcos, Ferdinand, 171
Marx, Karl, 90, 106, 175

Ma Yan, 74
May Fourth Movement: Confucian politics and, 172; Dewey and, 1–2; People's Movement and, 2–3; "scientific socialism" and, 2; Western modern state and, 22
McAdam, Doug, 41
"mean world" syndrome, 86
"Measures for Custody and Repatriation of Vagrant and Beggars in Cities" (C&R measures), 81, 148–50, 226n26
Measures for Managing Internet Information Services, 60
"Measures of Management of Urban Vagrant Beggars," 148
media: CCP policies on, 7, 91; commercialization of, 7; conflict resolution by, 46; SCIO and, 61
medical and health care sector: corruption in, 120, 120; costs in, 120; in rural areas, 163–64; SARS (see SARS)
MEI, 52, 53, 212n35
Meng Jun, 75
Meng Xuenong, 160, 163, 182
Mexico, "Zapatista Effect" in, 4
Meyer, John W., 19
Microsoft, 65–66
MII. See Ministry of Information Industry (MII)
military: control over, 158–59; functions of, 177; imperialism and, 21; Jiang Zemin and, 27; networks for, 52; online information on, 93; in Political Bureau, 182; regime change and, 172; SARS and, 158–59; social movements and, 177; submarine event, 162, 163; weapons for, 23
Ministry of Civil Affairs, 149
Ministry of Culture: on cyber cafés, 65; DOP, State Council, and, 55; organization of, 54–55; rules and regulations by, 61; Web site censorship campaign, 55
Ministry of Education, 55
Ministry of Electrical Power, 52
Ministry of Electronics Industry (MEI), 52, 53, 212n35
Ministry of Health (MOH), 156–58, 160, 182

Ministry of Information Industry (MII): on addresses, 65; creation of, 53; domains and, 61, 65; functions of, 53; ISPs and, 53, 61; network gateway of, 63; non-profit Internet data services and, 62; propaganda and, 54; responsibilities of, 50, 53–54; rules and regulations by, 61; Web site censorship campaign, 55
Ministry of Land and Resources, 121
Ministry of Post and Telecommunication (MPT), 50–53
Ministry of Public Security (MPS), 55, 57, 59, 61
Ministry of Radio, Film, and Television, 53, 216n6
Ministry of Railways, 52
Ministry of State Security, 55
modernization theory, 82
MOH, 156–58, 160, 182
Mongol conquest, 172
Mou Tsung-san, 20
MPS, 55, 57, 59, 61
MPT, 50–53
Mr. Democracy, 1–2, 18, 205n2
Mr. Science, 1–3, 18, 205n2
MSN Spaces, 66
Mu Chuangheng, 75
multinational/joint venture businesses, 34, 35
Mulvenon, James C., 10, 138, 173

Nanfang dushi bao (Southern Metropolitan News), 148
Nanjing: polls on SARS in, 159, 160, 162, 163; SARS, reaction to, 160
National Bureau of Statistics, 45
National Congress of CDP, 146
National Information Infrastructure Steering Committee (NIISC), 52, 53
National Party Congress: blocking and, 64; C&R system and, 150; functions of, 156; retirements at, 181; schedule of, 156. See also specific events
National People's Congress (NPC): blocking and, 64; C&R system and, 150, 226n27; functions of, 156; Internet use by, 37; legislation from, 150; Li Peng and,

240   146; Qiao Shi and, 180; rules from, 59,
        61, 150. *See also specific events*
national security: ISP records and, 64; MII
        and, 54; rules and regulations on, 59, 60,
        62, 63; State Secrecy Law on, 58
neiluan (internal chaos), 172
neo-technonationalism, 27
Net Ease, 65
networks: architecture of, 84; filtering
        software on, 65; ISP registration on, 60;
        for military, 52; official Web site, 64;
        political freedom and, 80; SILG and, 57;
        statistics on, 31; structure of, 109; wiring
        of, 63
"New Culture Forum," 64, 116
New Culture Movement, 205n2
New Life Movement, 22
news: online access for, 93; survey on use
        of, 95; on Web sites, 64, 109
News Center of China International Inter-
        net, 64
newspapers: in Guangdong province, 148;
        in Hunan province, 66; vs. Internet, 109;
        on SARS, 156; voters and, 83; Web sites
        for, 109
New York Times: Beijing Bureau, 66; block-
        ing of Web site, 64; on SARS, 160
NIISC, 52, 53
9/11 terrorist attacks, 171
1911 revolution, 22
1949 communist revolution, 22–23, 172
1978 Democracy Wall movement, 96, 174
1989 June Fourth Incident, 145
1989 pro-democracy movement: arrests
        and, 72–73, 76, 77; blocking and, 64;
        corruption and, 120, 121; Deng Xiaoping
        and, 27; entrepreneurs and, 183; Jiang
        Zemin and, 27, 183; May Fourth Move-
        ment and, 2–3; regime's response to,
        25–27, 99, 177, 180–81; rise of, 96, 174;
        Thirteenth Party Congress and, 26; Web
        sites on, 67, 117, 126
1997 Asian financial crisis, 43, 176
1998 CDP movement. *See* China Democ-
        racy Party (CDP)
1999 FLG movement. *See* Falun Gong
        (FLG)

1999 National People's Congress, 153–54
Ninth National People's Congress, 53,
        153–54
nongcun (village) issues, 178
nongmin (farmers) issues, 178
non-government organizations' Internet
        use, 38
nongye (agriculture) issues, 178
non-profit Internet data services, 62
Norris, Pippa, 80
Notice on Improving Internet Domain
        Management, 62

O'Donnell, Guillermo, 88, 98, 99–100, 168
OpenNet Initiative, 9, 65
Outlook Weekly, The, 175
Ouyang Yi, 75

Party Principle, 56
passwords, 68
Pearl River Delta, software parks in, 29
Peiping Academy, 22
People's Bank, 52
People's Daily, 117, 126, 178
People's Daily Web site, 64, 117, 178
People's Liberation Army, network for, 52
People's Movement: arrests and, 72–73,
        76, 77; blocking and, 64; books on, 126;
        corruption and, 120, 121; Deng Xiaop-
        ing and, 27; entrepreneurs and, 183;
        Jiang Zemin and, 27, 183; May Fourth
        Movement and, 2–3; regime's response
        to, 25–27, 99, 177, 180–81; rise of, 96,
        174; Thirteenth Party Congress and, 26;
        Web sites on, 67, 117, 126; Zhao Ziyang
        and, 99
People's Net Web site, 64, 117, 178
Philippines, regime change in, 171
Phoenix TV, 226n36
police, 177. *See also* judicial system
Political Bureau: DOP and, 55, 55–56; on
        Liu Yong, 125; retirements from, 181–82;
        SARS and, 157, 158, 160
political correctness, 156
political democratization: in authoritarian
        states, 100; civic engagement and, 103;
        definition of, 87–88; election systems

in, 184; events by social movements and, 101–2, 185; liberalization and, 167, 168, 186; *san ge dai biao* concept and, 183
political liberalization: in authoritarian states, 88–89, 98–101; beneficiaries of, 11; C&R system and, 148; characteristics of, 11, 186; civic engagement and, 103, 134; collective actions and, 168, 184; definition of, 87–88; democratization and, 167, 168, 186; early stages of, 99–100; events by social movements and, 101–2, 155, 185; exit activities and, 138–39, 141–42; hard- vs. soft-liners and, 98–99; IT and, 88–89; loyalty activities and, 137, 141; power struggles and, 182; regime change and, 171, 179–86; *san ge dai biao* concept and, 183; state empowerment and, 155; voice activities and, 138–41
polls, public opinion, 86
populism, 2
pornography, 59–61, 63, 65
post and telecom bureaus, 51
post and telecom enterprises, 50, 51
poverty, 43, 151, 214–215n77
pragmatism, 1–2, 6
privately owned businesses: Constitution on, 153–54; Internet use in, 34; legalization of, 183; political control of, 35; workers in, 153
propaganda: control function of, 36; decentralized development and, 108; directionality of, 36; MII and, 54; on NPC, 156; on official Web sites, 173–74
property rights, 36, 153, 183
"proxy" technologies, 94
public administration: efficiency of, 38; Internet use by, 32, 33
Public Pledge on Self-Discipline, 65
Public Security Bureau, 60
Putnam, Robert, 86, 104, 106
Pye, Lucian, 172

qiangguo luntan ("Strong Nation Forum") Web site, 117, 178
Qiao Shi, 180, 181, 182
Qing dynasty, 20
Qin Yongmin, 146, 147

Qi Yanchen, 71
Quan Huicheng, 75

rapid-reaction force, 177
rational choice theory, 105, 140
regime change: definition of, 168; by external forces, 171–74; by political liberalization, 172; by rebellions, 172, 174–79; reflection on, 186–87
registration of users, 59
Regulations on Administrative Protection of Internet Publications, 62
Regulations on Internet Access and Cafés, 61
Regulations on Internet Domain Management, 62
Regulations on Internet News and Bulletin Boards, 61
Regulations on Non-Profit Internet Services Provision, 62
religious beliefs, 60, 77, 227n2
Renmin, 65
Republic era, 22
"revitalizing the nation" strategy, 27
"Revolutionary Marxism" Web site, 64
"rich nation and strong army": information technology and, 24; Mr. Democracy, Mr. Science, and, 2; neo-technonationalism and, 27–28; Western modern state and, 21, 22
Robinson, Mary (Madame), 145
routers, filtering by, 66
rule of law: censorship and, 68; corruption and, 46–47; in liberal democracy, 228n2; Zheng Enchong trial and, 130
Rules and Regulations on Implementation of URL Registration, 59
Rules on the Administration of Internet News Information Services, 62, 63

Safety and Protection Regulations for Computer Information Systems, 59
sai xiansheng (Mr. Science), 1–3, 18, 205n2
san ge dai biao ("three represents") concept, 154, 183, 184
Sang Jiancheng, 75
san-nong issues, 178

242

SARS: arrests and, 67, 71, 74; Bush on, 227n40; in coastal areas, 159; first cases of, 154, 156; FLG and, 144, 164; Hu Jintao and, 161, 182, 227n40; interaction strategies of, 142; military and, 158–59; MOH and, 156–58, 160, 182; *New York Times* on, 160; polls on, 159, 159, 160, 162, 162, 163; regime's response to, 81, 101, 154–65, 176–77, 182, 185; in rural areas, 163; social movements and, 101, 155; social organizations and, 163; *Southern Metropolitan News* on, 148; *Time* magazine on, 226–27n36; WHO on, 154, 161

satellite dishes, sales of, 69

Schmitter, Philippe, 88, 98, 99–100, 168

Schram, Stuart, 90

Schumpeterian democracy, 83, 219n18

science, political influence of, 18

Science Society of China, 22

"scientific socialism," 1, 2, 4, 23

SCIO, 55–57, 55, 61, 62

search engines: Altavista, 64; blocking of, 64; Google, 64–67; key word filters, 65, 68; passwords and, 68; survey on use of, 95; use of, 94; Yahoo!, 65–66

secret police, 90

"self-strengthening movement," 21

servers, censorship and, 68

Severe Acute Respiratory Syndrome. *See* SARS

Shananxi province, arrests in, 77

Shandong province: arrests in, 75, 76; CDP in, 145–46; FLG members in, 143

shang fang, conflict resolution by, 46–47

Shanghai: arrests in, 75, 76; business use in, 34; corruption in, 128; "Digital Shanghai" plan, 37; home use in, 34; interpersonal relationships in, 115; news use in, 111; polls on SARS in, 159, 160, 162, 163; proficiency in, 35; SARS in, 163; urban redevelopment in, 128–29; Zheng Enchong trial in, 128–29

Shanxi province, SARS in, 177

Shi Tao, 66

Shi Yunsheng, 163

shopping, online, 92, 95, 109

short message service (SMS), 95, 159

Sichuan province, arrests in, 71, 73, 75, 76

SILG, 37, 57, 59

Sina, 65

Singapore: political survey of, 118, 119; SARS in, 156

Sixiang de jingjie ("Field of Ideas"), 64, 116

Sixteenth Party Congress (2002): on entrepreneurs, 154; Jiang Zemin and, 181; media coverage of, 56; propaganda on, 156; retirements at, 181, 182; SARS and, 156; Web site censorship campaign, 55

slavery, 149

small and medium-sized enterprises, 31–32, 34, 35

SMS, 95, 159

"social atomization," 92, 119, 133

social capital, 86, 106, 108, 133

social movements: arrests and, 100, 126; capitalism and, 175–77; causes of, 170; constraints on, 89–90, 177–79; corruption and, 46–47, 120; definition of, 41; digital divide and, 97; economic development and, 175–77; email from, 100; events by (*see* events by social movements); globalization and, 176–77; goals of, 178; industrialization and, 175, 178; military and, 177; modern state and, 41–43; organization of, 96–97, 100, 178–79; political reform and, 170, 175–81, 184; regime's response to, 97–98, 136, 177–79; rise of, 96, 174–75; SARS and, 101, 155; state-owned businesses and, 175

social organizations: CCP policies on, 91; conditions for, 146; decision making by, 163; Internet use by, 32, 38; registration of, 63; SARS and, 163

societal empowerment: civic engagement and, 10, 166; cooperation strategy and, 165; information flow and, 10, 166; "Internet nationalism" and, 137; political change and, 169; vs. state empowerment, 10–13, 135; voice activities and, 165, 166

soft-liners: cooperation strategy and, 140, 165; definition of, 98; exit activities and, 164; policies of, 185; political liberalization and, 98–99; voice activities and, 140, 165

software: downloads, use of, 95; searches for, 93
software parks, 29–31
Sohu, 65
Southern Metropolitan News, 148
South Korea: democratization in, 169; political survey of, 118, *118*, *119*; regime change in, 171
Soviet Union: August coup in, 17; collapse of, 26; democratization in, 169, 177–78; ideology in, 90; Maoist politics and, 23; power struggles in, 181
Spain, political survey of, *118*
SSB, 57, 60, 61
Stainless Steel Mouse, 125
state, modern: autonomy of, 41–42; composition of, 13; control in, 9, 91, 227n12; definition of, 41, 210n51; features of, 19, 227–28n2; globalization of Western, 18–19, 43, 173; goals of, 23; imperialism and, 19, 21; legitimacy of, 228n2; making of, 41–42; models of, 19, 23; policies of, 42, 90; political form of Western, 228n2; power in, 90, 227n2; social movements and, 41–43; technology in, 23
State Administration for Industry and Commerce, 55
State Administration of Radio, Film, and Television, 53–56, 55, 216n6
State Administration of Taxation, 37
State Bureau of Secrecy, 55
state capacity, democracy and, 12
State Commission for Development and Reform, 120
State Council: C&R system and, 149–51; Internet use by, 37; organization chart for media, 55; regulation by, 58; rules from, 59–60, 62; SARS and, 158, 160
State Council Information Office (SCIO), 55–57, 55, 61, 62
State Economic and Trade Commission, 37
State Education Commission, 52
state empowerment: coercion and, 8, 91; control and, 9, 91; cooperation strategy and, 165; economic development and, 32, 166; via "Internet nationalism," 137; political change and, 169; political

liberalization and, 155; from regulation, 8–9; vs. societal empowerment, 10–13, 135; from surveillance, 9; voice activities and, 165
State Information Leading Group (SILG), 37, 57, 59
state-owned businesses: Internet use in, 34; political control of, 35; social movements and, 175
State Planning Commission, 52
State Press and Publication Administration, 55, 56
State Science and Technology Commission, 52
State Secrecy Bureau (SSB), 57, 60, 61
State Secrecy Law, 58
State Secrets Protection Regulations for Computer Information Systems on the Internet, 60
"statist" paradigm, 41
stock market, online access to, 92, 95
"strategic interaction": conflict strategy (*see* conflict strategy); cooperation strategy (*see* cooperation strategy); coordination strategy, 94–95, 140–42, 221n57
"Strong Nation Forum" Web site, 117, 178
submarine event, 162, 163
Suharto, 4, 17, 79, 171
Sun Dawu, 142, 151–54, 165, 185
Sunstein, Cass, 86
Sun Yat-sen, 22
Sun Zhigang, 142, 147–51, 165, 185, 226n27
Supreme People's Court: on death penalty, 61; on Liu Yong, 124, 125
Suttmeier, Richard, 27
Su Xiuwen, 130–32
Sweden, political survey of, *118*, *119*

Taiwan: democratization in, 169, 177–78; elections on, 117; regime change in, 171; SARS in, 156
Tan Qiu, 75
Tao Haidong, 76
Tarrow, Sidney: on collective actions, 106; on print media, 47, 170; on social capital, 106; on social movements, 41, 42, 47; on state making, 41, 42

243

244

Taxation Intranet System, 37
technocracy: capitalism and, 6; decision
making in, 6; definition of, 5; elites in,
5–6; ideology and, 6; political legitimacy of, 182; problem-solving in, 6–7;
research on, 6–7; state-society relations
in, 6–7; virtues of, 5–6; voice activities
in, 140
Telecommunications Regulations of
PRC, 60
telephone: fixed-line subscribers, 29; ISP
records on numbers used, 60; lines for,
statistics on, 28, 29, 30; local switchboard
capacity, 28; mobile subscribers, 29, 30,
69; penetration rate for, 29, 30, 38; prepaid cards for, 69; text messaging on, 68
television (TV): community engagement
and, 86; in Eastern Europe, 79; vs. Internet, 109; Liu Di on, 126; SARS coverage
by, 160, 226n36; stations' Web sites, 109;
trust of data from, 86
Tenth Five-Year Plan, 27
Tenth National People's Congress, 156
terrorism, rules and regulations on, 60
Thirteenth Party Congress (1987), 25, 26
"three nos" concept, 149
"three represents" concept, 154, 183, 184
"three talks" campaign, 183
ti (substance, essence), 20
Tiananmen Square demonstration. *See*
People's Movement
Tian Fengshan, 121
Tianjin: CDP in, 146; FLG in, 142
Tian wang ("The Heaven") Web site, 64,
126
Tian Wenchang, 124–25
Tibet: social movements on, 100; Web sites
on, 173
Tilly, Charles, 41, 42–43
Time magazine, SARS coverage by,
226–27n36
totalitarianism, 90–92
township and village enterprises, 176
townships, election system for, 184
Truman, David, 84
Tu Runsheng, 151

2002 NPC, 53
2003 CPI score, 46
2003 NPC, 156
2005 NPC, 64
2006 NPC, 36

unemployment, 175, 178
Unicom, 52, 53
United Nations, 145
United States: CDP in, 147; Liu Di release
and, 127; political survey of, 118, 118, 119

Vietnam, IT in, 80
villages: election system for, 184; *nongcun*
issues, 178; township and village enterprises, 176
violence, rules and regulations on, 60
VIP Reference online magazine, 67
voice activities: on C&R system, 151; cooperation strategy and, 140–42, 165; coordination strategy and, 140–42; definition
of, 139–40; exit activities and, 138, 139,
141, 165; in FLG events, 144; hard- vs.
soft-liners and, 140, 165; political liberalization and, 138–41; in SARS event,
142; societal empowerment and, 165, 166;
state empowerment and, 165; of Sun
Dawu, 142, 153; in technocracy, 140

Wacker, Gudrun, 9
waihuan (foreign aggression), 172
Walzer, Michael, 104
Wang Donghai, 145
Wang Gungwu, 171–72
Wang Jinbo, 76
Wang Renchong, 56
Wang Renzhi, 56
Wang Sen, 76
Wang Xin, 76
Wang Xuebing, 121
Wang Xuefei, 76
Wang Yi, 64
Wang Youcai, 67, 145, 147
Wang Zhenyong, 76
warlords, 22
Washington Post Web site, 64

Weber, Max, 5, 24
Wei Jianxing, 181
Wei Jingsheng, 126
welfare state, 175, 178
Wen Jiabao: on C&R measures, 148, 151; class issues and, 183; leadership of, 181; Liu Di and, 127; policy agenda of, 3; "pro-people orientation" of, 183; on public opinion, 36; on redevelopment, 129; SARS and, 160, 161, 182; Zheng Enchong and, 129
Wen Yuankai, 3
WHO, 154, 161
Wilhelm, Anthony, 84, 86–87
working class movement, 175
World Bank, 37
World Health Organization (WHO), 154, 161
World Trade Organization (WTO), 27, 52, 173, 175
World Wide Web: blocking of sites, 64–65, 94; censorship campaign, 55; dissent sites, 10, 64, 67, 117, 126, 173; filtering of, 9, 64, 65; "guerrilla warfare" on, 117; Harvard Law School study on, 65; international sites, 127; ISP records on visited, 60; newspapers' sites on, 64, 109, 117, 178; official sites, 64, 109, 117, 173–74, 178; SCIO and, 61; Sun Dawu's site, 151; TV station sites on, 109. See also Internet
WTO, 27, 52, 173, 175
Wu Bangguo, 57
Wu Guoguang, 212n29
Wu Jichuan, 53–54
Wu Jinlian, 151
Wu Yi (Madame), 160, 161
Wu Yilong, 77

Xiao Gongqin, 225n23
xiaokang shehui ("comfortable society") concept, 183
Xici online bulletin board, 125
Xie Wanjun, 145–46
Xinhua News Agency: coverage by, 109, 216n7; DOP and, 55; Internet News Information Service Self-Pledge, 65; on Li

Peng on CDP, 146; organization of, 55; State Council and, 55; Zheng Enchong and, 129
Xinjiang province, arrests in, 73, 75
Xin wenming luntan ("New Culture Forum"), 64, 116
Xu Guang, 77
Xu Liangying, 3
Xu Wei, 77
Xu Wenli, 146, 147

Yahoo!, 65–66
Yang, Guobin, 10
Yang Baibing, 180, 181
Yang Huaiqing, 163
Yang Shangkun, 180, 181
Yangtze River Delta, software parks in, 29
Yang Zili, 77
Yan Jun, 77
Yao Xiangkui, 27
Yao Yue, 77
Yeltsin, Boris, 17
Yimin Food Products, strike at, 129
yong (function, utility), 20
Yu Jie, 127
Yunnan province, corruption in, 121

"Zapatista Effect," 4
Zeng Li, 64
Zeng Peiyuan, 57
Zhang Dejiang, 157, 158
Zhang Haitao, 77
Zhang Honghai, 78
Zhang Ji, 78
Zhang Pinghua, 56
Zhang Shengqi, 78
Zhang Wenkang, 160, 163, 182
Zhang Yuhui, 78
Zhang Yuxiang, 78
Zhang Zhitong, 20
Zhao Jing, 66
Zhao Ziyang: MPT accounting system, 50; on 1989 pro-democracy movement, 180; People's Movement and, 99; on political reforms, 25; problem-solving by, 7; Tu Runsheng and, 151

246

Zhejiang province: arrests in, 74, 76–78; CDP in, 145; Zhang Dejiang in, 157
Zheng, 78
Zheng Enchong, 128–30
Zhongguancun E-park, 31
Zhongnanhai, siege of, 97, 142–43, 155, 176
Zhou Yongkang, 125
Zhou Zhengyi, 128–29

Zhu Houze, 56
Zhujiang (Pearl River) Delta software park, 29
Zhu Rongji: on GOP, 37; Jiang Zemin and, 181; SILG and, 37, 57; WTO and, 52, 173
Zhu Yufu, 78
Zou Jiahua, 52